Tom Young is a Performance Psychologist (C.Psychol, HCPC) specialising in team dynamics and leadership. His academic study began at Lancaster University and continued at Liverpool John Moores University where he graduated from their globally recognised MSc programme in Sport Psychology.

Tom has worked with teams and individuals at the highest level of professional sport, providing psychological support to organisations and individuals from the worlds of rugby union, football, boxing, rallying, track and field, and golf.

Most recently he has been part of the coaching team to European and PGA Tour golfer Tommy Fleetwood and worked as a consultant to both the Belgian football team ahead of the World Cup in Russia, and the victorious European Ryder Cup team in Paris 2018.

Praise for *The Making of a Leader*

'Although elite athletes understand the keys to excellence, you rarely have the chance to get inside their heads. You're in luck: Tom Young has solved that problem. As a performance psychologist, he's worked closely with some of the world's best in both individual and team sports. In this fascinating book, he shares his rich experiences and his keen insights on the science – and the practice – of achieving and sustaining success'

— Adam Grant, *New York Times* bestselling author of *Originals* and *Give and Take*, and host of the chart-topping TED podcast WorkLife

'A valuable addition to the high performance literature. Read it'

— James Kerr, bestselling author of *Legacy*

D1649464

'There is no such thing as a single "recipe for success" . . . yet this book shows that in the world of professional sport these proven and renowned leaders all have their own rules of strategy, which have brought continued success and recognition. Especially, of course, Sean Dyche of Burnley FC!'

— **Alastair Campbell, bestselling author, strategist, communicator and lifelong fan of Burnley FC**

'I am always looking to learn from other sports and this book gives a unique insight into what it takes to navigate the challenges of high performance'

— **Tommy Fleetwood, professional golfer**

'Full of important lessons that you learn as a leader in sport that are as applicable to business environments as they are to elite sports'

— **Sir Bill Beaumont, chairman of World Rugby and former England and British & Irish Lions captain**

'A great insight into how leaders help shape and nurture high performance environments. Full of relevant lessons for any current or aspiring leader'

— **Heather Knight OBE, captain of the England women's cricket team**

'Sport, and especially golf, has so many elite, standout individual performers, but the key to building a winning team is understanding each individual within it. This book offers fascinating insight into man management and the attributes needed to be an effective leader, which is incredibly useful and relevant to me ahead of captaining the 2020 European Ryder Cup team'

— **Pádraig Harrington, three-time Major champion and captain of the 2020 European Ryder Cup team**

'Drawing on rich narratives of proven leaders in elite sports like rugby, soccer and NFL, this engaging book steers clear of the jargon and the buzzwords to leave readers with compelling lessons for their own leadership at the end of every chapter. If you want to be a leader or become a better leader, man or woman, in sport or any other sector, this book is for you'

— **Professor Andy Hargreaves, Professor Emeritus, Boston College and author of *Uplifting Leadership***

'*The Making of a Leader* provides a unique insight into the inner workings of established leaders' minds. Young draws common methods together while also allowing room for distinct individual approaches and opinions to come through . . . Well worth a read to gain useful leadership intel'

— **Rebecca Symes, senior performance psychologist, The FA**

'Tales from the trenches. Engaging, insightful and above all authentic'

— **Michael Calvin, award-winning sportswriter and *Sunday Times* bestselling author**

'Compelling, relevant and honest. A real account of what it takes to lead in team environments. I enjoyed reflecting on what was a brilliant part of my career at Burnley'

— **Joey Barton, manager of Fleetwood Town FC**

'Grounded in academic research, *The Making of a Leader* gives an authentic view of leadership, as seen through the eyes of those who do it'

— **Dr Martin Eubank, Liverpool John Moores University**

'A global account of what it takes to lead in elite sport: culture, relationships and resilience'

— **Mike Forde, executive chairman, Sportsology, and former director of football operations, Chelsea FC**

'First-hand experience inside the minds of elite sportspeople makes Tom a compelling storyteller and speaker. It is his humility and ability to turn that experience into relevant and applicable learnings to workplace leadership, at all levels, that make him unique'

— **Simon Potts, CEO, The Alchemist**

'The business world can take valuable lessons from top sporting organisations. This book pulls together the experiences of acclaimed sports coaches, and highlights strategies that are applicable across industry'

— **Barry McNeill, CEO Sportsology, and former Group COO of Catapult Sports**

'To bring out the best in a player who will always put the team first takes a unique skillset. This book highlights how seven different leaders understand and develop their people to do just that'

— **Andrew Trimble, CEO of Kairos, and former Ireland and Ulster rugby union player**

'I have been part of some special teams and this book gives an honest and authentic account of leadership at the highest level. Young writes with clarity and precision about what it takes to succeed as a leader'

— **Isa Nacewa, former Leinster Rugby captain**

'Packed full of real-life experiences and strategies, a must-read for anyone who wants to improve their leadership skills'

— **Blake Wooster, co-founder and CEO, 21st Club and 15th Club**

THE
MAKING
OF A
LEADER

What elite sport can teach us about leadership, management and performance

TOM YOUNG

ROBINSON

ROBINSON

First published in Great Britain in 2020 by Robinson

1 3 5 7 9 10 8 6 4 2

A CIP catalogue record for this book
is available from the British Library.

ISBN: 978-1-47214-507-9

Typeset in Scala by Hewer Text UK Ltd, Edinburgh
Printed and bound in Great Britain by Clays Ltd, Elcograf S.p.A.

Papers used by Robinson are from well-managed forests and other responsible sources.

Robinson
An imprint of
Little, Brown Book Group
Carmelite House
50 Victoria Embankment
London EC4Y 0DZ

An Hachette UK Company
www.hachette.co.uk

www.littlebrown.co.uk

How To books are published by Robinson, an imprint of Little, Brown Book Group. We welcome
proposals from authors who have first-hand experience of their subjects. Please set out the aims of
your book, its target market and its suggested contents in an email to howto@littlebrown.co.uk

For Bella and Henry, and the love of sport

Contents

Foreword

....

On 6 December 2016, I was honoured to be named as Europe's Ryder Cup captain, and to lead the team in Paris in 2018. For the next two years I immersed myself in the role of a sporting 'leader', giving me some insight into the scrutiny and pressures that are inevitable with such a position.

I have been fortunate to have played on three winning Ryder Cup teams and served as vice-captain to four other captains. As a player, you can focus on your own personal performance and what you contribute to the team. As a vice-captain, you support the captain in whatever way you can. However, as captain, rightly or wrongly, everyone is looking at you. Every pairing or selection decision is debated in the global media and now on social media.

Sometimes the importance of the captain can be a little overplayed. I have said time and again that it is, after all, the players who go out to hit the shots and hole the putts, and compete for that historic trophy. But as captain you have the ultimate responsibility to those players, that team and to the people of Europe who love this great game. During my time as captain, I had some sleepless nights, my own game suffered, and I certainly felt that pressure and expectation.

The Ryder Cup is a unique sporting scenario. We bring twelve individuals, who compete against each other all year round, together as a team. Some players qualify automatically and others are picked as the captain's 'wild cards'. For one week every two years, these players form bonds and friendships that last a lifetime. They are not playing for money, but for something greater and more significant than their own individual gain.

Throughout my time as captain I looked to implement, in my own style, many of the ideas discussed in this book. My first priority was to be myself, to do the job to the best of my ability and in my own way. Players know if you are faking it.

European golf is full of stories, history and tradition. Most people will be familiar with the emotional impact that the magical and mercurial Seve Ballesteros has on our team, but I was also keen to connect the players to other past captains and players, to make them realise what they are part of. I don't think they needed any more motivation than that.

I am wary about using the term 'culture', as I believe such a thing takes time to create. However, there may be an enduring culture within Team Europe, and I am fortunate to be the most recent custodian of that. What I can talk about is the feeling in that team room. Let me tell you, it was special. That atmosphere was not a result of a motivational speech or a picture on the wall. It was due to a group of phenomenal people who also happen to be very good at their jobs. That 'group', by the way, goes beyond the players and also includes the caddies, vice-captains, our families and the back-room staff.

Our team, like any other, was made up of different characters and personalities. I wanted to understand each individual and how to communicate with them in order to maximise their performance. At times, that meant adapting my own style. You can't treat them all the same, simply because we are all unique as human beings.

I also got a taste of the public scrutiny that a sporting leader can encounter. The wild card picks. I had some tough phone calls to make to those that missed out, but my choices were made on both talent and character, and what I believed those four individuals would bring to the golf course and to the team room. They didn't turn out too bad.

On 30 September 2018, we reclaimed the Ryder Cup. As golfers, we don't get to experience that feeling of 'team' very often, so when we do it is undoubtedly special and we make sure we enjoy it, as you could tell from the celebrations. Now the dust has settled and, after a taste of leadership, I can pass the baton on to the next captain, Padraig Harrington.

The people in this book don't do that. They lead teams every day under intense pressure, constantly responding to the successes and setbacks of elite sport and, for that reason, I have the utmost respect for them and their achievements, and even more appreciation for what we can learn from them.

Thomas Bjørn
Professional golfer and Ryder Cup-Winning captain

Introduction

I remember, as a newly qualified psychologist, walking into a state-of-the-art Premier League training facility to meet a high-profile manager. I was anxious, nervous and probably well out of my depth. This was football, the sport that I had been engrossed by as a youngster, and the sport I dreamed of playing, like many others, at the highest level. Now here I was, surrounded by people I had watched on television only a few years before.

This first brief foray into elite sport ultimately left me feeling unfulfilled. It was not what I expected, yet still I wanted more. The obsession with football and the acute awareness of being in the same room as some 'big names' quickly dissipated to be replaced with an intense fascination into what drives high-performance teams and cultures.

In my professional life I have since been privileged to witness first-hand critical moments within elite sport. Some of these are performances, played out in public for all to see: cup finals, triumphs against the odds, play-off successes, and spectacular victories after periods in the sporting wilderness. I have also been behind the scenes witnessing tension, arguments, preparation for major tournaments, team meetings, team talks, debriefs, jubilant celebrations and devastated silences. The highs and lows of sport in high definition.

I would love to say that this book is the result of a clear goal that I set myself, but that isn't the case. Not even close. It is also not the result of a well-executed publishing masterplan; it has taken long enough to write! In fact, the project started out as an academic study with Liverpool John Moores University, exploring elite-level leadership in professional sport.

My initial objective was to complete a period of research which would contribute to a growing body of literature within psychology and perhaps help give me some more letters after my name. However, as the process continued, it became apparent that the rich data I had gathered would offer far more as a book aimed at all readers with an interest in leadership, in sport, in business or, perhaps, in all three areas.

AN OFFER OF INSIGHT

The Making of a Leader offers an insight into the leadership principles, beliefs and strategies applied by seven individuals operating and leading within a range of high-performance environments across the globe. Drawing on first-hand experiences at the highest level in rugby union, rugby league, football, cricket and American football, this book details the personal accounts and perceptions of best practice for leading and managing teams in elite sporting environments, and examines real-life responses to specific situations and challenges.

STRUCTURE

The sections of the book closely mirror the in-depth interviews that took place with each individual contributor. We start with an examination of their own journey and their leadership characteristics before exploring their specific approach to leadership in more detail, such as their beliefs, philosophies and methods. The next sections of the book focus on big-picture thinking, the development of a culture and, crucially, how that is balanced and often conflicts with the unavoidable need for short-term results. The subsequent chapters focus more on person management, emotional intelligence and how leaders navigate specific challenges. Finally, I finish each interview by asking for three bullet points for a 'Leadership Masterclass', aiming to summarise the approach of each contributor.

THE REALITY: HIGHS AND LOWS

This project has been more than four years in the making, owing mainly to the practicalities of interviewing leaders on a global scale and co-ordinating busy schedules. Pinning them down was by no means an easy task. To put this into context, the first interview with rugby union coach Stuart Lancaster took place before he led England into the 2015 Rugby World Cup and his final interview was conducted in the build-up to Leinster's two cup final victories at the end of the 2018 season.

My initial interview with Roberto Martínez took place in 2016, when he was manager at Premier League club Everton. Our last conversation happened in the summer of 2018, following Belgium's successful yet agonising World Cup campaign. Michael Maguire and Ashley Giles have also both changed roles during this period. Maguire was released by the South Sydney Rabbitohs and took up a dual role as national coach of New Zealand and head coach of the Wests Tigers, while Ashley Giles opted to leave Lancashire and return to former club Warwickshire as sporting director, before taking up the role as England's director of cricket.

As Stuart and Roberto will attest, four years in elite sport is a long time, yet can also feel like no time at all. Such a period will require a coach or manager to face a range of scenarios and challenges – from euphoric highs to crushing defeats, enjoying the personal plaudits and confronting brutal and personal attacks. Across these experiences, an individual will need to deploy many different facets of leadership. In many respects, this is no different to any career – portfolio or traditional. Increasingly, our paths require a degree of flexibility and resilience to handle the inevitable ups and downs of modern life. You will find examples of this malleable approach throughout this book.

While their skill set and background may predominantly be as an effective coach, leaders will invariably find themselves utilising a multitude of leadership skills and managing a variety of stakeholders, including owners, governing bodies, boards of directors, players, fans, the media and player representatives. Furthermore, they are the ones who are ultimately held accountable for performance levels and the relative success and failure of the organisations and teams that they lead. To put that feeling into context, one of the contributors described the feeling of constantly living on the edge and 'walking round with a P45 in your pocket' each day.

Rather than indicating 'good' or 'bad' leadership, the fact that half of our sample have changed roles reflects the harsh reality and scenarios that leaders will invariably face during a career in elite sport. Crucially, it is their response to such scenarios that will ultimately drive the impact they have throughout their career. It is, in fact, the qualities of the leader that determine the quality of the response.

POSITION OF INFLUENCE

Elite sport is brimming with science, technology and data, yet leaders find themselves in the unique position of having the ability to influence both individual and organisational performance. As a topic, leadership in sport is now more intellectualised and scrutinised than ever before. Every day experts and practitioners dissect and propose models of leadership, be that in the form of autobiographies, academic textbooks, social media, online articles or at high-profile conferences around the world. Global organisations are spending hundreds of billions of US dollars annually to develop and cultivate high-performance cultures. We are constantly searching for lessons in managing talent, and exploring the fields of psychology and neuroscience to develop characteristics such as mindset, trust and resilience. In the internet age we seem to have developed a genuine interest in learning from other leaders, rather than relentlessly competing against one another. This more collaborative approach offers significant learning opportunities for established, novice and potential leaders, as well as people with an interest in culture, sport and performance.

I hope that this book enables the reader to learn from others by offering something slightly different: seven unique perspectives of leadership from a range of backgrounds, sports and nationalities. The aim is not to put these people on a pedestal as the embodiment of the perfect leader. How could they be, if they all differ in their approach? You will see as you read on that they do not always agree with one another. They will also be the first to admit that they are not perfect, they do not always get it right and they have made mistakes along the way. Each has enjoyed significant success, while also experiencing what they would perceive as failure. There is no single recipe for leadership and this book is not designed as such, but rather as a body of work for you to study, reflect upon and create your own eclectic approach, perhaps choosing to apply some of the principles outlined here.

During this process, I wanted not only to understand the characteristics that certain leaders possess, but to delve beyond traditional models of leadership and understand first-hand the human experience of leadership, examining how leaders deploy behaviours and strategies at critical moments.

After lengthy discussions spanning many emails, calls and meetings, the contributors all agreed that the book should provide an honest, logical and authentic account of leadership; identify areas of agreement and difference; cite real examples of leadership challenges; and leave readers with practical takeaways to apply.

My role in this project is that of scribe and co-ordinator, offering a mouthpiece for the voices of the real experts who, under constant scrutiny, live their leadership philosophies each day, experiencing the highs and lows of a life in elite sport.

The Interview Process

....

The interviews were carried out over a period from 2015 to 2019 using a combination of digitally recorded and face-to-face interviews. All the data was transcribed personally (a time-consuming but rewarding experience) and analysed to identify key areas for discussion. The chapters you will read throughout the book emerged from this process and do not follow a specific leadership model or theory.

As you read on, you will see that some leaders contribute consistently throughout, while others feature more with regard to specific areas of leadership. This is due to the dynamic nature of the interviews, regularly diverting from a planned topic of questioning. There are some lengthy quotes too. Reducing these direct quotes was considered but, ultimately, it felt that by losing words, the book would also lose context and some authenticity of the insights provided.

THE INTERVIEWEES

MICHAEL MAGUIRE — RUGBY LEAGUE

Michael Maguire is the current head coach of the Wests Tigers and the New Zealand national team. He previously held the same position at the South Sydney Rabbitohs and Wigan Warriors. Michael led Wigan to the Super League (2010) and Challenge Cup (2011) titles, and was gracious enough to give me some of his time as his South Sydney side, having won their first National Rugby League

Grand Final (2014) in more than forty years, prepared for their forth-coming victory in the World Club Challenge against St Helens. As a player, he represented the Canberra Raiders and Adelaide Rams.

STUART LANCASTER — RUGBY UNION

Stuart Lancaster, then England's head coach, gave an honest and extensive insight into his leadership approach during an inter-national training camp. Although the 2015 World Cup ultimately ended in disappointment, Stuart played a key role in leading a crucial transition within England Rugby, ushering in a new group of players, many of whom he coached with England Saxons and the Under 20s, and reconnecting English rugby with its fans. As well as his role with England Rugby, Stuart has also acted as an advisor to a range of high-performance organisations, notably the Atlanta Falcons, the Football Association and British Cycling. He is currently senior coach at Leinster Rugby, having helped them to victory in both the European Champions Cup and the Pro14 league title in 2018. Stuart gave a second interview to discuss his experience and transition from leaving England to taking on his role at Leinster.

GARY KIRSTEN — CRICKET

Gary Kirsten gave three Skype interviews from his home in Cape Town, initially drawing on his experiences as a record-breaking Test batsman for South Africa. He went on to detail key leadership lessons from his time as head coach of India, South Africa and the Indian Premier League (IPL) franchise the Delhi Daredevils. Gary led India to the pinnacle of the sport, winning the World Cup in 2011. His insights from that time, addressing culture and specific leadership challenges, are enlightening. He has also coached the

Hobart Hurricanes in the Australian 'Big Bash' T20 league, the Royal Challengers Bangalore in the IPL and, at the time of writing, has just been named head coach for Welsh Fire in the new 'Hundred' competition.

ROBERTO MARTÍNEZ — FOOTBALL

From a playing career in the English lower leagues, Roberto led Swansea to promotion to the Championship in 2008. In 2009 he joined Wigan, who he kept in the top flight until 2013, and where he made history by winning the FA Cup, beating Manchester City in the final at Wembley. Having joined Everton in 2013, he led them to their highest Premier League points total, before leaving the club in 2016. A move into international football followed, as Roberto took charge of the highly talented Belgian national team, and led them to third place at the World Cup in Russia 2018.

ASHLEY GILES MBE — CRICKET

I was introduced to Ashley Giles by former Lancashire captain Tom Smith. At the time of the interview Ashley was cricket director and head coach of Lancashire County Cricket Club. Previously, as cricket director, he led Warwickshire CCC to both the Division 1 and 2 County Championships and, from 2012 to 2014, he was head coach of the England and Wales Cricket Board's (ECB) limited overs teams. In December 2016, he returned to Warwickshire CCC as sporting director and in December 2018, he was announced as the ECB's new director of cricket, building on the great work done by predecessor Andrew Strauss which culminated in England winning the World Cup in 2019.

DAN QUINN — AMERICAN FOOTBALL

Dan Quinn is head coach of the Atlanta Falcons of the National Football League (NFL). I interviewed Dan in Atlanta in April 2018 at the Falcons' Flowery Branch training facility as he prepared for the forthcoming season. In 2017, the Falcons reached the Super Bowl where they were famously beaten by the New England Patriots in the game's final moments. He previously served as the defensive co-ordinator of the Seattle Seahawks from 2013 to 2014, whose defence led the team to two consecutive Super Bowl appearances and won Super Bowl XLVIII. In an NFL coaching career starting in 2001, he has been part of the coaching staff at the San Francisco 49ers, Miami Dolphins and New York Jets.

SEAN DYCHE — FOOTBALL

Sean Dyche has a growing reputation as one of the most sought-after English managers in professional football. Starting out as a youth team coach, Dyche's first senior role was as manager of Watford and he is currently more than five years into his tenure as manager of Burnley Football Club. At Turf Moor, he has created a side renowned for their resilience and team spirit, driven by a philosophy that underpins the entire club. He led the club to promotion to the Premier League in both 2014 and 2016 and his leadership was a key reason behind the club maintaining their Premier League status for the 2017/18 season. Our discussion took place during the 2017/18 season.

The Making of a Leader

....

THE MAGIC INGREDIENT

What makes a leader? This question has been debated countless times and, depending upon who it is you are speaking to, you will often get a different answer. As a global population, we are fascinated with the make-up of leaders, be that polar explorers, politicians, CEOs or sports coaches. What is it about these people that enables them not only to reach the pinnacle of their profession but to captivate and bring others with them on that journey?

For me, the key word here is 'people'. Leaders are fundamentally no different to you and me; they are, first and foremost, human beings. They are a product of their personality traits (some innate and some learnt), their backgrounds, conditioning and mindsets. Like us, they all have great strengths that invariably sit alongside some limiting weaknesses.

During my research, I was eager to find the magic ingredients that all leaders possess; the common characteristics that absolutely guarantee effective leadership. What a book that would make – it would surely fly off the shelves!

However, as each leader went on to provide a unique insight into their own backgrounds, it was clear that no such formula exists. Every leader draws upon their personal history and experiences to craft their own approach and brand of leadership. And so, it makes sense to examine each leader starting from that crucial point – their conditioning and beginning.

CONDITIONING AND BEGINNING

This first section of the book examines the early experiences and personality attributes that built the foundations of an individual leadership philosophy. It is these foundations that influence how leaders interact with people and eventually generate the belief and confidence in others to follow them.

While all participated in their chosen sport to an extent, only two of the seven can truly be described as having reached the very top of their sport. Gary Kirsten (101 Tests and 185 One Day Internationals (ODIs) for South Africa) and Ashley Giles (54 Tests and 62 ODIs for England) had successful domestic and international cricketing careers before going on to take up their respective leadership positions. In contrast and to different degrees, Michael, Roberto, Stuart, Dan and Sean will all readily admit that their athletic careers were solid rather than spectacular, especially when viewed in comparison to the levels at which they have led teams and organisations to success.

It is worth highlighting that these playing experiences, gained far away from major international or domestic success, perhaps provided a unique vantage point for them to experience different methods of working and to truly value the importance of maximising potential in the absence of exceptional talent.

ROUTES TO LEADERSHIP

It is somewhat comforting to know that the interviewees did not always have a clear goal and strategy in place to become an elite level head coach. They did not sit down with a neat piece of paper and write 'GOAL: LEADER'. However, you will see that they were all willing to take calculated risks and trust their instincts as they progressed in their respective sports.

On a daily basis our brains, fuelled by our perceptions, are constantly and quietly labelling ourselves and other people we encounter. 'Leader' is one such generalised label that we might use without due consideration, based on the assumption that leadership is a characteristic one either has or has not; for example, 'he or she is a born leader'. At the same time, we may also discount ourselves from a certain category – 'I am too quiet to lead' – owing to our conditioning and existing biases.

Of course, some individuals do naturally gravitate towards leadership positions throughout their lifetime. They proactively seek responsibility and the opportunity to lead. However, for others it is a longer, more drawn-out process and something that simply evolves over time. You may be someone who consistently questions your own knowledge and experience before finally proving to yourself that you are 'worthy' of leadership. You might have a subtle emotional intelligence and empathy that means you naturally build trust and rapport with others. You could have spent a sustained period of time observing and learning from other leaders. You may suddenly have an opportunity thrust upon you that you do not quite feel ready for. For some, it is a willingness to think differently, or the experience of a critical moment, like having the courage to challenge in a team environment. It may not even be in the guise of a formal position but, in all of these examples, almost quietly and before we know it, we are leading.

FAMILY BACKGROUND

Each individual human being is a unique and tumultuous combination of beliefs, thoughts, emotions, values and behaviours. We search for meaning throughout our lives and what we come to believe is shaped by an exclusive recipe of culture, biology and psychology.

3

A key part of this conditioning is made up of our formative experiences and, when asked about their biggest influences, it came as no surprise that the leaders were quick to turn the conversations to their upbringing and specifically the role that their parents played in their development.

Michael Maguire cites his parents, Patrick and Mary, as his biggest influence and the primary source of the family values that he now looks to instil in the teams that he leads. 'Family is a big part of what I believe in; footie and family are the two most important things in my life,' he tells me.

The second youngest of six children, Maguire grew up in a sport-loving Canberra family, alongside three sisters and two brothers, and recalls that they 'really enjoyed family life and were very close'. While he has acknowledged the impact of working alongside high-profile coaches such as Matty Elliott (Canberra Raiders) and Craig Bellamy (Melbourne Storm) during the early part of his coaching career, it is his father who the Australian coach credits as his number-one influence and the source behind his own drive, work ethic and desire to keep improving: 'His work ethic was unbelievable. He was a massive part of what I did.'

Patrick Maguire drove a taxi to support his family, and the late-night fares and early starts have clearly influenced Michael, who works around the clock in his pursuit of high performance, be that planning sessions, speaking with players, having calls with other practitioners around the world, or his dedication to his own fitness regime.

Patrick was a keen rugby union supporter. So when the young Michael, after finishing high school, decided to pursue rugby league instead, he was worried to tell his father – 'He came around in the end,' he says with a wry smile.

Roberto Martínez believes that every leader has an 'inner inspiration' and identifies his own as his father. Martínez Senior was a player and manager for Spanish third-tier side CF Balaguer in the small Catalonian town, nestled between the plains and mountains of Lleida and close to the Segre River, that Martínez still refers to as 'home'. He fondly remembers kicking a ball around on the pitch at CF Balaguer with his father and, as young Roberto grew, the two became fiercely competitive, something he believes prepared him early on for a life in elite sport.

Martínez Senior 'always brought his work home' and this proximity to the sport, Martínez tells me, exposed him to the principles of management at an early age, allowing him to start to 'understand what decisions were based on, and the importance of treating people the way he would expect to be treated'.

Roberto had the opportunity to witness his dad operate first-hand in three roles – as a father, as an athlete in a team sport and as a manager. Leadership and the pursuit of excellence can be lonely places to exist; the opportunity that Roberto had, over his formative years, to observe his father has surely been a key factor in his ability to motivate his players and staff, study teams on a tactical level, and adjust his style accordingly.

Parental guidance is not reserved exclusively for childhood. When Martínez signed his first professional contract for Real Zaragoza, his father was there to keep him grounded, remind him of the importance of fitness and encourage him to continue his academic studies, an area in which Martínez excelled. He heeded the advice and attended the University of Zaragoza, studying for a three-year degree in physiotherapy and exploring his interest in the appliance of science in football.

When interviewing Roberto, and having worked as a consultant to his teams at Wigan, Everton and Belgium, I wondered if this strong paternal figure in Roberto's life had given him the softly spoken, yet firm voice that has resonated so well with his players, and made him an effective leader in his own right. For many of us, it is typically the family environment, or in childhood more broadly, where we experience leadership for the first time. That is not to say we are ever too old to seek out mentors or inspiration from those we admire. One of the suggested actions to emerge from this research for aspiring leaders is to have a personal support network in place. Have people to turn to who exist independently from your immediate environment, to offer perspective, to listen and to challenge.

A FAMILY FABRIC

Family background is undoubtedly a key component in formulating who we are as individuals and who we grow to become as leaders of our own families. Business and sport are peppered with stories of individual success emerging against a backdrop of challenging family backgrounds, histories or experiences; often a testimony to those characters, their resilience and the people who supported them along the way. Whichever stable you might find yourself in, acknowledging your family fabric and taking these lessons into your life is a key ingredient that makes us all individual.

Martínez's managerial counterpart Sean Dyche grew up in a caring and supportive family, as the youngest of three brothers in the small English town of Kettering, Northamptonshire. His father was a management consultant for British Steel and his mother a machinist in a shoe factory. Dyche retains a keen appreciation for a well-made shoe! Throughout his contributions to this book, you will notice that he regularly tries to cut through the leadership rhetoric and communicate with common sense. The Burnley boss, at times warmly referred to as the 'Ginger Mourinho', is clear in his own sense of morals and values. These values have their foundations in his upbringing and can be seen in his leadership style, as well as his comments on contemporary issues such as personal development and player simulation.

RESILIENCE AND RESPONSIBILITY

Gary Kirsten was born in Rondebosch, a southern suburb of Cape Town, into a renowned cricketing family. His father Noel was a civil engineer who later became groundsman at Newlands Cricket Ground. Newlands is one of the most breathtaking settings in sport, set in the shadow of Cape Town's iconic Table Mountain and Devil's Peak, and the young Gary spent long hours playing on the historic pitch – 'the biggest back garden in the world', he says smiling.

Noel played first-class cricket, as did Gary's half-brothers Andy and Peter, and brother Paul. Peter Kirsten, thirteen years older than Gary, played twelve Tests for South Africa, making his debut aged thirty-seven due to South Africa's omission from international Test cricket during the period of apartheid. Gary, or Gazza as he was known, looked up to his older brother in an environment where sports, predominantly cricket and rugby, were a constant and where there were 'no freebies and no easy road'. His leadership skills were honed at high school, where he captained the cricket and rugby teams, and became a prefect. As a Kirsten, you made your own choices and lived by them:

My parents encouraged me to make my own decisions. I think I made a whole lot of wrong decisions along the way but at some point, you're drifting through life, especially as a youngster, and I had to make some calls about which direction I was going to go. I was very fortunate to have cricket as something that was very dear to me as a sport. I wanted to be recognised as a good cricketer. That stood me in good stead in the early part of my life.

These early experiences would have instilled a sense of choice and consequence in the young Kirsten, strong lessons for a growing leader. Cricket became a touchstone and a constant, transforming from a pursuit to a sanctuary – an excellent way to view a sport that Kirsten would go on to live, breathe and lead.

IMMERSION: DELIBERATE PRACTICE AND PLAY

Far from Cape Town, Ashley Giles – who would go on to play against Kirsten on the biggest stage – also grew up in an environment that was conducive to producing a talented young cricketer. As a young boy, he remembers watching his father play on the village green at Ripley Cricket Club in Surrey. The entire Giles family were heavily involved at the club, where his uncle, cousins, brother and both grandfathers played. Giles would regularly be at the club until dusk, either throwing the ball and playing in the nets, or exploring the surrounding forest on his bike or on foot. It all sounds idyllic and quintessentially English, but the upbringing also instilled in Giles a resilience and an appreciation of hard work, an attribute he now sees as non-negotiable in the players he leads.

Having a strong connection to the local club, Giles observed, interacted, trained and played in the cricketing world throughout his childhood. This exposed him to what psychologists refer to as 'deliberate practice': structured practice that targets specific areas of improvement, often overseen by a coach. This theory stems from the work of Anders Ericsson[*] in the fields of music, medicine and chess, and has since been popularised by American author Malcolm Gladwell[†] in the much debated '10,000-hour rule'. Sport psychologists have built further on Ericsson's work by creating a model that combines 'deliberate practice' with the notion of 'deliberate play', the idea of unstructured and unsupervised play that still requires an increased level of skill to achieve improved results.[‡] As an example, there is a long list of Brazilian footballers who have honed their skills playing in the street or on the beach.

Our leaders' sports – football, American football, rugby and cricket – are all perfect opportunities for deliberate play. If you think back to your own childhood, whatever sport(s) you enjoyed will likely have lent themselves to multiple variations and flexible formats, played in fields, alleyways, streets and playgrounds, irrespective of numbers, facilities and even the weather. Cricket in the street, touch rugby, or knockout football in the park until sunset – no coaches or referees required.

Those long summer days spent immersed in cricket, in the form of both deliberate practice and play, likely imbued Giles with the skills, language and cultural awareness that are now a crucial component of his ability to take on the leadership and helicopter-view roles as a director within the game.

[*] Ericsson, A., Krampe, R. and Tesch-Romer, C. (1993). 'The Role of Deliberate Practice in the Acquisition of Expert Performance.' *Psychological Review*, 100(3), 363–406.

[†] Gladwell, M. (2011). *Outliers: the story of success.* New York: Back Bay Books.

[‡] Côté, J., Baker, J. and Abernethy, B. (2003). 'From play to practice: a developmental framework for the acquisition of expertise in team sports.' In J. L. Starkes and K. A. Ericsson (eds), *Recent advances in research on sport expertise.* Champaign, IL: Human Kinetics (pp. 89–110).

Across the pond, I was struck by the American family experience, and how the father of one of our leaders may not have had huge quantities of time with his son, but instead emphasised the quality of the moments they shared together.

Dan Quinn enjoyed a particularly close bond with his father. One of six, he was nurtured by his parents, Sue and Jim, and grew up in New Jersey. Despite travelling extensively for work, Jim Quinn always attended his son's football games and track meets, no matter how obscure the venue, or fleeting the event. After all, throwing the hammer, as Quinn often did, is not the most exciting of events, but that was not going to deter Jim, or prevent him supporting his son.

A reassuring presence from childhood to adulthood, his father bonded with Dan over sports, attending the Quinn brothers' football, basketball and baseball games, and creating memories that would last a lifetime, perhaps most notably taking Dan to watch his first ever NFL game. Their close relationship has had a long-lasting impact on Quinn's approach to leadership. He credits his father for instilling in him the need for discipline and for hard work, but also the importance of being there and going the extra mile for others.

This is reflected in how Quinn's players, past and present, describe his leadership. In an interview with the former Falcons' outside linebacker on the NFL website,[*] Brooks Reed is effervescent with praise for Coach Quinn, specifically about how he cares about people:

[*] Wesseling, C. (2017). 'Why is Dan Quinn the NFL's most unique coach?' NFL. com, retrieved 8 November 2019.

He's a very personable guy. When you first see him, you're like, 'Oh man, this guy looks tough.' You might be intimidated. But the second you start talking to him, he is all about you. He cares about people, cares about his players first and foremost. You can see that in the way he talks about us and treats us.

In the same article, wide-receiver Mohamed Sanu references the importance of being there for others, referring to the sense of 'brotherhood' that Quinn has instilled throughout the team. Sanu says, 'I know I am going to do my job because I know the guy next to me is going to do his. So I don't want to let that guy down.' In a sport of multi-million dollar contracts, fine skill and brute force, supporting one another may just be the glue that holds it all together.

A SENSE OF HOME

All leaders need a place to recharge, reset and re-engage. For some, that will be a particular place or person; for others, it may well be a family home, or a place that offers a constant in a brutal and rapidly changing professional world. For Stuart Lancaster, his mentor and family home have combined to fill that role.

The important role of mentors is a topic discussed later in the book. For Lancaster, however, who regularly visits other high-performing cultures, the one true mentor was his dad, John. Sports-mad Lancaster grew up on the working family farm in Culgaith, Cumbria with his three siblings, Stephen, Fiona and David. The quartet were supported by John and their mother Ann, whose Scottish heritage enabled Stuart to qualify and play for Scotland's Under-19s.

The Lancasters' Lime Tree Farm was a small working dairy farm with just three workers. Stuart has fond memories of family

Christmases when, presents all opened, his parents would rush off to milk the cows before Christmas dinner. Lancaster returned home from boarding school each summer, filling his time with a combination of sport and manual work, tasks like painting fences or spreading silage. He laughs at the memory of naively piloting farm machinery on the public roads, with nothing more than a provisional driving licence to his name. He recalls 'driving this huge tractor with silage on the back and thinking, "This can't be right, I've not even passed my test!"'

The farm has long been a constant for Lancaster. He returned to these familiar surroundings, where he is known in the small farming community simply as Stuart, to reflect in solitude on his World Cup experience in 2015. By then in his forties, he still needed his family's support, in particular his father's, who he describes as his 'rock at the start, middle and end'.

In September 2018, John Lancaster passed away unexpectedly at Lime Tree Farm, but not before he was in the stadium to witness his son win the Pro14 Championship with Leinster and restore his reputation as one of the most revered and respected coaches in the modern game.

Leinster faced a stubborn Scarlets team in the final at the Aviva Stadium in Dublin as they looked to follow being crowned champions of Europe a few weeks previously. They eventually won the match 40–32, with tries from Devin Toner, James Lowe, Sean Cronin, Jordan Larmour and Jack Conan, and thirteen points from the boot of man-of-the-match Johnny Sexton. The images of the ensuing celebrations, under the floodlit Dublin sky, are a sea of blue; players sharing the moment with their families young and old, outgoing captain Isa Nacewa – who you will hear from later in the book – lifting the trophy, and Lancaster himself having photos with the crowd before being soaked with champagne among the madness of the changing room.

That night in Dublin, John Lancaster saw his son happy again, surrounded by a community of people who Stuart believes are, in many ways, like the people of Cumbria: close-knit, loyal, humble and hardworking. Many of those same people travelled to John's funeral, held at a tiny church in Cumbria. It was full to the point that not everyone could fit in. Stuart delivered the eulogy, focusing on the role of his father in shaping the personalities of the Lancaster siblings and describing what life was like through the seasons on Lime Tree Farm.

TEACHING

Bill Walsh, the legendary head coach of the San Francisco 49ers, once said, 'The ability to help the people around me self-actualise their goals underlines the single aspect of my abilities and the label that I value most – teacher.'* John Wooden, the renowned head coach of the UCLA (University of California, Los Angeles) basketball programme also referred to his teaching attributes as the driving force behind his successes. Wooden played down any special talent he might possess, saying:

> I believe effective leaders are, first and foremost, good teachers. We are in the education business. Whether in class or on the court, my job was the same: to effectively teach those under my supervision how they could perform to the best of their ability in ways that best served the goals of our team. Effective teaching is intrinsic to effective leadership, the kind that can build and maintain a successful team. I am unaware

* Walsh, B., Jamison, S. and Walsh, C. (2009). *The Score Takes Care of Itself: My Philosophy of Leadership*. New York: Portfolio.

of any great team builders who were not also great team teachers.*

Completing this triad of coaching greatness is Vince Lombardi, the leader whose name is engraved on the Super Bowl trophy. Lombardi, a strict and no-nonsense character, took his first steps into coaching as an assistant at a local high school. From then on, he held teaching at the very heart of his philosophy, saying, 'They call it coaching but it is teaching, you do not just tell them . . . you show them the reasons.' A recent BBC article offers a player's perspective, citing former offensive lineman Jerry Kramer's comments about his former coach: 'He was a wonderful teacher. He believed teaching was the greatest profession.'†

While coaching on school fields might seem light years away from leading a team at a major tournament, it should, perhaps, be no surprise that teaching and the development of young people arise as common themes in the backgrounds of our contributors. If you think back to your school days, you will probably remember two types of teachers. The 'good' teachers, the favourites who made you feel as though you could take on the world; and the 'bad' teachers, whose lessons you approached with trepidation.

There is a fantastic, emotional video of ex-England and Arsenal footballer Ian Wright reconnecting with his old schoolteacher, Mr Pigden. Pigden had seen that the eight-year-old Wright, then a disengaged pupil from London's Honor Oak estate, needed nurturing. Talking on the BBC's *Desert Island Discs*,‡ Wright describes the colossal impact his teacher had on him:

---

* Wooden, J. and Jamison, S. (2005). *Wooden on Leadership*. New York: The McGraw-Hill Companies.
† Bysouth, A. (2020). *Super Bowl 2020: Vince Lombardi, the story behind the name on NFL's biggest prize.* bbc.co.uk, retrieved 30 January 2020.
‡ *Desert Island Discs: Ian Wright.* BBC Sounds, 16 February. 2020.

I know he loved me. I don't know why he chose me. I'm glad that he did. Once he come in, everything was so much better. I used to collect the registers from the teachers. Then they made me milk monitor. I really liked that. It was really good. I just felt important. Then what he'd do, he'd put me back into the classroom, and then my writing got better. He wouldn't let me play football if he'd heard I'd been naughty in class. He just gave me a sense of feeling like I had some use.

The two met again when Wright was filming a documentary about his career. The footballer, mistakenly believing Pigden had died, breaks down in tears on seeing his old mentor. Recounting the meeting at Arsenal's Highbury stadium, Wright continued, 'He said how proud he is of me. Then I hugged him and because he was three or four steps up, I felt like I was seven again.'

The superstar footballer is transported back to being that same young boy from the estate. Wright's voice breaks even more when describing the bond that he and Pigden, who was a pilot in the Second World War, shared:

He was one of the youngest pilots in World War II. He was one of the pilots chosen to do the flyover at Buckingham Palace. I remember him saying he was more proud of the fact I played for England than him flying over Buckingham Palace. I love that man. When he said that, he changed my life just by recognising, I don't know what it was when I was standing outside that classroom, that I needed more – and he gave it to me.

Importantly, we don't actually remember everything they taught us but, as Wright's words so powerfully describe, we do remember how they made us feel. The best teachers are able to quickly identify how to coax the best out of an individual, how to speak to them, how to push their buttons and how that person wants to receive their information. This is a rare and unique skill set. Perhaps at times we fail to identify teaching as a valid stepping stone to leading, yet teachers are able to build up hours and hours of leadership experience on the ground, and deal with a broad range of challenging situations.

I interview Michael Maguire – or Madge as he is often known – in a hotel in Leeds, Yorkshire. The South Sydney Rabbitohs, owned by Hollywood superstar and fan Russell Crowe, are fresh from their first NRL Grand Final victory in over forty years. The hotel lobby is buzzing as players come and go, the green and red of the Rabbitohs dominating against a drizzly, grim Yorkshire evening. They are here to play the World Club Challenge against the Super League champions, St Helens, and Maguire's stock is high. He has created history with the Rabbitohs and his name has been written into their folklore forever.

The sport of rugby league was founded in Australia in 1907 by a group of rebellious players discontent with the amateur status of rugby union. Since then, it has become one of the most watched sports in Australia, with the coveted Grand Final a highly anticipated event in world sport.

While the UK Super League does not enjoy the same financial backing or profile as it does in Australia, it is entertaining, tough, uncompromising and physically demanding. In the UK, the majority of teams that make up the Super League come from the north of England (Wigan, Leeds, Huddersfield, St Helens, Warrington, etc.) and are predominantly made up of players from working-class backgrounds.

Maguire is physically imposing, tough, strong, authoritative and by no means an extrovert. He is competitive and does not tolerate poor standards. Make no mistake, he is here to win. Yet underneath the tough demeanour is a leader who places the development of people and the improvement of players at the very top of his list of priorities.

Having played fewer than twenty NRL games for the Canberra Raiders and the Adelaide Rams, Madge's own playing career was cut short by a neck injury in 1998. Upon hearing the news, he recalls how he instinctively 'made a decision to stay in the game'. His teaching qualification, achieved thanks to his parents' insistence that he continue his studies at university rather than become a full-time athlete – something he describes as the 'best thing they ever did' – enabled him to teach Mathematics, Science and PE at Lanyon High School in Canberra, alongside his burgeoning coaching ambitions.

Michael describes his rise through the coaching ranks from the youth teams in Canberra to his position as head coach of the South Sydney Rabbitohs as a journey that began with some initial uncertainty:

I wasn't quite sure how I was going to do it, but I decided to head back to where I started at school-boy level. I coached them for two years and grew into the grades. I coached the young Canberra teams while also being the strength and conditioning coach. From there an opportunity arose to become a first-grade coach at Canberra, an assistant coach, so I took that role on for about three years.

Despite being 'a born-and-bred Canberra man' he made a tough call to leave the club, as he 'didn't agree with where they were heading at the time'. He took a position as assistant coach to Craig Bellamy at the Melbourne Storm: 'I was there for five years and through that journey I learnt a lot. From there, I became the head coach at Wigan Warriors for two years and then in Sydney with the Rabbitohs.'

Now a successful and experienced head coach across two continents, it is clear that the passion for 'developing young people and seeing them grow' that Maguire satisfies through coaching has teaching at its core.

A brilliant and effective teacher has the knack of being able to bring out the best in a pupil by finding a way to reach into their true character. A key component of leadership, in any setting, is exactly this, a level of emotional intelligence that allows the leader to understand what drives the people that make up their teams. Madge's mission early on in his career was to help junior athletes mature and grow as both people *and* players. A constant and genuine focus on helping others to develop and shift out of their comfort zone is the essence of leadership. Done effectively, irrespective of talent, results with naturally follow. One player might go on to play for their country and another might develop the crucial life skills that equip them for an effective transition to an alternative career. To the leader, there is equal value and satisfaction in both such examples.

'THE PUREST FORM OF COACHING'

My interview with Stuart Lancaster takes place in the evening, during an England training camp at their headquarters at Surrey's Pennyhill Park. Viewed from its quintessential English country garden, the imposing nineteenth-century building, with ivy creeping up its vast stone walls, combines traditional features, such as heavy oak panels and towering ceilings, with the modern facilities that are a requisite for elite sport: high-tech meeting rooms, state-of-the-art pitches, a bespoke sprint track, a spa, a fully equipped gymnasium and even a golf course. The facility is polished and impressive, with the physical environment reinforcing key cultural messages, leaving me in no doubt that I am in the inner sanctum of English rugby.

Lancaster enjoyed a longer playing career than his rugby league counterpart, turning out for Wakefield, Headingley and Leeds Tykes. He represented Scotland at junior level, before retiring through injury at the age of thirty. Academically, Stuart went on to complete a degree in Human Movement Studies and a PGCE (Postgraduate Certificate in Education) in PE before going into teaching full-time.

> I taught PE until 2000, so I was thirty at the time. I then took a job as Academy Manager at Leeds and did that for five years, then the Director of Rugby resigned, and I took the job. We got promoted to the Premiership and I was Director of Rugby in the Premiership. The RFU approached me and I took the job as Head of Elite Player Development for the RFU which was responsible for the academies, the England age grade teams and coaching England Saxons. I did that for three years until 2011 when Martin Johnson resigned. I got the interim job as Head Coach and became Head Coach on a full-time basis in April 2012. Within that also there was a restructure of the department and I became also Head of International Performance, so I was responsible for all the other England teams, as well as the England senior team.

This sounds like an orderly and planned progression but, for Lancaster, his initial goal was to simply be the best teacher he could be. He took up a leadership role when out of the game with injury and, in his words, 'it evolved rather than it was planned – my plan at the time was to take a more senior role within the school'.

Both Maguire and Lancaster cite their early teaching experiences as vital to their development as coaches. Maguire relates it to the 'big satisfaction' he gets out of coaching and identifies 'the growth of young people and seeing them develop' as a personal driver. Lancaster believes that teaching provides a strong foundation to excelling as a coach and cites the time on the ground as beneficial to a career in coaching. 'It is the purest form of coaching and you do it five times a day, five days a week and thirty-five weeks a year. You get tremendous practice at planning, doing, and evaluating on a daily and weekly basis . . . you are going to become a better coach.'

In contrast to his teaching experience, Lancaster's role with the Rugby Football Union (RFU) was arguably one of the most multifaceted in sport, as he spent less time on the field coaching due to the nature of international sport, where time is restricted to training camps and fixtures, and the broad demands of the role. Lancaster estimates that his time with England could be roughly divided as 50 per cent management, 40 per cent leadership and only 10 per cent coaching. As a next step, he wanted to redress the balance.

Following his departure from his role with England, Lancaster returned to his roots and spent time coaching schools and clubs in Yorkshire. The image of the former England coach teaching rugby on the fields of Leeds will have turned heads, but all the while he was planning his next move. That move came when he joined Leinster as senior coach, a role that allowed him to spend more time coaching the players, leaving the other aspects of leadership to the head coach, Leo Cullen. He now estimates that 90 per cent of his time is spent coaching and he finds the role both invigorating and rewarding:

'I don't mind what level of player we are talking about. At Leinster we have a lot of internationals away at times, but I enjoy coaching the younger players who are filling those holes just as much, to make them better.' He brings the conversation back to teaching: 'You know I really enjoyed teaching and, if someone told me I could not coach rugby any more, I would be happy to go back as a teacher. I enjoyed the lessons, the variety of sports, I enjoyed helping kids get better, when you are doing it day in and day out, you are outside, running around, you are not in board meetings and committee meetings and wearing a suit, it wins every day for me.'

In the critical moments, when individuals and teams are under-performing, perhaps results are slipping, and negative momentum begins to force a group into a downward spiral and a fixed mindset, a leader's reaction is crucial. Before we know it, it is easy to slip into catastrophic and generalised thinking, mislabelling situations, letting our biases run riot, and attempting to solve challenges with sweeping changes or searching for miracle cures. It is an interesting concept, in the heat of the moment, to attempt to shift towards a true teaching mindset. Returning to this foundation of personal develop-ment can enable us to see things somewhat differently, to take a rational and specific approach, asking pertinent questions such as 'how do I communicate with this individual player to get the message across?', or 'when does this certain situation occur, and when does it not?'

Although at times we perhaps undervalue teaching as a profes-sion, be aware of how much leadership shares with teaching and consider bringing it into your own practice. The results may well surprise you.

TEACHING AS A PERSONAL DRIVER

On the other side of the Atlantic, there are limited options for American football players to continue their athletic careers after high school and college. If you are a real prospect you enter the draft, where the thirty-two NFL clubs strategically select from the best collegiate talent. If a player does not make the draft, they might make the decision to play in the Canadian Football League (CFL) or perhaps in a European country like Germany. The opportunities to forge a career in the NFL are few and far between. To put this into perspective, in English soccer, a small geographical area compared with the vastness of the USA, there are ninety-two professional league clubs. Mention this to an American and their reaction is often one of disbelief and shock, especially if you then tell them about promotion and relegation. If a player is released from a Premier League academy there is still a chance for them to join a club in a lower professional league and make their way back to the top. Stateside, many good players finish after high school, which can still be high profile, and many more call time on their playing career after college, where some of the larger programmes, like Alabama, Tennessee, Georgia and Florida, regularly play in front of crowds of over 50,000.

Dan Quinn, Head Coach of the Atlanta Falcons, played American football at high school in Morristown, New Jersey before spending three years at Salisbury University (a Division 3 Programme):

After college was done, I got right into the college ranks and for us that is an important part of the guys' development. I did that for seven years at the college level. After that there was an opportunity to move into the NFL in a development role, which is more like an assistant to an assistant, the most entry-level position that you can have. So I worked through that way and over the next ten years I worked in the NFL [at clubs including the Seattle Seahawks, San Francisco 49ers, New York Jets and the Miami Dolphins] in that regard. I then went back to the college game for two years in a bigger leadership role, then came back to the NFL for two more in a defensive co-ordinator role. The last piece was the opportunity to come here to the Falcons, as Head Coach.

While Quinn did not train or qualify as a teacher, it is this element of the profession that he identifies as driving his passion for coaching. 'Number one I love the coaching. At the core, I think that is what we do. It is our job to use every tool we can to help teach the guys to be at their very best so, at the core, that is what I would say I am first – a teacher.'

Quinn looks to 'understand that each guy has different spots and different needs that need to be met to help them develop. We like taking every single guy as far as we can. Some are only here for a short time, and some are here for a long time, but knowing that there is a spot to hit to gain and improve, I love that.'

Sean Dyche, like Quinn, is not a trained teacher, but with both leaders an enthusiasm for teaching and a desire to improve their people prevails. Dyche enjoyed a long career as a player and took his first steps into coaching within the youth teams at Watford, a developmental phase where he relished the teaching element of the profession. 'Winning is still sort of a mindset in the youth team,' he told me, 'but you are teaching them the game and I really enjoyed that.' A key pillar to Dyche's leadership is to try to take what he has learnt and 'impart that on to others, to give them a better chance'.

His physical appearance – tall, imposing, shaven head and gravelly voice – together with the perception of him as a tough, no-nonsense centre half in his playing days, often lead to misconceptions of his leadership style. He passionately wants his players to be better than he was.

I am not judging other people but, you know, there is the odd coach who is like, 'Ah, you don't do it like I used to do it.' I don't want them to do it like I used to do it! I want them to do it ten times better than I did it. I want them to be miles in front of me. I am like that with my kids, I will give them every chance to be better than me. I always have the mindset that it is about them, not about me. How much can I impart on them to help them have a better chance of having a better career than me.

He contrasts the short-term nature of the elite level, where 'you are judged purely on winning and losing at first team level', with the developmental nature of his role. 'There is so much more to it. I love it when players move forward. Some move forward with us and help us be successful and some go on to new situations. I really like that. I really like seeing players develop and mature.'

For over ten years Sydney Finkelstein, management professor at the Tuck School of Business at Dartmouth College, has studied the practices of world-class leaders, looking to identify the characteristics that make these 'super-bosses'* truly exceptional. One common thread emerged from the research: the art and ongoing practice of individual teaching. In Finkelstein's words, these super-bosses 'did not just build organisations; they spotted, trained, and developed a future generation of leaders'.

These leaders did not necessarily teach in a traditional or formal manner, stood at the front of a classroom or boardroom, or in the guise of personal development plans and annual appraisals. Instead, they imparted their wisdom in informal settings, often spending time on the job with their direct reports. Finkelstein summarised the lessons they taught into three succinct categories:

1. Professionalism – focused on personal conduct and values
2. Craft knowledge – role-specific knowledge, skills, experience and techniques

* Finkelstein, S. (2018). 'The Best Leaders Are Great Teachers.' *Harvard Business Review*, January–February 2018 issue. hbr.org, retrieved 17 August 2019.

3. Life lessons – going beyond the work environment and holistically developing the person

Equally as important as *what* a leader teaches is *when* they deliver the message. This sense of timing is a craft, grounded in emotional intelligence and an understanding of individual drivers. Leaders will seize critical teaching moments that present themselves on the job (or on the training field) and consciously create teaching opportunities by taking an individual into a different environment.

If you reread the words of both Quinn and Dyche earlier in this section, you will note the prevalence of words such as 'develop', 'mature', 'impart', and 'improve', all terms that link to the sense of growth that is associated with teaching. Dyche refers to the satisfaction he takes from players 'moving forward'. However, what is most notable here is that the sense of fulfilment is consistent, whether that player remains at the club or goes on to continue their development elsewhere. The ongoing battle for talent in elite sport dictates that player turnover, demonstrated in the most extreme by the Premier League transfer window, is inevitable. A leader with a genuine teaching mindset will accept when people go on to bigger and better things, often maintaining the relationship, and using the transition as an opportunity to recruit fresh talent into their own organisation.

Finkelstein's work also found that these super-bosses were responsible for the development of a future generation of leaders and CEOs. From sport, he cites Bill Walsh as an example. In 2016, twenty of the thirty-two head coaches in the NFL had trained under Walsh or someone he had worked with closely. This finding, published nine years after his death in 2007 and twenty-two years after his final head coach role at Stanford University, truly demonstrates that Walsh was a man of his word and that the role he did indeed value most was that of a 'teacher'.

The ongoing application of these methods or strategies does not require special talent or training, but simply an awareness and willingness to apply the principles outlined here, in order to deliver relevant, timely and individualised development. In Finkelstein's words, 'teaching is not an extra for good managers, it is an integral responsibility'.

If you are not teaching – are you really leading?

PLAYER–COACH TRANSITION

An athlete's transition from a playing career to leadership roles can take many turns. For some a sense of purpose or duty kicks in. For others an injury may accelerate the process, together with trepidation about walking away from the sport they love. Some athletes may gravitate towards mentoring and captaincy during their playing careers, breeding a burgeoning instinct for leadership.

Gary Kirsten, Roberto Martínez, Ashley Giles and Sean Dyche all moved almost immediately into coaching following their respective playing careers. Despite the short transitions, it was not part of a long-term master plan for Kirsten, whose only senior leadership experience was as vice-captain to the South African national team of the nineties:

I just wasn't sure. It wasn't like two years prior to retiring I was clear in my head what I was going to do – absolutely not. Like any retired sportsman, I asked myself, 'What comes next?' It is quite a process for a professional sportsman when you go from being on a contract for seventeen years to nothing, and starting again and you know that's the time when most working people are on their way up. In elite sport, it is the other way; you have this incredible opportunity to earn good income and it just drops off when you retire. I really didn't know what I was going to do, literally, months before I retired.

A SENSE OF PURPOSE

Throughout his career, Kirsten naturally focused on cricket and his performance within the sport. He did not follow a clearly defined pathway to a position of leadership. Instead, it seems that leadership was somewhat thrust upon him, his experiences within international and domestic cricket, against the political backdrop of South Africa, bleeding into him leadership qualities over a period of time.

Making his international debut in 1992, Kirsten enjoyed a playing career spanning over ten years, making more than one hundred (101) Test appearances and forging a reputation as a pragmatic batsman with the ability and resilience to dictate the tempo of an innings. At one time, he held the record for the most runs and centuries in a Test career, a record now surpassed by the great Jacques Kallis.

To be an international batsman of this calibre requires a certain poise, consistency and resilience – all qualities required of a leader. It is almost as if Kirsten absorbed these by default, rather than a hard-and-fast intention. As a player, these qualities enabled him to offer his skills, and runs, on the field. As the end of his playing career approached, the contribution of these qualities continued in such a way it would lead him down a path to leadership.

When he retired in 2004, Kirsten immediately stepped into coaching. Here he offers some context about the political and sporting climate in South Africa at the time:

I felt I had something to offer young South Africans coming through, partly because we had been in isolation for so long. I was one of the new breed of players who had some exposure to international coaching. So I felt there was a gap, from a coaching perspective, to add some value. Cricket has been part of my life since I was four years old and to have put seventeen years into playing, it was almost in many ways, a natural progression.

This quote reveals the sense of purpose felt by Kirsten, to fill the 'gap' he describes, grounded in his experiences as an international sportsman amid a tumultuous and critical period in his nation's history. In certain situations, an emotional pull or purpose can bring out leadership qualities in someone that they perhaps did not know were there.

LEADER-TO-LEADER LEARNING

During their early years as coaches, both Kirsten and Ashley Giles called upon the experiences and lessons learnt during their playing careers. Giles, who represented Warwickshire for the entirety of his domestic career, enjoyed an international career spanning eight years and including the historic 2005 Ashes. Having gone into coaching after a recurring hip injury caused him to retire, he now gets a genuine satisfaction from working with people and believes he is a better coach than he was a player. 'My playing career prepared me for being a coach. I worked with some of the best coaches technically, worked with some of the best players in the world and if you are a sponge you are absorbing all the information. I don't think anyone is born a natural coach or leader – we are all mimics to a degree.'

Apple co-founder Steve Jobs once gave an interview[*] referencing Picasso's famous quote 'good artists copy, great artists steal' and

---

[*] *Triumph of the Nerds* (1996). Channel 4 Television, 14–21 April.

describing how Apple are 'shameless about stealing great ideas'. Jobs talks candidly about 'trying to expose yourself to the best things humans have done and bringing those things in to what you are doing'. Given his well-documented history with rivals Microsoft and Google, the use of the word 'stealing' may raise a few eyebrows. However, I doubt Jobs is referring to blatant stealing, but rather a deeper understanding and appreciation of what makes something special and worthy of incorporating into one's own approach. Our leaders, as alluded to by Ashley Giles above, will have noted countless lessons from the influential people in their own careers.

Gary Kirsten believes his playing background provided key learning opportunities for his career in leadership. 'During my playing career, I listened to a lot of leaders, I listened to a lot of coaches, motivational speakers, psychologists, people that would intervene in our team space and my own space to add value, trying to throw something out there that could make a big difference to you.'

Leadership is about embracing the lessons that fuel us, absorbing what others do, combining different elements, and adding a dash of personal wisdom to create a unique and eclectic approach. If you approach leadership with this mindset, you will deliver your message in an authentic and impactful way. Crucially, you will believe and model that message. A failure to do that can be evident and damning, as highlighted by Kirsten. While he appreciated some key interactions that went on to influence his own leadership style, he felt that some fell short of the impact that was required at the top level. 'There was much of it I felt people were saying just to tick a box. I didn't feel it made a significant difference to me when I was crossing the ropes when I used to go and play in pressure environments where your performance was being scrutinised every minute of the day.' As a result of that reflection, when he moved into the leadership space, he 'did not want to make the same mistake, saying things to tick a box', and vowed to be more focused in the interactions he selected for his sides.

THE EVOLVING LEADER

In the world of football Roberto Martínez began his playing career at Real Zaragoza, winning the Copa del Rey in 1994, before heading to the UK and joining Wigan Athletic as one of three Spanish players who became affectionately known as the 'three amigos'. Spells at Motherwell and Walsall followed, before he captained Swansea City to promotion to League One in 2005. After a brief spell at Chester, he retired from playing in 2007 and returned to Wales, becoming manager of Swansea City and leading them to the League One title and promotion to the Championship in 2008. In 2009, he joined another of his former clubs, Wigan Athletic, and helped them maintain their Premier League status for three consecutive seasons. Martínez made history at Wembley, as his side beat favourites Manchester City, with a last-minute header from midfielder Ben Watson, to win the FA Cup in 2013. A move to Everton followed and, after initial success, he left Merseyside and was appointed as head coach of the Belgian national team, leading them to third place in the 2018 World Cup.

Roberto experienced a short transition from player to manager as he was thrust into the role of the leader at Swansea, in an environment that was familiar to him. Such a scenario can prove to be challenging to the evolving leader, particularly in terms of role clarity and team dynamics. Players who are used to interacting with the newly installed leader as both a peer and teammate must now respect them enough to follow their guidance and direction. However, Martínez, as ever, saw this opportunity in a positive light:

My journey started in the best possible way, which is managing a group of players that I was the captain of six months
before. So I knew where they were partying, how they get
stimulated, what drives them. I knew the place and the club
inside out.

Roberto's recollection of this critical period in his career espouses
two fantastic leadership traits – an optimistic outlook and the ability
to see true opportunity in any scenario. In this case, the prior knowledge of the group provided him with a unique insight into the
motivations and lifestyles of the team. It cannot be easy to move to
the top of the hierarchy and command more respect, but the
knowledge and instincts it can engender can prove priceless.

Another distinct leader who has had a unique evolution through
football is Sean Dyche, who enjoyed a varied playing career, starting
out at Nottingham Forest for three years – 'I didn't quite make the
grade', he acknowledges – before heading to Chesterfield on loan,
where he signed and stayed for seven years. A period at Bristol City
followed – 'a tough time for me as an individual, but I learnt probably the most I've ever learnt both on and off the pitch, particularly
how to treat people' – before enjoying a loan at Luton that, in his
words, 're-birthed' him as a player. Next came three-year stints at
both Millwall, where he played alongside the likes of Tim Cahill, and
Watford before finishing with Northampton Town. His is a real journey through the professional leagues that brought about a multitude
of learning opportunities for Dyche, lessons he is now applying in
his role as a Premier League manager:

I just think you can learn so much from all these people you
encounter, particularly after the event. When you are in that
moment it is not as easy, but when you reflect back, especially

with what I am doing now, dealing with players and dealing with situations. You might remember how another manager dealt with it but then you put your own version across, deliver it in your style and your way of doing things.

His first coaching job came as a youth coach at Watford, working with then manager Aidy Boothroyd, to whom Dyche is grateful for the opportunity, especially as 'it is really difficult to get back in when you want to coach'. At Watford he learnt from Boothroyd, Dick Bate (who he describes as 'a bit of a guru'), Davy Dodds, Malky Mackay and Brendan Rodgers. He had the opportunity to follow Mackay to Cardiff but decided not to for both family and personal reasons – 'it didn't quite fit together' – and as a result, he got his first taste of first-team management at Watford.

While Dyche knew he wanted to go into coaching, he was also aware that it would not happen in a straight line:

> People go on about knowing where you want to go, but it is not that easy in football. Football is a weird game and a weird profession. I always say to go A to Z in the right order is unlikely in football, you are going to have to dart and weave to get there, so I am quite open-minded in that respect. The point is when I started coaching, I was in the youth system and I was really enjoying it. Because youth players are still malleable, still flexible. With first team players, some are, some aren't, and the pressure is whole-heartedly on winning. When the doors started opening for me along the way – and there is the difference – I was not pushing them open, they were just opening along the way. I wasn't treading on people or pushing people out of the way or trying to dominate my way to being a manager . . . it slowly opened up the right doors at the right time.

Recalling his decision to remain with Watford rather than move to Cardiff, Dyche believes that was the first time he 'really had to make a decision, rather than a door opening' for him due to circumstance. At the time, he asked himself, 'Are you going to step away from it or are you going to go towards it?' Dyche recalls that 'this situation was the one where I thought, "Right, I am going to take the bull by the horns, I want to be the manager of this football club,"' effectively completing his transition from player to coach to leader.

His time at Watford was brought to an abrupt end ('I was cruelly sacked', he laughs) due to 'a business change and a different model' being brought in by the new owners, who replaced Dyche with Gianfranco Zola. After five months out of the game, he joined Burnley where he has enjoyed a sustained period of stability and relative success, while leading the club through a number of challenging phases.

Dyche captained teams throughout his playing career and, upon retirement, was drawn immediately into coaching. Despite these early experiences and the fact that fellow players and friends saw something a little different in their teammate, it was by no means a given that Dyche would end up in the big leagues. He points to the 'darting-and-weaving' approach he applied early on in his coaching career – allowing doors to open and trusting his decision-making instinct. The ability to be fiercely driven while, at the same time, having the awareness to be flexible and open-minded about where your career could – or could not – go is a combination to apply to your own leadership. Leadership does not stop at the dressing room either. It is about making decisions for the team, but also for your career and your family. Dyche has done that, in the critical moments, to great effect.

DIFFERENT WORLDS AND COMMON THEMES

Born and brought up around the world – in Cumbria, Cape Town, Surrey, Catalonia, Canberra, New Jersey and Kettering – the background of each leader, enlivened by the characters that supported, influenced and moulded them not only through childhood but to the present day, is unique and exclusive to them. That said, there are common themes running through the course of the interviews.

Unsurprisingly, all played their sport to an excellent standard. While Lancaster and Maguire had their respective rugby careers cut short through injury, and Dan Quinn simply ran out of opportunities in the American system, the others – Martínez, Kirsten, Dyche and Giles – all enjoyed long-term careers as professional players.

Irrespective of their playing careers and different characters, a genuine interest in developing others emerged early on in our discussions. For some, like Lancaster and Maguire, that interest was formalised in the shape of a teaching career or qualification. For the others it was more informal, through the frequent and perhaps unknowing observation of their own coaches and, as was the case with Martínez, Kirsten and Dyche, regularly taking on the role of team captain – another precursor of their propensity to lead.

Another standout theme to emerge from the conversations was that of family. Each of the seven contributors highlighted the family unit as a crucial component in conditioning their adult selves. This is no shock revelation, and neither should it be assumed that each enjoyed a consistently idyllic childhood from start to finish. There were challenging times too. However, one would expect the home environment to play a significant role in shaping the identity of children as they develop through adulthood. The workings of a family as a social group can have a significant impact on an individual's self-esteem, character, beliefs and values. In our examples, the themes we explore further in the book, including work ethic, reliability, authenticity, honesty, desire, resilience and empathy, can all find their origins in the leaders' formative experiences.

THE LEADERSHIP INGREDIENTS

I was keen to explore what the interviewees felt were the key characteristics of their leadership styles. In the world of performance, organisations are constantly searching for metrics to measure output, identify patterns and examine trends. Analytics in sport is big business. However, one thing that is essentially intangible, and therefore difficult to define, is the complex behaviour of human beings.

We are unpredictable; each one of us a unique and exciting synthesis of emotions, experiences and genetics. For this reason, it can be tricky to get people functioning together. That is why groups of highly skilled, intelligent, world-class-talented people can and will fail to perform to their potential on the biggest stages. The chemistry simply isn't there.

While human behaviour is complex, the use of behavioural profiling or 'psychometrics' has long been commonplace in industry – in terms of both personal development and recruitment. I venture that many of you reading this book will, at one time or another, have completed a profile either as part of a job application or a training course. These analytical procedures are nowadays predominantly online, and range from simplistic to in-depth, looking to provide key information across a range of areas, including behavioural style, leadership style, flexibility, decision-making, strengths, areas for development, and energy.

Human beings are not orderly. We cannot be defined or reductively labelled into one box. Our behaviour shifts across contexts. We are, by our very nature, chaotic and this is what makes leadership so dynamic. However, in a leadership position, the subtle and regular application of this information can be key to communicating effectively with a range of different personalities.

THE BIG FOUR

The 'big four' of personality traits that these profiles typically measure are often derivatives of the same four attributes which can be traced back to the early work of psychologist William Moulton Marston.* Marston's 1928 publication of his book *Emotions of Normal People* developed the DISC theory that we know and use today. In a truly eclectic career, Marston is also credited with the invention of the polygraph or lie detector test and the creation of the 'Wonder Woman' comics.

Back to the psychology. The first of these four attributes can be referred to as 'assertiveness' or 'risk': the tendency to move towards challenging situations, take control, and make proactive decisions in order to achieve a goal or objective. The second is 'sociability' or 'influence', the measure of an individual's desire to proactively interact with other people. In other words, the extent of their introversion or extroversion. Let's call the next attribute 'patience', which measures the tendency to remain calm, controlled and accepting, as well as the pace at which someone prefers to operate. Finally, we come to 'conformity', which measures the degree to which an individual complies and follows the rules (or cultural norms) of a given situation, striving to do things right, avoiding error and censor.

From birth up to the age of around eighteen, we develop a relatively stable self-perception of our own behavioural style. This is

* Marston, W. M. (1928). *Emotions of Normal People*. London: K. Paul, Trench, Trubner & Co. Ltd.

what psychologists refer to as our 'self-concept', made up of the perceptions and beliefs we hold about ourselves. In his theory of personality, humanistic psychologist Carl Rogers* proposed that our self-concept is actually made up of three different components: the view we hold of ourselves (the self-image), our self-esteem, and what we would really like to be (our ideal self). Another theory interwoven into the application of behavioural profiling is Self-Consistency Theory†; the hypothesis that people will naturally tend to accept ideas that are perceived as consistent with what they believe, whilst rejecting concepts that are incongruent with their beliefs.

During this period of early development, we also begin to develop *perceptions* of what our environments demand from us. Crucially, this interaction between the self and the environment determines our behaviour.

On a daily basis I work with teams and individuals from a range of industries, exploring existing team dynamics or leadership styles. During these conversations, we often discuss the common misconception that the majority of effective leaders are assumed to be both highly assertive and extroverted. In my applied work I have profiled leaders across sport, business, and the military, and encountered many successful leaders who do not display what we might assume to be traditional leadership profiles. The tub-thumping leader may be great in one-off crisis situations, but often effective leadership comes from a gradual and consistent approach, rather than one of emotional firefighting. The motivation of teams and individuals is a skill set not solely reserved for extroverts.

* Rogers, C. (1951). *Client Centred Therapy: Its Current Practice, Implications and Theory.* London: Constable.
† Lecky, P. and Taylor, J. F. A. (1945). *Self-consistency, A Theory of Personality.* New York: Island Press.

Indeed, during our conversation Stuart Lancaster directly challenged the stereotypical image of the 'charismatic leader':

> There are charismatic leaders who are great orators who can inspire and motivate but I would say they are actually quite rare. And if they are very good at that, they are usually not as good at other things: empathy and understanding of other people. You know, so they might inspire and take people with them but, ultimately, when it comes down to the day-to-day, week-to-week leadership qualities that people need, I think that style is limited in the long run.

While assertiveness and extroversion will naturally be prevalent in some more than others, there is no way of identifying with any real certainty a one-size-fits-all personality of leadership. The contrasting examples are endless. Carlo Ancelotti, the Italian World Cup winner who has managed a plethora of European giants including Real Madrid, Bayern Munich, AC Milan, Chelsea, Juventus and Paris Saint-Germain, is respected for his 'quiet' and reflective leadership style. His book, written alongside Mike Forde and Chris Brady,* is aptly titled *Quiet Leadership* and describes the Italian's approach of calmness, serenity and stoicism. In the introduction, Ancelotti introduces his style in his own words:

> A 'quiet' approach to leadership might sound soft or perhaps weak to some, but that is not what it means to me. The kind of quiet I am talking about is a strength. There is power and authority in being calm and measured, in building trust and

* Ancelotti, C., Forde, M. and Brady, C. (2016). *Quiet Leadership: Winning Hearts, Minds and Matches.* London: Penguin Random House UK

making decisions coolly and being professional in your approach. When you watch Vito Corleone in *The Godfather*, do you see a weak, quiet man or do you see a calm, powerful man in charge of his situation?

This approach can be juxtaposed with the high energy and effervescent style of Liverpool's Jürgen Klopp, the German who is held in high regard across Europe. In an interview with club sponsor Western Union,* Klopp, who refers to his team as 'my boys', explains that he uses his natural energy as 'the reserve tank' for the team, saying that 'if the energy level goes a bit down, then I am still there, for whatever they need'.

Both, it should be noted, appear to have 'looking after their people' high up on their list of priorities.

When profiling individuals and teams, it is valuable to examine the differences that exist between an individual's 'self' (their natural behavioural style) and their 'role' (what they perceive the need to be like, in order to be successful in their role). A degree of flexibility is normal here. We all make subtle adjustments to our behavioural style at work, don't we? However, you may also be able to think of times when you have felt the need to be something that you are not or to 'put a mask on' at work in order to complete a specific task or project.

The use of behavioural profiling, or psychometrics as they are commonly referred to, is prevalent in organisations around the globe and the practice can provide great value in terms of driving team dynamics, performance and recruitment. Crucially, it can highlight the role perceptions and biases play in influencing our

* Williams, S. (2019). *Western Union presents: The world according to Jürgen Klopp.* liverpoolfc.com, retrieved 16 August 2019.

behaviours and attitudes. Take an example of a team working towards a project deadline. One individual might be highly assertive and another, working in collaboration, more cautious in their decision-making. The more assertive individual might, mistakenly, *perceive* his or her colleague as lacking drive or motivation. Conversely, the risky and dominant style could be *perceived* as being overly aggressive or controlling. Both of these perceptions have the potential to influence the working relationship and the way each individual is labelled within a group dynamic – after all, mud and labels stick, and we instinctively make judgements on others based on what we already know about them.

It is important not to fall into the trap of labelling individuals in an overly simplistic and generalising way. For example, a socially confident individual with a high level of extroversion could also be a cautious decision-maker, experiencing anxiety, or someone who requires a high degree of detail. By simply labelling ourselves and each other, we ignore the things that make us unique as individuals and leaders. With teams, leaders have to be ready to look past the obvious traits, challenge their own biases and look to understand a little more about what is really happening under the surface, or behind the mask.

It became apparent during the interviews that the leaders seemingly possessed a heightened level of self-awareness. Each leader was comfortable reflecting on their own personality and behavioural style. Sean Dyche was happy to discuss his own profile in detail. In fact, he shared the same document with the team at Burnley to demonstrate trust and why it can be a useful tool within elite sport. A manager with a 'no-nonsense' reputation, Dyche's regular use of profiling betrays his appreciation for the nuances of human behaviour. By gaining a snapshot of players' individual behavioural styles, he can tweak his communication and coaching specifically to get the most out of their performance at an individual level.

It does not require a psychologist to identify that Dyche's own behavioural style is fast-paced and impatient. However, 'that is improving, I have calmed down a bit', he assures me, and he actually listens more than people might think. He is high on the extroversion axis, as you can possibly tell from his contributions to this book and in the media. Kevin Davies, the former Bolton Wanderers centre forward, who played with Dyche at Chesterfield, affectionately referred to him as 'loud and ballsy'. Dyche chuckles when I mention this but acknowledges that Davies' assessment is 'probably not a million miles away, I do talk a lot and listen a lot', he explains. His level of risk and assertiveness is also relatively high: 'I say it, then do it, rather than say it, think about it, then do it. Once I have made a decision, that is it, we are in it to win it. I am pretty high on that, let's have it.' His conformity is low and he likes to focus on the bigger picture, but his level of self-awareness enables him to appropriately gauge the demands of a situation: 'There are certain times I have to conform, then there are certain times I choose not to, and there are certain times when I am definitely not going to!'

Ashley Giles gives his perspective on his own personality: 'Most people think of me as quite extroverted. I'm not. I am an introvert; I like my own space to think. I can have a proper party, but I have to feel comfortable with those people. If I go into an environment where I don't know anyone, people probably think I'm rude because I will probably go and try to find one of the corners!'

The introversion–extroversion axis is one that people are especially drawn to. Extroversion is often perceived as the most desirable of personality traits. However, if you allow yourself to dig a little deeper and perhaps think of someone who you would class as more of an introvert, you might consider their strengths such as creativity, analysis and problem-solving. While they may not be the loudest person in the room, they might just have a game-changing thought or idea. You will find a range of personality traits described by the interviewees. While some of these will not come as a surprise, others may evoke more interest and debate, and perhaps force you to consider the people that make up your teams from a different perspective.

RESILIENCE, GRIT AND DRIVE

One characteristic that a leader must undoubtedly possess is resilience, typically defined as the ability and optimism to recover from a specific setback or failure. The intangible term is used extensively in modern sport, as individuals or teams are regularly lauded or criticised for the level of resilience they display. The All Blacks, following their 2007 World Cup defeat to France, quickly identified it as an area for immediate improvement. Fundamentally, the most talented rugby team in the world could not perform under pressure, when it mattered the most. What followed in the coming years was a group-wide, concerted effort to target this fragility through brutal honesty, reflection, and scenario planning, culminating in New Zealand winning both the 2011 and 2015 rugby World Cups.

Research from the University of Central Lancashire and Gloucester Rugby Club* found that a 'fanatical reaction to challenge' was a key component in elite performers – individuals that the researchers refer to as 'super-champions' and those who have performed over a sustainable period at 'premiership' and international level in their chosen sport. Whilst this clearly relates to athletes rather than leaders, it is an interesting component of success that may be applicable across sporting contexts.

* Collins, D., MacNamara, A. and McCarthy, N. (2016). 'Super Champions, Champions, and Almosts: Important Differences and Commonalities on the Rocky Road.' *Frontiers in Psychology*, 6, p. 2009.

Another term, 'grit', popularised by the work and publications of American psychologist Angela Duckworth[*] and defined as the 'passion and perseverance for long-term goals', is also a key part of this conversation. 'Grit' is essentially a close relative of 'resilience'. While resilience is the ability to respond to a setback, grit is the enduring motivational drive that enables an individual to pursue goals over a sustained period of time.

Our leaders have, at key moments, all displayed their own levels of personal resilience and grit. To illustrate this, during the time it has taken to conduct and finalise these interviews, Lancaster, Kirsten, Maguire and Martínez have been sacked (a stark reality of elite sport) before successfully taking on new roles elsewhere, Ashley Giles (who was released by Surrey aged eighteen) has taken on two new roles, Dan Quinn was tasked with bringing a team back from a devastating last-minute Super Bowl defeat, and Sean Dyche has navigated relegation from and promotion to the Premier League. Every leadership position has its ups and downs but in elite sport these extremes are much more visible – stark, exposing and dangerous. That type of pressure demands a certain type of response.

Resilience is 'massive in football management', says Dyche, describing how the role of the media can have a significant impact. 'I speak to people who are not managing any more and they say that it is now ten times what it used to be. You have the normal media streams, but now you've also got your social media and they are battering people on there because social media has no governance. They can put what they want. They can put stuff about your family, about your kids . . .'

---

[*] Duckworth, A. (2016). *Grit : The Power of Passion and Perseverance*. New York: Scribner.

The prevalence of social media dictates that the opinion of others is readily available at the click of a button or the tap of a smartphone screen. Fans often genuinely believe they can do a better job than the person in the hot seat. As Dyche describes, 'Everyone has an opinion ... they say "I would do this" and "I would do that" ... so you can't be naive enough to think it is going to be easy, you have to be ready to take the hits that will come.'

Across industries, leaders at all levels will have to navigate and manage different levels of office politics and subversion. If people are not happy with decisions or changes, they communicate that in different ways: face-to-face, via gossip, online or all of the above. During these times, when tension is high, personalities clash and emotion hits a tipping point, it is crucial that a leader demonstrates their own level of resilience. With an authentic and genuine approach, most situations can be dealt with.

In Gary Kirsten's case, the family name and their sporting reputation drove the development of an inner resilience and toughness that, in his words, 'proved to people that I could be good enough to go out there and do things in my own right' from a young age. He showed this resilience when his father Noel, who he had been living with at the time, suddenly passed away from stomach cancer. The eighteen-year-old Kirsten had to deal with his father's passing and find a new place to live. He lodged with one of his teachers for six months and then moved around, before going on to settle and thrive at university. Adversity is not reserved exclusively for sporting situations and does not discriminate between the personal and the professional.

I asked Kirsten what it was really like to go out to bat in the cauldron of international cricket. In response he outlined the two attributes that, in his opinion, a truly elite batsman possesses. The first was a foundation of technique able to withstand any type of bowling.

The second was a 'determination or resilience to go through tough times'. As a batsman Kirsten, dogged and pragmatic, personified this. He recalled a specific innings against England in 1999, at Kingsmead, Durban, where his resilience was tested to the extreme:

> I was in such turmoil in my batting at that time. I was battling to make any headway and was in bad form, and was probably down to my last innings before I was going to be dropped permanently from the team, so that innings dealt with a lot of things for me. One, it made me realise I could still score runs at the higher level of the game. Two, it was defining in the test series because we were in a spot of bother. And finally, it really got my career going again.

Kirsten batted for fourteen hours (878 minutes) and posted a total of 275 runs. Impressive numbers, but his personal experience of batting is dominated by rather dark accounts of resilience and struggle. These recollections illustrate a somewhat contrary and foreboding enjoyment of the process rather than the glory. He seems to revel in the moments of battle, and his experiences provide him with a unique and unparalleled insight for leadership:

> For me, batting was always a bit of a hack, it was tough. I enjoyed the challenge and the ability to get over a very difficult period to score runs. I think I enjoyed that. Batting only really became fun when I got past fifty runs, so before that, it was always hard work. For me batting is more around dealing with failure than it is dealing with success. So you spend a lot of time not doing well, and that means you have to work it out, you know, how to get to the next innings where you can have some success. I think batting was almost, when I did well, it

was a sense of relief that I could do it. It was always a challenge for me. I had this love-hate relationship with batting. When it was good, it was unbelievable but when it was bad it was dark – really, really dark.

Kirsten's sense of determination, forged throughout childhood and his playing career, is deeply embedded in his leadership style. This is echoed by Michael Maguire, whose playing career was curtailed by a neck injury after only eighteen top-flight appearances, missing out on a Grand Final appearance in 1994. That setback acted as a driving force for his future success. 'I thought, "I *am* going to be part of a Grand Final." I guess having that goal of wanting to be a head coach, I didn't know it at the time, but I knew I wanted to be a part of a Grand Final in a big way. I didn't know how it was going to be but obviously now I have been part of some special times in Grand Finals.'

Maguire's disappointment over missing out in 1994 and his subsequent reaction to that setback is a clear example of the 'fanatical reaction to challenge' we referred to earlier. After the initial period of disappointment and reflection, he found an intense level of motivation emerged from the setback, an opportunity lying under the cloak of failure.

As you get a sense of Maguire's personality, it will not come as a shock that he describes himself as a bad loser, citing his competitive upbringing and will to win and how, at times, that leads to him confronting and challenging those around him and holding people accountable:

I don't like losing. It is one thing I've had from a young age . . . I always wanted to win. I guess that's where sometimes people see my personality as quite intimidating at times because I do

not accept losing. That is my expectation inside the organisation, everyone has got to be winning at their roles. If they are
not, well I am honest about it and I'm very open to a discussion with whoever it is and just making sure that they are
getting the most out of themselves.

Stuart Lancaster describes his sense of self-belief and his opinion
that you don't have to be an extrovert to be confident: 'I think I've
always had the self-confidence and self-belief to stand for something,
to think through my reasoning and act on it. I wouldn't say I was a
massive extrovert, but I've got enough self-confidence and belief to
have my voice heard.'

The words of both Maguire and Lancaster express a sense of
inner confidence. In Madge's case, it is a confidence to admit the
events he cannot bear. For Stuart, it is the confidence to accept who
he is.

ACROSS THE DETAIL

Taking on a leadership role is a good sign you have been successful
to date. However, from that point on it can become difficult to navigate. The role of a leader is not just about getting your own work
done, but juggling wider demands, communicating with stakeholders and remaining aware of the bigger picture and the variant
components of performance.

One of the biggest challenges for a leader, particularly early on in
a career, can be the prospect of delegation: the willingness to trust
someone else to do a job to the same standard as you would – or, to
be more specific, as you *think* you would.

This can be a leadership red flag, indicating the blessing and
curse that is perfectionism. I say this because I have seen so many

perfectionists in sport who have great drive, who are always looking to the next challenge, and are consistently searching for new ways to improve. The flip side of this is the fact that in our careers we rarely achieve perfection. That is the very nature of the beast. It can lead to people becoming highly self-critical, never satisfied and with a real propensity to stress. Think of a golfer who shoots sixty-eight but comes off saying 'it should have been sixty-six if only I hadn't three putted on the fifteenth hole', or a team member who surpasses their sales target but bemoans the deal that got away.

As a result of his perfectionism and high standards, Michael Maguire described a need for control or at least an awareness of what is going on within an organisation, despite also acknowledging that his real skill set and passion lies firmly on the field: 'I tend to put myself across all parts of an organisation. So, I know exactly what the CEO is doing, what the administration department, the marketing department are doing, all those sorts of things. Whilst I am not making decisions in those areas, I am very aware of what goes on in those departments because I utilise those in driving our whole organisation forward.'

Maguire describes his approach as 'extremely thorough in all areas of what I try to do. I guess people take that in many ways. I am going to make sure I get the best out of every single player.' However, this attention to detail appears to be driven from the pain he experienced of having a career cut short:

I learnt that if it doesn't come around, a career might finish just like that— [he snaps his fingers]. I make sure that every player will get everything out of themselves because it comes and goes very quickly. As a young kid you do not understand that and that is probably what I have learnt. To suddenly wake up one day and it is not there any more. I make sure that every player is doing everything that they can possibly do. I guess people sometimes take that as intimidating, but I know the hurt on the other side, so I just make sure that the players do not go anywhere near that.

Maguire's words illustrate the fine line that exists between a finger-on-the-pulse awareness of the bigger picture and excessive micro-management. His approach is intense, driven by a fierce inner drive and desire to be in control – something, I expect, he will always be trying to balance.

Sean Dyche describes his contrasting approach, as he looks to balance an overall awareness of what is going on across the club with the confidence to step back and let his staff do their jobs. He points out that, at Burnley, he has 'grown with the club', making it easier to know 'where everyone sits and what their roles are'. Dyche chooses areas, like the youth system, not to get involved with: 'I don't step on their toes, it is up to them to run it how they want to run it.'

Delegation is a skill that comes more naturally to some than it does to others. Think back for a moment to our earlier section on behavioural styles. Delegation is often more challenging for someone who is highly detail-oriented or conforming; they want everything to be in order, to be 'just so'. It is an easier task for someone who is at the lower end of that scale, and therefore is more focused on the bigger picture. This, however, is a key example where behavioural styles and preferences should not be used as a lazy excuse to prevent a leader from delegating. All leaders are able to delegate; for some it may simply require more conscious effort and energy. Effective delegation communicates trust to people and teams, empowers and engages staff and, ultimately, helps to drive high performance.

To illustrate, Dyche is selective in his interactions and interventions. 'I can park certain moments, although I can still have a very big say if I choose to or if the board ask my opinion, which they do, about many different things. So, it is more a case of dipping your toe in and knowing enough to understand and push and pull where needed but not too much so you dominate. I think that has been the key to it. You have got to allow the people to work, allow the departments to work. I have a rough guideline on it all, but I'm not running in and out of every department.'

When I sit down with Dan Quinn at the Falcons' Flowery Branch training facility in Atlanta, it is clear that his time is tight. Sarah Hogan is Quinn's co-ordinator of head coach operations and briskly manages his schedule to the second. Our interview is tight on time. I push my luck and squeeze an extra ten minutes from his schedule, but still leave Hogan with some additional questions for Quinn to reflect on before sending over his answers. The logistics and detail behind an NFL organisation are astounding. Around ninety players attend a pre-season training camp, and this is reduced to a playing roster of fifty-three when the season comes around.

The delineated structure of an NFL team means that the ability to delegate is an unavoidable prerequisite of the job. Quinn's staff is vast. He has over twenty technical coaches alone, with roles including assistant head coach, offensive co-ordinator, defensive line coach and specialist coaches for the quarterbacks, special teams, wide receivers, running backs, tight ends and linebackers. We haven't even considered the administration, medical, athletic performance, equipment, scouting and analysis departments.

Quinn's offensive co-ordinator at the time, Steve Sarkisian (or Sark as he is known), sits in on our interview. It is Sark who provides an insight into the intense levels of focus and energy that Quinn displays:

The thing he does better than anyone else I have been around is focus, then shift focus and re-establish focus. If he is having a conversation with you, you get 100 per cent of his attention. Then someone else comes in the door and it's on to the next one, 100 per cent focus there and it is that ability to do that for the entire course of the day. That is the energy you are talking about.

'Or I have ADD [attention deficit disorder],' Quinn interjects.

In each case, the leaders demonstrate an ability or at least an awareness of the need to let their colleagues and co-leaders breathe and work freely. They consciously strive to avoid micromanaging and suffocating their respective staffs. Equally, straight talking and immediate red flagging of any suspected under performance is key.

EMPATHY

While competitiveness and assertiveness can be construed as more aggressive and task-focused tendencies, it became clear early on in the discussions that there was a real warmth and people-focus present in each of the interviewees. An ability to empathise with their athletes was described as a key component of effective leadership. Stuart Lancaster discussed the importance of understanding the people within a team dynamic: 'I think I have always been good at understanding myself but also understanding other people and how teams work and understanding how the dynamics of operations work.'

Lancaster's words point to the fact that a large proportion of leadership is about understanding people and, in fact, a somewhat 'hard' job title is actually comprised of what might commonly be referred to as 'soft skills' – empathy, collaboration, listening and questioning. In reality, these skills are not only fundamental to leadership but to all of us who are looking to thrive and develop in the modern world.

Maguire described how his formative experiences, and having a doctor tell him he could no longer play the sport he loves, help him to identify with his players, whilst appreciating that all of them bring different qualities in creating a team dynamic. This element of his style most likely softens his more ruthless and aggressive side:

> I completely understand the emotional ride that players go through in their careers. I was never one of those great players. I was someone who had to work extremely hard to have my opportunity. To sit in that position, I know not everyone is a natural, not everyone is a superstar. It is like every other job, you have good days, you have bad days, you are not always going to be turning up at 100 per cent. Understanding the psychology of how we all work in a different way, from the superstar in your team right down to the youngest kid coming into the organisation. You have to be across so many different personalities, and the personality of your team is key when you bring everyone together.

Madge's deep passion for the sport and the fact that he would 'do anything to go out on the field and play a game now' drives him to keep doing what he is doing. He believes the players sense that fierce passion for improvement. 'I love being in the middle with them trying to work out how to get better, dealing with different personalities, you get to know them very well.' A key component of leadership is the ability to manage emotions, even in the most ruthless of performance environments.

Gary Kirsten, having performed at the highest level in his sport, understands the pressure of performance and how important it is to tailor your communication to the people you work with. 'I understand when people are really battling in that space and I have an empathy towards that. I don't believe in a one-size-fits-all approach. I would never come and impart a philosophy on a group of people and it just be that those who fit in fit in and those who don't, don't. It is not my style; I am trying to get the best out of people in whatever way I can intervene around their individual set of circumstances.'

I have seen first-hand leaders carefully flex their style in order to select the right communication tools to resonate with an individual player. In Premier League football, I remember a young player, new to the first team who, at the time, appeared to be playing down his natural level of assertiveness and making a real effort to be more sociable. As a young player, he was trying to fit in to the group's established norms. By using a combination of profiling and observation, the manager identified the player's need to belong to a group, his dislike of micromanagement and his positive reactions to challenge. As a result, the manager was able to implement some effective coaching strategies: outlining challenging targets and expectations, but allowing some freedom and autonomy; taking a gradual approach to building trust with the player, rather than overpowering him with extroversion; giving him responsibility within the team and encouraging him to speak up in team meetings.

Taking another example, this time from rugby union, I was part of a discussion about maximising the impact of a senior player. The head coach, who was detailed and analytical, adapted their style to the player, who preferred to focus on the bigger picture. In this instance the leader had to check their approach, resisting the temptation to provide thorough data and analysis, and instead communicating in a straightforward and confident manner, focusing on the opportunity to achieve and allowing the player to take ownership of their role.

Leaders know they need to subtly change their approach in order to motivate and coach different individuals. However, under pressure or tension, it is easy to respond on 'auto pilot', allowing our impulses and instincts to take over. Before you know it, the moment has passed and the damage is, potentially, done. It is during these critical moments that the most effective leaders are able to press pause and catch themselves in order to tailor their approach to the demands of the situation and individual in question.

PERSONAL VALUES

Many organisations strive to have a clearly defined culture, demonstrated by consistent and reinforced behaviours. Contrastingly, some have 'words on the wall' that are simply that. We will explore team culture in due course, but it is also important that leaders are clear and congruent with their own personal purpose and values.

Dan Quinn's personal values are heavily influenced by the military. It is a way of life that he has a close affinity to, to the extent that Quinn and his wife now run a charitable organisation supporting military families. He also involves Navy SEAL training in the Falcons' pre-season camp and it is a profession he thinks he would have entered into, had he not built a career in elite sport. 'I have always wanted to be part of a team. The military have done "team" better than anybody has, so I have a good connection to the military and my regard and respect for them is really high.'

Steve Sarkisian (the offensive co-ordinator who we met earlier) believes that Quinn's person-management reflects his values of honesty and authenticity. At one point in our conversation, Steve interjected: 'Instead of asking Coach Quinn what he is good at, let me tell you what he is good at . . . he is sincere and he is genuine, so all the messaging gets through to people because they know it comes from a truthful place and everybody, from the staff to the players, can see that.'

In a similar guise to Quinn, Sean Dyche tries to use open and honest communication to get the best out of his teams. He believes that one of the misconceptions about him is that 'Dyche just talks all the time'. However, he also places a great emphasis on listening. 'I listen a lot more than people think. I don't know about how effectively I deliver it but, in my internal thinking, I am always honest, and I try to be respectful. I try to help guide players, guide them rather than just tell them all the time, I try to be open-minded, I try to have open discussions, open lines of communication. I think communication is important. I think I am a reasonable communicator. I think I know the balance between seriousness and laughter. It's a fine line but it's an important line.' Even Dyche's choice of language in this instance indicates a dual commitment to his personal values and those of the club – an indication of the 'fit' that exists between them.

Roberto Martínez's treatment of people is always based on respect. The Belgium coach described how he will always try to treat people the way he would like to be treated: 'I would not expect people to embarrass people in front of others. I never want to let anyone down and that can be from a purely professional or a human point of view.'

Gary Kirsten found the question of personal values a difficult one to answer, despite having been asked it a great deal during his career to date. 'I think as an individual, from a values perspective, people often ask me, "What has been your mantra or reasons for success?" It is always a difficult thing to answer. I think every one of us has a trait, or characteristic or an attitude that helps us through, helps us manage the direction that we move into.'

A solid pillar of Kirsten's values and purpose now lies in his clear sense of faith, something which first impacted him as a young boy at Rondebosch Boys' Prep School. While his early experiences as a young professional athlete led him away from these beliefs temporarily, a reconsideration of his own purpose led him to make a long-term commitment to the Christian faith. The night before his marathon innings at Kingsmead, where Kirsten contributed 275 runs, a conversation and prayer with his wife Deborah reaffirmed his faith. It is this faith that underpins Kirsten's approach to leadership, an approach based on what he can offer to those around him, and allows him to embrace the experiential qualities of the rigours of leadership.

To illustrate this further, Kirsten steers our conversation towards the commercial side of sport and how, for him, 'it has never ever been about the money'. This rebuttal may provoke some scepticism, but Gary talks about the financial element with a sense of clarity that demonstrates a healthy relationship with regard to his role, his remuneration and his priorities:

> 'The money for me is a by-product of what you can do. I am not driven by the money. In fact, I have negotiated one or two of my contracts down, where I think I am being paid too much. I understand where my values sit financially and if an organisation wants to pay me more, I am not comfortable with that. I would rather sit in a space where I know where my value is.'

A leader's self-awareness enables them to acknowledge their own personal drivers. If financial terms are important, there is nothing wrong with that, but it should never impede a leader's judgement and commitment to the organisation.

During his time as England head coach, Stuart Lancaster was widely known for placing great emphasis on values and standards. When describing his own values, he reflected succinctly, 'I would say that I am honest, hard-working and authentic so what you see is what you get, and I have got good integrity and good moral values. I do what I say I am going to do.' I don't think anyone, even his fiercest critics, would argue with that.

Ashley Giles relates one of his key values, authenticity, to his ability to make tough calls: 'It is about being true to yourself. If I can wake up in the morning or go home at night and look in the mirror . . . I have to hire and fire people, that is not a nice position to be in because I have been on the other side of that . . . so you have to do it right.' Giles references the duality of leadership. Invariably, there will be days when you don't like what you have had to do, but if you are safe in the knowledge that your actions ultimately align with the values you set at the start, it will make it that little bit easier.

Interestingly, he also provides a caveat to the importance of authenticity, describing how a leader may need to be selective in their communications:

> You do have to be authentic, but sometimes you put on a show because there will be situations when you are paddling like hell under the water but you can't show it to the players – 'oh we're cool, we're fine, don't worry about it' – and that can be quite wearing as well.

This proves an interesting insight from Giles. I believe what he is saying is that there are times when protecting the team comes before a leader's personal preference for authenticity. The leader shields the group from external issues, allowing them to focus on their performance. Not sharing information can cause deep issues in any environment, sport or otherwise, when a team is faced with times of uncertainty or change. A leader, in a misguided attempt to protect their people, may not be completely honest. This conveys uncertainty and, as a result, the leader appears as if they are either lying, deluded or untrustworthy. In the end, the truth will almost always come out. In such instances, leaders must openly communicate the information they *can* share, even if they can't share everything.

Maguire describes how his values and sense of family dictate both his coaching methods and his outlook on life – 'I am big on family. I think that is what a club is all about, a sense of family. You have your good times and your tough times, whatever it might be, but you are all going through it together. The tightness of that family or team, the tighter that becomes, the stronger the bond and the more you are willing to do for each other. That is what I work hard on and that is how I look at life.'

Continuing the subject of family, several of the interviewees described the change in perspective and values that occurred when they met their partners and started a family. Giles described his own experience of meeting his Norwegian wife, Stine: 'I definitely went through a transition as a player and a person when I met my wife and had kids. Suddenly your perspective just changes to what is important.' Gary Kirsten described the impact of his wife Deborah on his Christian beliefs: 'From a values perspective, I think meeting my wife guided me in a direction to understand my life outside of sport. She gave me some good direction in terms of my values system as a human being. She played a strong mentoring role in that space. It was massive for me.'

As individuals, we all have different components of our identity that make up our self-image and self-esteem. As an example, one person alone can be a lawyer, a leader, a mother, a sister, a daughter, a friend, an athlete, a coach and a Christian. A common pitfall of a life in elite sport can be the dominance of the 'athlete identity', where an athlete (or leader in this case) becomes solely known for their profession and absorbed by its demands. There are countless examples of an athlete becoming a parent and their outlook changing overnight. In the quotes above, Giles and Kirsten are describing the sense of perspective that relationships, and the diverse 'roles' that come with family life, can provide.

A leader who aspires to be congruent with their personal values is arguably more likely to inspire others to loyally drive a high-performance environment. Scattered throughout the interviews you will see words like open, honest, genuine and authentic. These words can, at times, seem at odds with the cut-throat and seemingly mercenary nature of elite sport. However, as in business, the values of a leader can set the tone for an entire organisation, therefore having an impact on long-term performance and results. It is the actions of a leader, not the words on a wall, that represent their true character. Leaders must make tough calls and effectively communicate those decisions. If those decisions are made from a solid foundation of personal values, of respect and sincerity, then even the most disappointed athlete must ultimately reciprocate that respect.

CHAPTER 1: LEADERSHIP LESSONS

- There is no clear road map to leadership. Whatever route you take, trust your instincts and be prepared to take a risk when the time comes. It may not happen in a straight line.
- You do not need to be the most talented or skilled person in order to lead – be vulnerable enough to delegate, trust and empower those around you.
- Embrace your background and the people that support you, however varied or untraditional they might be. The traits you develop during your formative experiences will form the bedrock to your own leadership style.
- Many of the most effective leaders are teachers at their core. Consider the lessons you impart, and how and when you deliver your message. This does not necessarily require 'talent', but rather the willingness to consistently apply a teaching mindset.
- Effective leaders possess myriad personality characteristics – there is no right or wrong profile – but resilience and empathy, delivered in your own way, are non-negotiables.
- Regularly reflect on the leadership lessons (good and bad) you take from others: absorb, listen, write, learn, mimic.
- Consider your own personal values and where they come from. They play a crucial role and will guide you when making decisions in the critical moments.

CHAPTER 2

Approaches to Leadership

....

THE INTRIGUE OF LEADERSHIP

In the modern world we can access a multitude of sources – from academic research, books, social media and blogs to speeches, TED talks and podcasts – that enrich our discussions about leadership, and that might lead us to consider it a contemporary issue. But this is not a new phenomenon. The study of leadership has long been of fascination to the wider population. There is something curiously compelling about attempting to understand the set of traits and qualities that inspire others to action.

TRAIT THEORIES

Early theories focused predominantly on the identification of individual characteristics and traits that were to become associated with successful leadership. This way of thinking can be traced back to the mid-nineteenth century and the philosophies of historian Thomas Carlyle. The 'great man' theory* suggests that history is shaped by the presence of extraordinary leaders, and that these individuals are highly influential due to genetics and the natural presence of wisdom, skill or charisma. Charisma, after all, is the Greek word for 'gift'. In other words, leaders are born and not made, and their

---

* Carlyle, T. (1840). *On Heroes, Hero-worship and the Heroic in History. Thomas Carlyle's Collected Works.* London: Chapman and Hall.

possession of such traits allows them to impact events in a way that ordinary people simply cannot. Only 'great' people – the likes of Gandhi, Lincoln and Napoleon – were deemed to possess such traits.

Over time, such a narrow focus on the prevalence of individual characteristics has been refuted as research and experience has evolved. Despite this, the trait theory* of leadership, which is effectively a more considered and systematic approach than the great man theory, remains influential, as illustrated by enduring intrigue about the ingredients of effective leadership. In its definition of leadership, trait theory acknowledges a wider range of personality, social, physical and intellectual attributes. It is also important to note that the specific attributes we debate in modern society have also evolved. In the past, the likes of Thomas Carlyle and his contemporaries may have identified things like ambition, dominance and authority, whereas in today's literature, you are more likely to find words like trust, authenticity and emotional intelligence. Irrespective of this advancement, these theories have been found to hold little predictive value, as there is no universal trait that can anticipate leadership in all situations.

AUTHENTIC LEADERSHIP

More recent theories of leadership look to acknowledge the role of both the environment and the group in establishing the effectiveness of leadership. You may well have heard people using the term 'authentic leadership'. In 2004, as a response to the constant stream of emerging corporate scandals, Harvard Business School's professor of management practice, Bill George, emerged with a theory

---

* Zaccaro, S. J. (2007). 'Trait-based perspectives of leadership.' *American Psychologist*, 62(1), 6–16.

grounded simply in doing the right thing. Stemming from discussions with 120 leaders across a range of organisations, George's work identified the importance of a leader's purpose, values, heart, relationships and self-discipline. In other words, their inner compass, their morals, their true north.

While George's book, *Authentic Leadership*,* has brought the term into the public consciousness, in reality the concept of authentic leadership has been around for a number of years – in Hamlet, Shakespeare penned the famous line 'to thine own self be true' – and is more an ongoing discussion than a structured theory. The authentic leader focuses on improving performance by building open and trusting relationships with others and puts the organisation before their own personal ambition.

TRANSFORMATIONAL AND TRANSACTIONAL LEADERSHIP

In sport psychology, research has focused on the transactional and transformational theories of leadership, with both exploring the importance of relationships in improving performance. Transactional leadership, however, depicts the exchanges that occur between 'leader' and 'follower', by placing the leader in a position of power, at the top of a hierarchy, and using reward and punishment to galvanise the group. This approach is still widespread, as businesses and organisations regularly use incentives to encourage certain behaviours and make clear to those who fail to comply that there will be consequences. Consider the case of a head coach who entices athletes with the promise of a social event, a night out or, amid the affluence of elite sport, an end-of-season trip. On the flip

* George, B. (2004). *Authentic Leadership: Rediscovering the Secrets to Creating Lasting Value.* New Jersey: John Wiley & Sons.

side of this, there have been examples where such events (think Christmas parties) are cancelled due to poor performances. In this instance, the coach holds the power and it may well drive the desired result in the short term. This is an example of a transactional approach to leadership.

Contrastingly, transformational leadership outlines that it is the leader's ability to inspire group behaviours through the communication of an aspiring vision and the creation of relationships that are the key drivers of high performance. In the aftermath of the 2019 Rugby World Cup, England's head coach Eddie Jones talked about how his own style – which is typically direct and tough, more transactional – has had to be balanced with a constant awareness of what he referred to as 'performance relationships', the need to understand the individual people within the group.

SOCIAL IDENTITY

Most recently, researchers at Staffordshire University[*] have focused on the application of the social identity approach to leadership, with specific reference to sport. They contend that effective leadership is formed as a result of leaders and athletes sharing a sense of belonging and, crucially, an emotional and meaningful attachment to the group. This feeling of being in the 'in-group' contributes to our sense of identity and, in turn, impacts the mindset and actions of both the individuals and the collective.

Danny Kerry is the current head coach of the England and Great Britain men's field hockey teams. He was also the head coach of the

[*] Slater, M. J., Coffee, P., Barker, J. B. and Evans, A. L. (2014). 'Promoting shared meanings in group memberships: a social identity approach to leadership in sport.' *Reflective Practice: International and Multidisciplinary Perspectives*, 15(5), 672-685.

women's team that claimed numerous titles, including the Olympic gold medal at Rio 2016. He is the most successful coach in British hockey history and, perhaps unsurprisingly, is someone other coaches are keen to meet. Eddie Jones and Gareth Southgate, the current leaders of English rugby and football respectively, have both sought him out and publicly referenced Kerry's work. In 2008, however, Kerry found himself at a professional cross roads. During a post-Olympic review of his performance in Beijing, Kerry had to digest some brutal feedback from the people closest to him, his colleagues and players. They told him in no uncertain terms that, at his worst, he was intense, grumpy and unapproachable. As a result of his own reflection over the ensuing years, he switched his leadership style from one that focused on information and analysis, which therefore lacked engagement, to one that now focuses on common purpose, distributed leadership, collective ownership and collective review.*

Throughout the following chapters, you will see clear examples of some of the theories summarised here. Yet despite the multitude of theories that have been proposed and the increasing coverage of effective leadership, we have still not settled on one defining model. The reason being, perhaps, that each individual 'leader' is a unique mixture of characteristics, experiences, beliefs and values.

---

* Richardson, B. (2015). 'How High Performance Coach of the Year Danny Kerry has put the Great into British hockey. community.ukcoaching.org, retrieved 26 November 2019.

LEADERSHIP PHILOSOPHY

TO BE . . .

A well-defined 'philosophy' is often cited as a prerequisite to effective leadership. In light of this, I sought to explore the interviewees' perceptions and interpretations of the concept. A philosophy can be defined as a cohesive way of thinking about a specific role and is often an extension of the leader's own personal values. In the fast-paced, volatile and dynamic environments where these coaches operate, a clear philosophy can help guide them through the difficult decisions and tough calls that they invariably need to make.

The use of the rather grandiose term 'philosophy' is a nod to the sometimes over-intellectualised aspect of sports leadership. Perhaps we are guilty of overcomplicating it at times. As Richard Gillis examines in detail in *The Captain Myth*, golf's Ryder Cup is a suitable example, as every two years the United States and Team Europe compete in the sport's premier competition. At the risk of overgeneralising, if a captain leads a team to victory it seems as though they are quickly classified as a 'good' captain who has successfully united a team of individuals, and every intervention and idea is cited as an example of elite-level leadership. Everyone wants to know their philosophy. Having worked in these environments, it is usually not the captains themselves who promote this view, but rather it is another symptom of our ongoing fascination with leadership.

If a captain does not return with the coveted trophy, they are placed in the 'bad' category, all of their ideas defunct, and often confined to history. Those who have witnessed such an environment first-hand might point to specific examples where a captain has led the team effectively but they have ultimately been beaten on the scoreboard by a superior opponent, or a captain who perhaps struggled to unite the team but benefitted from a talented group of players in great form who claimed the all-important victory. This is another illustration of one of the inevitable realities of leadership – to the victor go the spoils.

The 2012 Ryder Cup provided drama like no other – the 'Miracle of Medinah' – where a final-day fightback from Team Europe produced a scintillating victory over the US team, who held a four-point lead going into Sunday's single matches. Over the course of that day, we witnessed a remarkable turnaround, a piece of sporting history, and a curious switching of leadership narratives.[*]

José María Olazábal's leadership had been questioned over the first two and a half days of the competition. He had dropped one player, Peter Hanson, for an afternoon session, yet only communicated this fact twenty minutes before Hanson thought he would be teeing off. Other selection decisions had also been questioned, and this was all before Rory McIlroy almost missed his tee-time due to poor timekeeping for his final-day match with America's Keegan Bradley. With a four-point deficit to overcome, one can imagine the looming media onslaught.

Simultaneously America's leader, Davis Love, had seemingly executed a structured plan perfectly. He was sitting pretty, looking likely to dispel the lingering rumours of a lack of team spirit within Team America. Suddenly, as the match began to turn, so did Love's narrative. McIlroy, arriving in a police car, delivered his point. Justin Rose holed a preposterous putt that he had a 1 per cent chance of making, before Martin Kaymer sealed Europe's victory. With that shift in momentum, it was Love's decisions that were being critiqued and Olazábal's inspiration lauded.

---

[*] Gillis, R. (2016). *The Captain Myth: The Ryder Cup and Sport's Great Leadership Delusion*. London: Bloomsbury.

Sitting in an office at Burnley's impressive state-of-the-art train-ing ground, where the first words any visitor sees are 'Legs, Hearts, Minds', Sean Dyche visibly recoils when the word 'philosophy' is mentioned; he doesn't like to overcomplicate his approach and gives his thoughts accordingly:

> It is still football. We are a football club. Using the word 'philosophy', I mean it's pseudo-intellect, isn't it? It is putting yourself in a bracket of deep, guru-type thinking. That is the word philosophy in my head – life philosophy – and that's when I go 'no, no, hold on a minute'. I just think you have to be careful. The thing that annoys me: if you haven't got a philosophy nowadays, you are almost deemed a dullard. How is that right? You can still be a really good planner and have ethos, culture, environment and all those words, but when you talk about philosophy . . . it is just a bit of a grand term for someone who is talking about football. It can be a little bit heavy for me.

Despite Dyche's views and the intellectual connotations, 'philoso-phy' is still a widely accepted term to describe an individual's beliefs regarding their approach to building the culture that enables a team to thrive in an elite sporting environment. What is refreshing here is Sean's openness around pursuing leadership on his terms, and shunning the more populist demand for a convoluted 'philosophy'. In a convex way, his dismissal of an overarching philosophy is a part of his own leadership philosophy.

OR NOT TO BE . . .

The leaders, when asked to describe their own philosophy, often found it a difficult task. Their responses were largely reflective and unstructured, some talking about their philosophy in leading people and others describing their beliefs of how their sport should be played. This variance hints at the intangible nature of a philosophy, a notion that underpins the behaviours and actions of a leader, that is undeniably present but yet is not always easy to articulate.

Stuart Lancaster clearly differentiates between his philosophies on and off the field. 'There are two philosophies really. One is on-field philosophy, so how you play the game and the type of game you want to play. The second is your off-field philosophy and how you lead people. I think I would say that my off-field one is based on the principles of honesty, integrity, people being authentic, and inspiring people with a vision for the future.'

He describes the long-term and transformational approach he took as England Head Coach. 'I picture a vision for the future and lead people towards it. I am always thinking ahead to the next thing, the next stage, the next week, the next month.'

This need to have a present view, keeping an eye on short-term results, but also maintaining the pursuit of a long-term vision, can be applied to life in both elite sport and business. The dual approach that Lancaster references here also prevails in the world of cricket. Ashley Giles, like Lancaster, described his desire to genuinely impact an organisation in the long term, linking it to the concept of leaving behind a legacy, 'not just improving them as cricketers but trying to improve people, trying to improve culture, trying to improve and leave behind something better than what you take on'.

Discussions around leadership often refer to this notion of legacy, and the value of leaving a long-term impact upon a group. While this is a topic we will examine in more detail later in the book, purpose-driven and long-term thinking gives the position of leader a unique degree of pressure: one that requires a cool head and the ability to manage personal stress, particularly when fans or customers start to show unrest or dissatisfaction with results.

Roberto Martínez spoke about his unwavering on-field philosophy, something that has gone both for and against him over the course of his career. During his time at Everton, Martínez led the team to European qualification and their best ever Premier League points total. However, the following year, despite two semi-finals, supporters became frustrated when the same style of football failed to produce the results they had started to expect at Goodison Park.

The foundation of Martínez's steadfast philosophy can be traced back to his Catalan roots. As a youngster, Martínez recalls having divided loyalties when it came to football. His mother, who ran the local shoe shop, was a Catalan, supporting Barcelona, while his father hailed from Zaragoza. Roberto was caught in the middle, until Johan Cruyff arrived at FC Barcelona, captivating Martínez and making the decision of who to support that little bit easier. Incidentally, Cruyff's early years in Barcelona did not bring immediate success, but the style of football and his fierce long-term commitment to it not only laid the foundations for a sporting dynasty that endures to this day, but hooked the young man from Balaguer who would go on to lead and manage at the biggest competition in the world.

Cruyff's philosophy of possession football and numerical advantage remains the driving force behind how Martínez sees the game. He is firm in his beliefs, adding the layer of resilience that allows him to withstand critics' calls for a change in style. In order to achieve this on the field, he looks to instil in his players a strict level of personal responsibility. If they are going to meet his demands, the players must have the self-belief and confidence to play in a certain way. 'I want the players to be thinkers, to take responsibility. I want to control the game, get on the ball, break things down and score goals. To do that you need to feel good about yourself. You need to trust yourself and your team.' In order to achieve this emotional state, off the field he focuses predominantly on individual engagement with his players: 'I am always intrigued by trying to engage with a person on a one-to-one level in order to get the best out of them. That is very stimulating.'

Martínez seeks to impart his philosophy within the team, with the aim of seeing his preferred methods prevail on the field. It is an interesting approach that places clear emphasis on the players, investing them with a level of responsibility that shows, rather than tells them, that they are trusted and respected by their leader.

Michael Maguire's on-field rugby philosophy is simple and almost romantic, harnessing a love of the game and making players feel like kids again. 'It is easy to lose perspective and it's actually about bringing the players back to the understanding that if you can play under pressure like you played in the backyard and you have got a free mind, you are just enjoying doing what you do. You are at your best when you are back in the backyard.'

Here Maguire – like Dyche – describes almost an anti-philosophy. At times, he will reject the complexities, the pressures and the stresses of the big game, in favour of something more basic and inherent. By reminding players to enjoy their rugby and reconnect with the 'backyard' mentality, he builds a sense of freedom. Maguire combines this awareness with high standards of behaviour which sometimes might feel like a contradiction, but their co-existence has achieved results. By contrast, over in the NFL, we see something more deliberate.

CRITICAL MOMENTS

In training sessions, Dan Quinn is always looking to replicate the critical moments and scenarios that players will face in the heat of competition. He looks to implement his team philosophy on a day-to-day basis. 'I think it is all the things that go into coaching that makes it unique. It is the strategy, it's the connection with the players, it's the intensity of the moment, you know in the game, in practice, those are the moments when you feel most alive, when the game is on the line, the toughness of it all, I like those environments. We try to create them as often as we can in practice so when we get in to those spaces, we can perform.' Psychologically speaking, by embracing the emotions and mindsets of tough moments, our brains are better prepared to respond appropriately when we encounter them in a competitive environment.

Of all the coaches it is Quinn who focuses predominantly on the on-field application of his philosophy, actively trying to replicate in-game situations in practice scenarios. Whilst all of our leaders will look for their players to embody their approach on the field, it is perhaps the stage-by-stage, play-by-play nature of the NFL that allows Quinn to foster this in more detail. With carefully constructed offensive plays and more regular coach co-ordination, teams can rehearse scenarios so that when they occur in real time, they are as prepared as they can be. The other sports, by contrast, are more dynamic and reactive, relying on players' real-time responses on the pitch.

Two sacrosanct qualities that Quinn demands of his team on the field are *competitiveness* and *toughness*. 'We would hope someone would say "they are a really competitive team, they really work at it against one another", and "they are a really tough team, their physicality, and the way they compete against each other".' These on-field attributes are non-negotiables for Quinn, and things he looks to actively track and measure with his staff, reflecting his own intense level of commitment, energy and desire in driving the environment he has created within the culture of the Falcons.

RESPONDING TO CHALLENGE

A leadership philosophy comes under increased internal scrutiny when dealing with specific challenges. Stuart Lancaster describes the role his own beliefs and values play when making high-profile decisions:

> When I get faced with a decision about what direction to take, I often fall back to what I believe, what is my personal philosophy, where do I stand? And I am constantly checking and self-checking where I sit on one position or another and often it's, maybe it's from another manager or another sport, I am looking and thinking what would I do in that situation?

Lancaster, speaking ahead of the Rugby World Cup in 2015, went on to describe his high-profile situation at the time:

> In this job, it is real because now I am really in the sharp focus of the media and even some of the decisions I've made in the last week or two ... you are now getting questionnaires in newspapers or people can get a chance to vote 'Would you have done the same thing?'. So every decision you make gets scrutinised, so you have got to be clear in what you believe. I do not think I could do this job if I wasn't clear on my own personal philosophy.

He provides an insight into the much-debated subject of selecting foreign-based players to play for England – a decision that was made by the Rugby Football Union (RFU), not by Stuart alone:

> Perhaps we would have gone down a different route and just picked everyone we can and not worried too much about the long-term consequences, but that has never been my belief, so if you go back to what you believe in, then you have got to act on your beliefs and my belief was I wanted to create a team that would win in the short, medium and long term. And I was acutely aware that we have all played a huge role in developing a strong sense of team and team spirit.

Here, Lancaster is telling us that while the presence of an ingrained philosophy (a clear set of values and way of doing things) does not necessarily mean that making the tough calls becomes easier, it does become a more congruent and resilient process. Knowing you are acting according to your own long-established principles lends a confidence and psychological safety to decision-making, which ultimately leads to more authentic and effective leadership.

CONFIDENCE IN CHAOS

Gary Kirsten illustrated how his philosophy has helped him to deal with the unpredictable nature of elite sport. The South African offers perhaps our most 'philosophical' philosophy, describing the importance of failure in long-term development and improvement:

> Over time, I have been able to understand the concept of winning and losing and the idea that the result, whatever it is, helps in the learning process of life. Rather than the result is

just an end to itself, the result is a way to take your journey of life forward and it is a question of how you manage yourself in that result. I have often found that, if you are open to it, you can learn a huge amount from failure. To the point where that has almost become more relevant, how you manage your journey through the failure.

Where it would be easy to catastrophise failure – especially in the stark visibility of elite sports – Kirsten is ready and able to take a step back and look at failure as an opportunity to learn and actually gain something from a negative experience. This ability is closely linked to our explanatory style (how we attribute something that has happened to us) and Kirsten takes a much more rational approach that will, in turn, lead to more solution-based, specific and controllable thinking. In contrast, catastrophic thinking can lead us towards fixed, uncontrollable, generalised and problem-based modes of thinking.

Kirsten's philosophy is grounded in the idea of learning from both defeat and victory. From that central facet he is in a position to build a philosophy that he can rely upon as a leader. He warns of the dangers that can come with 'living the results' as this can, he tells me, 'eat you alive'. He strives to stay level-headed after victory or defeat, always reflecting ('it's about the journey') on the lessons learnt. Perhaps surprisingly, he enjoys 'the process of getting to the match' much more than the match itself. This cornerstone of his philosophy allows him to control as much of his teams' experiences and mindsets as possible.

INTUITION

Sean Dyche views leadership as 'knowing what to do when you don't know what to do'. There are times when you have to trust your intuition and allow natural instincts to play their part. 'In football, it is not always about structure and strategy, it is about feel. Sometimes you have just got to feel what is needed. You can't write it, you can't go and read it in a book. You have just got to smell it, trust yourself and know where it is going to take you, because it is you that has to make the decision.'

Despite Dyche's staunch opposition to the word, it can be argued that it is the presence of a clear 'philosophy' or method that allows someone to trust their gut, and act accordingly in those critical moments when the textbook doesn't provide the answer. In the book *Blink*,[*] the Canadian author and journalist Malcolm Gladwell discusses the concept of 'thin-slicing' – an expert's ability to make rapid-fire decisions and inferences based on little information. Indeed, effective decision-making is not always directly correlated with the time taken to make such a choice. If you travel back in history, our ancestors had to develop the ability to trust their instincts and make split-second decisions in order to survive. Gladwell provides a perfect example of this phenomenon from the world of art – specifically, an expert who can tell a piece is a forgery at first sight. At times, the expert cannot provide a direct rationale for their decision, instead referring to a feeling of instinct or intuition.

The key point here is that decisions can still be made effectively in the absence of data and information. Judgements, on the other hand, are made as a result of accumulated experience and knowledge in a specific field. The same can be said of leadership. Sometimes, you just know what to do – so back your judgement.

[*] Gladwell, M. (2006). *Blink. The Power of Thinking Without Thinking*. London: Penguin Books.

CONSISTENCY OF APPROACH

A philosophy is by nature relatively high-level, providing an over-view of an individual's approach. But it can also inform the precise methodologies and behaviours that leaders employ in their roles. The presence of a clear philosophy forms a key component of a leader's identity and purpose. It provides the guiding principles and internal congruence to influence decision-making and is a source of confidence to work in a robust, consistent manner over a sustainable period of time. While it does not guarantee results, it helps to provide clarity and focus to a method of working. Longevity and persistence of approach is a crucial part of authentic leadership.

Roberto Martínez vividly described his steadfast commitment to his leadership method, offering an insight into his approach which both delighted and frustrated the supporters of his teams at Wigan and Everton. He works 'with the same principles, the same philosophy, the same staff and with the same ideas'. He is acutely aware of his methods and style of play and his commitment to them remains steadfast, enabling him to work with players in a focused way.

I have never ever changed the way of working in ten seasons. It is true that the demands, the commercial aspects, the travelling and probably the type of player affects the way you work. But the method has never changed. The hours I spend on the training ground now are the same as I did ten years ago. The way of working should be the same, you shouldn't lose your role within the organisation.

Roberto's philosophy and personal approach is unwavering, allowing him to use his core tenets to focus on the team at hand, successfully applying them, rather than constantly resetting and shuffling the pack. This consistency of approach allows him to establish his position quickly and not get lost within vast organisations. It must be said, however, that the nature and time constraints of international football, in his role as manager of the Belgian national side, have challenged this approach and encouraged Martínez to flex and adapt his core style.

MANAGING EVOLVING TEAMS

The need for consistency in leadership is supported by Gary Kirsten, who notes that this is particularly crucial through the constant and evolving experiences that teams encounter over a period of time. Talking ahead of his final year with the Indian Premier League (IPL) franchise the Delhi Daredevils, Kirsten says, 'You always need more time. I am in that position now; we have had two poor seasons and I have got one more year on my contract and I am going to pick the players up one week before the season starts. It is a refocus on where we want to go this year but if you can create some continuity from year to year it makes the job a lot easier.'

Particularly in sport, there are times when you have to pick up and lead teams swiftly. Knowing your own mind and approach allows you to do this confidently and instinctively. By constantly reflecting upon your own philosophy, you can use that and the methods it breeds to generate behaviours and results.

As an organisation, Burnley Football Club have successfully navigated one relegation from and two promotions to the Premier League. By his own admission, it is easy to make assumptions about Dyche's methods due to his physical appearance. He assures me that this 'is just the way life works, six foot skinhead, gruff voice, so people immediately go to labels like aggressive and dominant . . . well my players will probably tell you I am not that aggressive, now and again when I need to be, but not really. Dominant, no. I think they would say "he will talk to us, he'll listen". I think I am modern enough to know where we are going and know what's needed to get there. And I think I am old-fashioned enough to know it still takes hard work, grit and determination.'

Dyche's awareness and sense of self is unwavering. He seems to lead without doubts, or that is how it appears, and this breeds confidence in his team, granting the manager a sense of assurance or, dare I say it, swagger. He has repeatedly shunned the stereotypes and continued to focus on the important job of leading on a daily basis.

He works with what he terms as 'positive realities', something that can also be referred to as 'authentic optimism' – the ability to balance ambition and belief with the brutal facts of a given situation.* Dyche tells me clearly that 'you are not going to "positive" your way to winning the league, there has to be reality within it. So accept the reality of the tough times, but what are the positive ways we can take some control and go and take on the challenge? I am all for positivity but if it's not built on reality then where are you going with it?'

This sense of realism and pragmatic leadership infuses his team culture. He knows what his team is and, crucially, what they can aspire to be. He uses this concept to question and challenge his staff:

So where are we at? I use that with the staff, I ask them, 'Where are we?' Let's see where the reality line is and then ask how we can build beyond that. How can we make it better? So we are not *accepting* the reality, I must make that clear, so what are we going to do that is going to form a new way of working to take

---

* Collins, J. (2001). *Good to Great*. London: Random House.

us beyond that reality. It's just a bit of common sense to be honest.

He defines the role of a Premier League manager as 'part soft-psychologist, part motivator, part organiser, part strategist, and part media spin doctor'. Throughout their journey, Burnley have had to adopt different mindsets, yet the approach to good practice has been consistent and simple, as Dyche describes: 'A lot of how we work is just good common sense. Alignment too. I go "this is reality, this is where we are, this is where we need to go and this is how we are going to get there" – simplistic really in its thinking.'

Simple, maybe, but effective? Definitely. Dyche does not over-complicate his philosophical standpoint, but he has an established identity and knows who he is as a leader and as a person, which allows him to lead from a platform of common sense, responding to changes within the team environment with a simple look-assess-respond model.

WORK-LIFE BALANCE

REJECTING THE BALANCE IDEA

Given the nature of elite sport, it was fascinating to gather the leaders' contrasting views on the need for achieving the much-coveted 'work-life balance'. Each leader cited the all-encompassing and twenty-four-seven reality of elite sport, with Roberto Martínez vehemently telling me that he does not actually want to switch off. Even now, as head coach of the Belgian national side and without daily on-field interactions with the players, he is in constant contact with his staff, travelling to games, thinking, planning and observing. It is a refresh-ing perspective in a leader to accept that he or she does not desire a traditional work-life balance and that they welcome the nature of the role. Perhaps ultimately, leadership is so rewarding and encapsulates so much of who they are as a person, that to try to neatly categorise it under the label of 'work' is futile and actually energy-sapping. Why, after all, pursue something that may be out of reach?

Martínez recounts regularly encountering young coaches who ask him about achieving this sought-after balance. 'If they ask me that, they are not going to last. Football, for me, is not a job. It is a passion. It has to be a way of living. And you have to accept that it will bring with it both good and bad moments.'

By seeing leadership as a key part of an existential experience, rather than attempting to constantly separate difference elements of life, we can perhaps remove the burden and guilt associated with the pursuit of balance and instead breed personal and professional success via a consistent and flexible approach.

CONSTANT 'ON' SWITCH

Leaders accept that the role engenders a 100 per cent commitment that realistically, during key moments, means that there is no downtime. Gary Kirsten describes his approach to leadership as 'twenty-four seven' and something that can deplete his mental and physical energy – 'it works you over', he tells me knowingly. He describes how 'waking up every morning and asking, "How can I add more value to a group of people?" can become pretty exhausting.' There is an almost reluctant acceptance that leadership brings unpredictable challenges, leaving us emotionally and physically fatigued. During these moments, a philosophy can help the leader to maintain their ability and their sanity.

Ashley Giles asks, 'Do we ever switch off? No, I don't think we do properly.' His role in cricket, which at the time of the interview was with Lancashire County Cricket, brings varying demands. The seven-month domestic season is 'non-stop' and 'manic', demanding a constant focus on results and how to effectively manage a certain player or match scenario. When the season ends Giles tells us that he can 'sort of switch off', but there are still committees demanding his time.

Now, as director of cricket for the England and Wales Cricket Board, some of the challenges may be different, but the intensity and scrutiny will be greater than ever before. Giles' coaching and leadership journey is perhaps the most pertinent to demonstrate the array of demands that can be placed on a leader – the technical, tactical, physical and psychological components sit alongside the commercial, organisational and strategic elements. Even if you switch off from the training ground, the nets, the practice field, you may have to switch on and divert that energy elsewhere.

FAMILY LIFE

Many leaders are open about the challenges of combining family life with the demands of elite sport. Aside from the obvious emotional aspects, such as a lack of time spent with loved ones and missing important family milestones, it can be a big ask for a family to adapt to a leader living away from the established family home. This is even more pronounced when one considers the fleeting nature of sports posts and the considerable turnover in such roles.

Returning to football, Sean Dyche describes 'life meets professional football' as his biggest personal challenge. Upon joining Burnley, he relocated to the north-west, while leaving his wife and two children at home in Northampton. In his previous role, at Watford, he only lasted for a year before being sacked owing to a change in ownership. That experience impacted his decision when taking charge at Burnley: 'I thought I am not going to move my family, the same thing could happen here, who knows. Of course, five and a half years later, you think it could have been different, but we make it work, we make sense of it.'

In his early days at Turf Moor, he found the situation 'really difficult to make sense of' as he tried to 'keep it all together whilst being stretched', and his resilience and persistence were much needed. He goes on to say, 'I found that time really complex. Trying to win games. Trying to change the culture of the club and the confusion that brings, and you work with it and you get booed off and you think, "How is this making sense?" Keeping that all together and living to fight another day, that is probably the hardest thing, getting stretched all over the place, your private life, your professional life.'

Michael Maguire acknowledges that he also struggles to switch off, identifying it as an area that he needs to constantly work on, as he regularly takes his work home. 'The job is twenty-four seven. It might be a phone call you need to make or a Skype call. I thrive on learning, so I am trying to find people from the other side of the world that I have been involved with on various things – it is definitely a challenge.' The obsession and intensity that make Maguire an effective coach also lead to him seeming distracted in his family environment. This does not signify a lack of desire to be present in the moment with loved ones, but more a constant conflict between the need to switch off and the all-encompassing nature of sport.

Taking on a high-profile role in elite sport creates challenges for other areas of a leader's identity, specifically their family life. Maguire describes himself as a 'workaholic with three kids' and reflects that he has 'missed a lot of their life'. He goes on to say, 'There are two things that I have in my life: family and the sport. I don't want too much else. Because they are the two things that I love. Whenever I am not at work, I'm with my kids and my family.' In this, Maguire displays remarkable clarity of thought and self-knowledge.

There were serious conversations in the Kirsten household when Gary was offered the job as head coach of India. While the opportunity was compelling, Gary and his wife Deborah, with two little boys and a newborn baby, were keen to achieve a balance with their family life. They agreed he would only be in the role for a maximum of three years, allowing the family to travel while the kids were still young and not in school. They also, with India's agreement, implemented a 'twenty-one-day rule', meaning that if Kirsten was unable to return home in that time, Deborah would fly over with the family.

> The balance was tough, but we were fortunate that we had young kids at the time and it was easier to travel with them. Deborah commuted in from South Africa. It was tough initially, but we got into a routine. We actually ended up having lots of fun as a family at that time.

While leadership can put a strain on the strongest of family units, Kirsten's words here remind us that such positions also bring opportunities and, as is the case here, the chance to travel and make everlasting memories across cultures. Kirsten's firm promise of three years was to be tested when, having delivered the World Cup, he was offered a new lucrative contract:

> I said to my wife it would be a max of three years in the job and that would be it. So on my last day we won the World Cup. So of course, it was tempting to stay on and I was offered a really good contract. But it didn't deter me from my commitment to the family that I would only do three years so that was it. We moved on after that, it was never going to be an issue. That

was always going to be the end. In a way it worked out for the better.

A hero in India, Kirsten the leader could have been tempted to commit to another contract. Kirsten the father, however, had made a commitment to his family and was happy to honour it. After all, there are worse times to leave than after winning a World Cup.

Stuart Lancaster, talking in the build-up to the 2015 World Cup, referred to the impact such a high-profile leadership role can have on a family unit, saying at the time, 'It is one of the biggest coaching jobs in sport in this country now. I would say it does dominate because you don't have many other areas of your life anyway – the only other area of your life is your family and it clearly has a big impact there because you are away from home a lot, when you are at home you're dealing with issues or thinking things through and you're aware that there is this ticking clock of a major competition coming around the corner. The pressure and scrutiny that is going to come, not just on me but on the family, and the challenges that will bring to the family dynamic, if we are successful or we are not. So, it really is all encompassing.'

A leader's awareness of their own thoughts and emotions helps to navigate their role, as a parent and/or partner, within the family environment. As Lancaster's words attest, the impact on family life is unavoidable and, despite the unconditional love and support that work both ways, sometimes the family can but look on. Fast-forward four years and Lancaster has had time to reflect on the World Cup and the impact it had on his family unit:

You just felt the pain. My mum, I could see the pain I was causing my mum. She said, 'It doesn't matter how old you are, you want to be able to defend your son, and even though you are forty-five I want to be able to defend you and I can't – because the bullets were flying in. They were feeling my pain and I could not do anything to make it go away for them. Normally as a dad to your kids or husband to your wife, you can find a solution to make problems go away, but I could not find a solution to this one. That was the bit I really struggled with. So while my personal pain was tough, I felt for my family.

It was this pain and a burning desire to be present for the family that contributed to Lancaster taking up his role as senior coach at Leinster, which brings an easier travel schedule between Leeds and Dublin:

The family went through a lot of sacrifice when I was coaching England. Not just the physical time I was away, but the pressure, so I am very aware that the kids will be grown up and gone to university soon. As the kids grow up and establish themselves in their own way, then you can go back to just me and my wife plus the leadership and coaching element of things. At the moment, the family is definitely part of it. I have missed so many moments . . . living in Leeds and working in London, I've been away from home a lot and I've missed a lot of small conversations and big moments in their lives and I want to make sure I am there for them before they leave.

Lancaster's account of this period of his life and its impact on his loved ones provides a unique insight into the sacrifices made by all involved. In talking openly, he displays the authenticity and vulnerability that will also help him to manage the relationships he holds dear through difficult times.

TIME AND SPACE

In many aspects, elite sport almost forbids a leader from switching off. When the players go home, the leader's pursuit of excellence continues. However, the presence of a reliable philosophy and clear beliefs can go some way in enabling them to create a small space where they can step back – albeit briefly – from the daily reality of a fiercely results-based business.

While agreeing on the struggle they face to achieve a work-life balance, leaders sought out different activities that allow time for reflection and add an element of perspective to their lives. Ashley Giles describes the need 'for a bit of me time'. He gives an example of how he might fit in some time for reflection: 'Today I woke up before six and I am thinking about the day and practice, who I am going to play, who is available, what our formula is going to be. So, I just went for a walk, just an hour but my brain is still ticking over. I am trying to help myself on that.'

Dan Quinn loves to travel while Gary Kirsten described a range of keen interests: 'I have a lot of outdoor interests. I'm a keen runner and cyclist, mountain biker and fisherman. I love that as an opportunity just to break away from the space a little bit and just to have some good down-time. I think that has been very important for me.'

His commitment to a work-life balance is also evident in his approach to player management. The leader sets the tone for the environment and Kirsten, in valuing personal down-time, encourages his players to do the same. 'I think it is important for them too. I have been criticised on a few occasions, in some of the teams I've been with, of creating down-time for my players as well. People say, "We should be in the nets training," and I am standing there saying, "Hey, let's just take a break."'

Sean Dyche has seemingly settled on some element of balance, having initially found it difficult to be 'engaged when I am at home because mentally I am always thinking. That can be draining and hard on the family, because you want to be there and they know deep down if you are really there. They can tell.' He now uses his travelling time wisely: 'With technology you can be in the car and it is like a floating office so you are not actually missing too much. The club have learnt how I work and I know how they work, so it works pretty well overall and there is some balance to life now.'

Returning home for a few days allows Dyche to reflect and enjoy the simple pleasures in life. A meal out and a few drinks with his long-standing group of friends, who know Sean Dyche the person not the manager, often proves to be the best tonic to the persistent scrutiny of the Premier League. Spending time with those who are unmoved by status and reputation allows leaders to protect their authenticity and maintain the values and beliefs that propelled their ascendancy in the first place.

Gary Kirsten and Michael Maguire both talked passionately about the sense of perspective that their charity work provides, with Kirsten describing his foundation in his native South Africa. 'It is a massive component for me. I think we live in a country where there is tremendous need and if you are an individual who has had a significant amount of opportunity and privilege in life, there is a massive responsibility in our country to understand the need that is out there.' He continued to talk about his cricket academies in the townships of South Africa, and the opportunity to impact those around him on a wider scale:

We are doing our little bit in whatever capacity we can from a cricketing perspective to say, 'let's take a whole lot of schools in the communities and get a system going within that school'.

And by that I mean a cricket system. So you start by building some infrastructure, we need to build some nets and then give them some equipment and then you place a coach. Anyone that shows a little bit of talent, you can work with them and ultimately our goal is to produce township schools that can compete with the more privileged schools in South Africa.

Kirsten's work in the townships of South Africa is his way of giving back to the nation whose spirit lies at the very core of the man and the leader. Wherever in the world he finds himself, it keeps him connected to home and allows a sense of perspective that is perhaps uniquely different from the others. Striving for a work-life balance is not always about rest and recuperation. A fleeting window of time has the potential to allow leaders to use their position to add real value to important causes, while also continuing their own personal development.

Maguire recounted a trip to Papua New Guinea, where he enjoyed the physical challenge of trekking for seven days straight to a place that has 'no power, no phone, nothing – you are back to the bare bones'. He describes how these environments help him to appreciate 'sport at its purest, no money involved, they just loved it. It strips the game right down. It was a bit of an eye-opener. It is what the game is all about. I say to my players, "When you were running around at five or six, you didn't think about money and the fanfare, you just loved doing it." I went from an incredible ride of a Grand Final to realising there is so much happiness here, they just love life and they are so happy to see you. It is humbling and it probably keeps my feet locked on the ground, gives me perspective about what I get to do and ensures I don't take it for granted.' You can see how this offers significant benefits to Maguire as a leader but, more importantly, as a human being.

It is easy to view the pursuit of work-life balance as a chore, something we think we *should* do. Note how some of our leaders opt instead for activities that indirectly build into their leadership mix. This shift in mindset allows them an element of time to step back from their professional role, while simultaneously developing the very qualities that drive their approach to leadership and performance.

Leaders in elite sport are sometimes deemed public property, with everyone having an opinion on their results, their decisions and their actions. 'It is part of the territory,' as Sean Dyche explains reluctantly, but it is also important to remember the other aspects of their identities; as parents, partners and people who, like all of us, strive to achieve some element of balance in their personal and professional lives. Whether it is returning to the family unit, busying themselves in new initiatives, or retreating to the solitary, our leaders have a distinct means to pursue such a balance.

A LONELY PURSUIT

Picture the scene. A leader leaves their meeting and their phone buzzes. They have three voicemails and ten emails to attend to. All are marked urgent. A family picture is on their home screen, but it is hidden by the hoard of notifications dominating the screen. The next meeting is in five minutes, just long enough to grab a coffee for a much-needed caffeine boost. The phone pings again, another fire to fight, and still the day's to-do list remains untouched . . .

You may have noted I didn't specify whether this was a business or sporting setting. I'm assuming your brain painted that picture for you; that is what it is there to do. I didn't specify because it simply doesn't matter – scenes like this play out every day in organisations around the world.

Such a picture goes some way towards highlighting a great

paradox of leadership, and one that we have not yet covered. It is that even surrounded by a constant buzz of demands, messages, people and energy, leaders can simultaneously feel lonely and isolated. And while we might seek out time and space to think, we also crave connection and belonging.

Positions of leadership often dictate that as 'the boss' you are always one step removed from the in-group. As the leader, you are treated differently. You have to watch your step. Too friendly and you may get too close; too cold and the relationships become difficult to build.

Despite the chaotic and dynamic nature of the role, characterised by the 'twenty-four seven' and 'no off-switch' approaches described here, it is the individual leader who shoulders the ultimate responsibility for the success of the team. Looking back now, as I write this, I wish I had probed the topic of loneliness more. Perhaps that is a sign of the lingering taboo that surrounds such areas. Maybe I didn't want to go there. Yet Stuart's words, outlining his experience following the World Cup, and Gary's account of the time spent away from loved ones, are perhaps a nod to some of these emotions.

These feelings are entirely normal, understandable and human – and are particularly relevant to leadership. This is not a new phenomenon. We have been writing about loneliness in leadership for years. In *Henry IV, Part II*, William Shakespeare writes 'uneasy lies the head that wears the crown'. Hundreds of years later, rapper Stormzy, referring to his own position as a 'next generation leader'* uses a similar lyric: 'heavy is the head that wears the crown'.

While loneliness is a perfectly valid human emotion, it can also

---

* Eddo-Lodge, R. (2019, October). "It's My Purpose to Shine a Light Where I Can." How Rapper Stormzy Is Championing Black British Culture.' *Time, Next Generation Leaders.* time.com, retrieved 13 February 2020.

chip away at resilience levels and contribute to mental health issues, increasing the likelihood of depression, stress or anxiety. Being vulnerable and talking about emotions might still feel like a weakness to some in elite sport. In reality, it is the complete opposite. If an element of vulnerability is key to building a high-performing team, then this must start from the top down.

In the next section, you will discover the steps leaders take to continue their personal and professional development. These are highly effective strategies employed concurrently with their day-to-day work that continue the learning process and go some way towards tackling the loneliness that all leaders experience at some point in their careers.

PERSONAL DEVELOPMENT

As with many leaders in business and sport, the coaches I interviewed displayed a willingness and desire to continue their own process of learning and development. They achieve this via several mechanisms, either proactively as an ongoing experience or as a response to a given situation.

MENTORS

Elite sport is fundamentally aspirational, as individuals and teams relentlessly pursue their next goal. Athletes and coaches are always looking to *win*, competing with others, be that opponents in the traditional sense, their own teammates for a starting position, or other coaches who want their job.

The role of a mentor, offering an independent and non-biased ear, is a welcome source of reflection for a leader. The presence of such figures, either formal or informal, emerged as a common theme from the interviews. For a leader, there may only be a few people who can fulfil this vital role. Crucially, effective mentors do not just nod and agree, but rather listen, challenge, probe and question, offering a perspective that is one step removed from the intensity of the sporting environment.

Stuart Lancaster described his own mentors as 'hugely influential in shaping my philosophy and getting me through tough times' and Dan Quinn cited the significant influences of both Pete Carroll (head coach of the Seattle Seahawks) and Steve Mariucci, who gave Quinn his big break in the NFL at the San Francisco 49ers, on his approach to leadership. In each instance, mentors offered a sense of values or inspiration; in Quinn's latter example, his boss opened a career door and became someone to admire and aspire towards.

Gary Kirsten acknowledged how these sounding boards can 'play a big role in helping outside of sport'. Mentoring, he tells me, has given him 'direction in life' and played 'a massive role' in his development. Giving an insight into the role of a mentor, he went on to describe his relationship with mental skills coach Paddy Upton, who Kirsten has worked with regularly throughout his leadership career, in more detail:

> In him I found someone who helped me understand who I was as an individual and who I was as a player on the field, you know, and what my strengths were and what my weaknesses were, what I was comfortable with, not comfortable with. And I found that what he was saying made real sense.

Kirsten, not easily impressed and guarded and selective in his interactions as a player, found someone in Upton who was able to reach him in a way that others could not.

Sean Dyche spent the early part of his playing career at Nottingham Forest, under the leadership of the revered, iconic Brian Clough.

Despite the fact that 'as a player you couldn't help but be affected by the powerful force that was Brian Clough and the way he worked', he actually built a stronger and more enduring relationship with John Duncan, his manager at Chesterfield:

> He was amazing. I still speak with him about various things and decisions I have to make, as an outside ear if you like. We were a group of 'all-rightness' at Chesterfield, and yet we had great success so I was always intrigued by how he pieced it together and the things he stood for and the things he believed in and some of the simplicity and the depth mixed in you know, I was always intrigued by that. He is a lateral thinker so I can go to him for a view and he doesn't just say yes like some people tend to do, he might say, 'Have you thought about this and have you thought about that?' So he will give a different view of things.

The essence of leadership is how you reach others. In Dyche's case, the 'celebrity' name was not the one who impacted him the most.

Dyche also recalled the influence of his Sunday league manager, Jim Hoover, for whom he played as a seven-year-old. At this point I can't help but imagine a young Sean Dyche. Whilst Hoover cannot perhaps be classed as a mentor in the traditional sense, his simple message has endured to this day and is reflected in Dyche's own values and approach to management: 'He always said "a great attitude is everything" and it stuck with me, I have never ever forgotten it. I remember being seven and hearing him say it. He explained how people who just keep going, keep working, stay dedicated and all those things, they prevail in the end. That stuck with me, that has been just as powerful as anything.'

While he may not call Hoover up for advice on Premier League management, a seemingly simple interaction can have the most profound of effects. By the same token, we should never discount leadership lessons from our youth or upbringing. A message delivered and consumed on a smaller stage can resonate powerfully on the biggest stage of all.

LEARNING OUTSIDE YOUR SPHERE

The leaders noticeably sought out learning opportunities wherever possible, whether that be conducting their own research, visiting other high-performance cultures or attending relevant conferences across a range of fields, including the military, business and sport. A thirst for knowledge seemed to be a common factor across subjects.

Roberto Martínez, who recently travelled with other leaders to Atlanta to observe the NFL Super Bowl, discussed the importance of experiencing other environments, and temporarily escaping the goldfish bowl of professional football. 'I think you need the stimulation. I think sometimes we get clouded with too much of the same and sometimes getting away from that environment helps you, refreshes you, and gives you a different approach, a different angle.'

Michael Maguire highlighted the need for a leader to look outside their own sport, or even sport in general: 'I enjoy talking to business people and how they manage their staff, from a thousand staff to fifty staff, dealing with different people. But all sports, I am always looking to learn. I really thrive off educating myself. It might just be one little thing, but you have seen something that you might be able to use.' Being open-minded and willing to learn from all sources can provide interesting and sometimes unexpected lessons that a leader can apply to their own practice.

In today's leadership climate, the sharing of ideas and experiences is commonplace. We have seen, in recent times, an explosion of coverage of 'the leader' and huge analysis to go with it. Swapping notes has become an important part of leadership, and cross-pollination is more possible than ever. The most progressive leaders of today have the humility and vulnerability to accept learning from all angles and to relish the use of different prisms to drive performance. For instance, Gareth Southgate, in his preparation for the 2018 World Cup as head coach of the England national team, visited the NFL Super Bowl (with Martínez) between the New England Patriots and the Philadelphia Eagles. He took in a leadership conference on the same trip stateside and has also spent time around the England Rugby environment. This more meaningful approach to watching other sports allows leaders to draw lessons and inspiration in a new, refreshing way.

Stuart Lancaster, another who has spent time with Southgate, has 'studied and practised leadership for twenty years' and feels he has a 'good concept of the things that work' and, more importantly, is happy to share them. Lancaster has seized the opportunity to visit high-performance environments around the world, spending time at Hawthorn Football Club (Australian football – 'Aussie Rules') and swapping notes with Maguire at the South Sydney Rabbitohs, visiting the England cricket team and consulting with Southgate at the Football Association. He was even invited over to the USA to lead a technical tackling session with Dan Quinn's Atlanta Falcons. Following the World Cup in 2015, Lancaster again travelled to the southern hemisphere:

> I went to eight or nine different organisations, different sports, to speak to their coaches and to pass on what I had learnt from my experience coaching England. But also, to pick up from them, to hear their stories and where they are at and get some reassurance that it wasn't just me it had happened to and other

coaches had been through the same thing.

Leadership is a constantly evolving beast and a deeply human endeavour. Learning from the lived experiences of others is a key part of forming one's own approach.

The trip provided some headspace and allowed Lancaster to speak with other coaches about his own experience following the World Cup, taking some impactful lessons along the way, and absorbing how others deal with adversity. Lancaster recalls a conversation he had with Alistair Clarkson of Hawthorn Football Club, in which Clarkson described a time when his own job was on the line:

> Alistair said, 'I was one tackle away from losing my job. You've got to put everything into context, Stuart. Sometimes things happen that are out of your control as a coach. This player made this tackle, it wasn't anything to do with me, but he made a tackle that saved the goal and saved my job.' It was good to know it wasn't just me!

This sense of shared endeavour can lend a dash of camaraderie to leadership, a pursuit that in its darkest moments can seem solitary and remote. As awareness of mental health increases, we encourage people to ask for help or to check in on others. There is no reason this should not apply to leaders too.

Wayne Bennett of the Brisbane Broncos advised Lancaster to 'make sure, wherever you go next, you 100 per cent want to go and they 100 per cent want you to come'. At times, leaders need to admit their vulnerability in order to grow and move forward. For instance, Lancaster's willingness to take on his role as Leinster's 'senior coach', as opposed to that of a head coach elsewhere, has allowed him to return to his coaching roots and also given him the time to dedicate to his own continuing personal development. Leinster certainly made it clear they wanted him. The Irish club's desire to recruit Lancaster was evidenced by high-profile fly-half Johnny Sexton personally texting Lancaster, encouraging him to make the move to the Emerald Isle.

Sean Dyche gave an example of his experience of a study visit to the Oxford University boat crew, which he completed as part of his coaching qualification:

> I learnt so much. I only had one day but I had complete access. I got there at six in the morning [and] they let me see every-thing. I spoke with the coaches, saw the launch boats, saw the detail they go into in their technical work, the sheer hard work on the ergo rowing machines, the will and desire of people who don't get paid to do it – they are taking P.hDs at the same time, so [it's] a huge workload mentally and physically.

Two lessons in particular resonated with Dyche. Sean Bowden, head coach at Oxford, talked about the concept of 'maladaptive learning', where athletes who have previously been successful, some having been to the Olympics, enrol in university to study for a doctorate degree and win the Boat Race. Upon joining the team, they have to completely deconstruct and reconstruct their rowing stroke, undoing years' worth of habits, before putting it all back together. Although the culture, training and competition of rowing is vastly different from football, Dyche identified a deeper opportunity for learning.

The concept fascinated Dyche as he compared the situation with managing talented young football players who are given big contracts despite being 'nowhere near ready for the first team'. In this example the young player is the rower, arriving at university with a set of skills that have seen them achieve success, but in order to overcome the next challenge, they need to adapt. In football, it can be easy for an athlete to mistakenly assume that they have made the big time. However, according to Dyche, in reality what got them the contract in the first place will likely not be enough to make the next step to the first team, 'because they are not doing the things they need to do, their brains are telling them, "But you've just been given a big contract for doing what you've been doing," and you go, "That's not the point, you need to change, you're going to have to do this," hence the maladaptive part, they have not actually adapted to what they are going to need to do to move forward.'

The second lesson Dyche took was 'simplicity mixed with the detail', a balance he aims to achieve with Burnley. 'There are certain requirements that are going to have to be there, you can't cheat the system, hard work is going to have to be there, and they certainly work hard to try to win the Boat Race. That was a really good day that I still reflect on now.'

While the teams at Oxford now have access to some high-calibre facilities and elite-level coaching and support, the images evoked remain light years from the glamour and affluence of the Premier League. Hard work, teamwork and persistence, taken as a given at Oxford, are closely aligned to Dyche's own non-negotiables. This learning experience has given Dyche a pillar to reinforce his own beliefs and to endorse his leadership philosophy.

READING

Having an open mind and an appreciation of leadership lessons from multiple sources is vital to the development of a leadership approach. In our examples, none of the leaders let their ego impede the need for ongoing learning.

Stuart Lancaster reflected on the research and reading he does in his own time. 'I've studied. Reading books of great leaders. They have shaped my philosophy a lot. Some of whom are not alive but I've read the books and thought, "Yeah, I agree with that."' This viewpoint was supported by Gary Kirsten, who has thrown himself into learning and research. 'Understanding how different people are doing things across various platforms, and obviously, a lot of reading. Being invited to sports conferences, I have been very fortunate to get invited to a lot of different things.'

He went on to describe in detail how he has learnt from other leaders and their responses to certain situations, specifically referring to Pep Guardiola's time with FC Barcelona:

> I was fascinated with how Guardiola tried to reconnect the club with the Catalan way of life and what the football club stood for in that community. He tried to reconnect the players, especially the international players, to understand what that meant and what it stood for. And then he needed the right individuals to buy into that. I think that, what he was able to do, was move the more senior, rock-star individuals that he realised he wasn't going to win over, but he was able to bring in a new group of superstars that bought into his way and they had incredible success.

Kirsten also took key lessons from Manchester United under Sir Alex Ferguson:

> The club and the badge was always bigger than any star that arrived there. And the moment they shifted out of that space or out of what the bigger purpose was, they were just shut out, which a club like that can afford to do. I don't think we can always do that in other clubs.

REFLECTION

Regular reflection, either introspective or with a mentor, is crucial to effective leadership. Listening to the opinions of the leaders, it was clear that a heightened level of self-awareness had developed within them and become more important over time. Ashley Giles recalled finding himself in a challenging position when coaching the England T20 and one-day sides: 'I was not able to field the teams we wanted to field. I didn't feel I could have full control of the environment, it wasn't my management team, those sorts of things. That was a big learning experience for me because I learnt that actually you need to have control over those big decisions.' Giles was able to step back, analyse what wasn't working, and understand what was missing for him. A leader of any merit must employ an element of reflection in order to take the lessons from their experiences, and crucially implement future actions.

Michael Maguire's approach is another spin on reflection, facing more directly the idea of learning from failure. Leaving the Rabbitohs in 2017 was tough for Maguire. The club was (and is) close to his heart. He is part of their history and they are part of his. Together they made history, winning the 2014 Grand Final and ending a forty-three-year wait. The man and the club are perpetually intertwined, so the ensuing separation was inevitably painful. Now head coach of Wests Tigers and the New Zealand national side, he has had the chance to self-reflect and, in his words, consider 'what works, what I could have improved and how I might have changed things to follow a success like the Grand Final'. For Maguire, this can put a leader in a stronger position for the next role: 'You take the learnings. It is terrible going through it, but, in some ways, it is a great experience for the next opportunity that comes along.'

Following the World Cup, Stuart Lancaster's reflection started almost immediately. 'I am reasonably self-aware and the process started straight away. I felt I needed to get from "What is the problem?" to "What is the solution?" so it was immediate.' He travelled north to Cumbria, spending time at the family farm in Culgaith. Removing oneself from the professional environment can encourage a deeper, more focused level of reflection:

> In the immediate aftermath I took myself away. I made sure the family was OK and that they realised I was OK. I went back to the Lake District and spent a bit of time on my own, thinking through and processing the chain of events that had led to us being knocked out of the World Cup. I also wrote down what lessons I had learnt. So a little bit of clearing my mind of the chronology of the events but also understanding why things had happened the way they happened. So quite a lot of time on my own in a little caravan in the Lake District, climbing mountains.

To aid this reflection, in the ten months that followed the World Cup, Lancaster openly recounts that he visited a psychologist who 'was a long way disconnected from rugby, she didn't know much about rugby at all, but she knew how your thoughts affected your mindset'. A key aspect of leadership is to trust oneself enough to be vulnerable and, in Lancaster's words, this process (with 'the one person outside of sport I spoke to') helped him to 'download and offload' so he 'wasn't dragging the World Cup experience around forever'.

A leader's ability to authentically reflect on their experiences should also dictate that they are more likely to create a team dynamic with the ability to survive healthy conflict and have open conversations in the aftermath of sporting performances. Lancaster's ability to use reflection to make some sort of peace with his World Cup experience can only reinforce his future approach to leadership.

Whatever the specific method, investing in regular reflection helps leaders to become increasingly comfortable with their thoughts. It is natural to want to push seemingly unhelpful and negative thoughts away, but this fruitless endeavour is both energy-sapping and unproductive. It is much more effective and rational to acknowledge these thoughts: write them down, vocalise them, and challenge them. Becoming proficient at identifying irrational or limiting beliefs also helps people to work towards a more rational and solution-based way of thinking. This process is a habit like any other and a skill that needs to be worked on over time.

COPING WITH THE DEMANDS

Later in the book, we examine how the leaders manage their people through periods of sporting success and failure, but at these times leaders must also tackle this unavoidable aspect of sport on a personal level. Of course, they do not enjoy losing, but a sense of perspective and the ability to balance both the short-term and long-term aspects of their roles enables a leader to navigate the tumultuous nature of sport.

Ashley Giles referred to winning and losing as 'the danger of coaching', describing how he enjoys winning but 'it lasts a lot less time than the disappointment and frustration of losing. Whenever you lose, you carry that for days. Particularly the long drives home, you are just ticking over the critical moments. When you win, you might have a couple of beers but you are already thinking about the next game, you're moving forward.'

'The danger of coaching' is something Giles acknowledges is an area for him to work on. By his own admission he takes results and performances 'very personally'. He diverts our conversation on to the subject of social media: 'I'm on Twitter now, but I am seriously considering just coming off it, there is just no need, I don't need to know what someone says about our team on there really, if we are doing the right things and things are moving the right way, it's fine. The trouble is when you lose a game and you might go on it, and whatever people say, it gets under your skin. I've bitten. Sometimes, there is some good banter. The trouble is, you always read the idiot.'

It is not just Twitter that can be 'wearing' to Giles, as he describes interactions with the public: 'People want to come and speak to me and I find that quite tiring when I am out of my bubble.' It is important to point out that this feeling is not born out of ignorance. As we know, Giles views himself as an introvert, so interactions such as these can be energy-sapping, effortful encounters. Leadership is a relentless pursuit and coping with its demands is key. Maintaining a healthy internal relationship with feedback is essential for Giles' approach, as is the opportunity for reflection, and the time and space to ensure clarity of thought.

Sean Dyche is unashamedly driven by winning – 'It kept me going as a player and it keeps me going with what I do now. I sacrifice to win in many ways: private life, personal life, not seeing my kids, so therefore [losing] doesn't sit right with me.' However, his experience to date has helped him to take a more balanced approach to both winning and losing. 'I know how to balance it, so not to get too high with the highs and not too low with the lows.' The nature of the Premier League means that his position and decisions are discussed across the country and that is something that he has come to accept:

'You are in a position that is hugely opinionated from the outside. Now, if you are managing in most businesses, people are not walking down the street telling you what to do. Seriously, football management, everyone thinks they can do a better job than me, everyone. You wouldn't walk in to the doctors, and when they say, 'You have got a chest infection,' you go, 'No I haven't' – you just wouldn't do it, but people are happy to say to a football manager, 'Why aren't you doing that?' . . . and you go, 'Well, this is why,' and they go, 'Well I disagree,' so that is one of the complexities of it.

Dyche displays a realistic pragmatism here in accepting all he can do is hold a measured position in a noisy world of criticism and excessive comment.

In 2017, Dan Quinn's Atlanta Falcons were on the wrong side of one of the greatest comebacks in sport. The New England Patriots, led by Tom Brady, recovered from a twenty-five-point deficit in the third quarter to force overtime against the Falcons and ultimately emerge victorious in the Super Bowl. Think Manchester United versus Bayern Munich in 1999. For Quinn it was brutally tough to take, but he points out that to dwell too much would do a disservice to his current squad of players. 'It is not like I don't think about it or it doesn't leave a bad mark on me, within my heart, but ultimately it doesn't drive me to the next moment. This year is all for this team, for this season.'

He strives to achieve the same sense of balance and perspective as Dyche. He doesn't like losing, but is driven by those critical moments that end in either victory or defeat. 'It sucks, losing, but that is the life of a competitor, although that doesn't make it easier to take, that's competitive sports man, you get your ass off the mat. That is what is fun about being in pro sports, it is the competitive lifestyle we have chosen. We are addicted to it.' Again, we see a realistic admission and a home truth – that leadership is a choice.

Stuart Lancaster rather prophetically reflected on the 'tenuous nature of coaching', describing the limitations of a leader's role.

Reading his words, one can't help but think back to the night, under the Twickenham lights, that led to England's World Cup elimination:

> You can do everything you can to set the team up to be success-ful but ultimately the players have to deliver on the day, and you need the bounce of the ball sometimes and referees' deci-sions to go your way, and if you don't get that the reality is, no matter how long your contract is, it is going to be over and that's the unpredictability that you learn to live with. But it's not a nice feeling.

At times, Lancaster too struggles with the ever-present opinions of the media and public. 'If you've lost a game, you do typically want to avoid public situations because inevitably people have an opinion, sometimes misinformed, and it can get in the way of your thought process and start to wind you up a bit.'

Michael Maguire and Gary Kirsten interpret their leadership roles through the lens of pride – and putting the team before their own employment status. Maguire discussed the notion of pressure.

> People talk about pressure. I guess I feel pressure, but I can look in the mirror and know that I've done everything possible that I can possibly think of for us achieving to where we are right now. I take the pressure as a privilege. I know in myself that, if I'm not satisfied how we are travelling or how the team is performing, I'd probably sack myself. So, it is not about anyone else, it is about how I would judge it. I would walk away from a position if I didn't think we were achieving what we need to.

This acute self-awareness and sense of pride in a role were echoed by Kirsten who says that if he feels he is not adding value to a team, he is 'more than happy to move on. In fact, they wouldn't have to fire me, I would just leave anyway.'

This idea of self-sacrifice may well be met by scepticism from some readers; why indeed would someone walk out of a highly paid and high-profile dream job? Yet having spent time with both men, I am confident their burning sense of personal pride would come before financial reward. The willingness to self-sacrifice allows a leader to reflect on their impact and performance with indisputable high expectations but without excessive emotion. There is no linear equation or clear-cut formula for leadership. It is an ongoing and evolving process, playing out in an ever-changing landscape. Leaders must possess the coping strategies that allow them to accept the uncertainty, relish the choices they have made and own the unpredictability of a life in leadership.

Chapter 2: Leadership lessons

- Don't be put off by the term 'philosophy' – ask yourself, 'How am I going to do this?' and, 'What do I stand for?' Stay true to your answers when making the big decisions.
- There will be times when data and analysis cannot provide the answer. Back your judgement and trust your gut.
- Sometimes progress is more important than perfection.
- Prepare for the critical moments. Scenario planning allows you to react appropriately when the moment arrives.
- Simple is not always easy. Keeping it so is often the hardest thing to do when under pressure.
- A sense of balance is key. What are the most important areas of your life? Never lose sight of them; you will need them during the tough times.
- Never stop learning within and beyond your field. Be vulnerable and open enough to develop. Ask the questions, listen, observe. Leave your ego at the door.
- Ask yourself the right questions. Reflection helps you learn from the good times, and the bad. Both will make you stronger.

Creating a High-Performance Culture

An effective culture is consistently said to be at the core of the world's most successful organisations. It is a term regularly discussed and debated, and we often attribute teams' successes and failures to this somewhat ambiguous word. Indeed, it is not the culture that is actually high-performing, it is the people within the culture who are performing. So, how clearly do we understand the different elements that contribute to the creation of a culture that inspires high performance?

There are many unrefuted parallels between the leadership challenges of sport and business. However, elite sport, largely due to the intense media scrutiny and our ongoing fascination with sporting achievement, is the highest profile of talent development industries. Each sporting organisation brings with it its own unique tapestry of history, traditions, expectations, achievements, people and behaviours.

The culture of an organisation can be neatly summarised as the aggregate of behaviours that are both accepted and promoted within an environment. Essentially, it is the way in which people think and act collectively. Shifting a culture can be a seemingly insurmountable task, requiring critical thinking and genuine vulnerability, and encompassing the establishment (or resetting) of purpose, strategy, behaviours, mindset, roles and environments. Beliefs, habits, values and cognitive biases must be challenged, perhaps unlearnt, and often rebuilt. There is evidently more to the process than buzz-words, speeches and cleaning the changing rooms.

The Japanese football team left a thank-you note and a sparkling changing room after valiantly exiting the 2018 World Cup. A photograph of this scene went viral and the team were lauded as examples to everyone else. These much celebrated (and tweeted) instances of good behaviour are symptomatic of a positive culture. They are things we as onlookers and outsiders can actually observe. However – and I am not talking specifically about Japan here – such imagery can also be an attempt to find a shortcut to a desired culture. Changing a culture is not for the faint-hearted and this is why many organisations ask, 'Is it worth it?' and opt instead, either consciously or subconsciously, to remain in their existing comfort zones.

Make no mistake, every team has a culture but not every team's culture is a positive driver of performance. Within a weaker culture, we might expect to see people who fail to act in the best interests of the team, instead preferring to look after their own individual agendas. Cliques begin to form, and people move away from a sense of trust and responsibility towards a preservation of individual positions, power and prestige. Taking an example from elite sport, you might see a tendency for one group (e.g. the medical department) to make excuses and pass the blame to another subgroup (e.g. the sports scientists), who in turn blame another department (e.g. the coaches). Conflict is part of a healthy environment; excuses and blame are not.

In comparison, a strong and authentic culture is able to attract, engage and retain talent. Research from the world of business[*] has found an engaged workforce is linked to increased productivity,

* Harvard Business Review Analytic Services (2013). *The Impact of Employee Engagement on Performance*. Brighton, Massachusetts: Harvard Business School Publishing.

growing profits, improved staff retention, enhanced customer service and significant savings in terms of absenteeism and attrition. In the sporting world, it translates that such engagement will lead to a higher level of performance over a sustained period of time. Culture can be a key differentiator between sporting organisations, especially if their levels of talent are comparable.

Group culture is a constantly evolving beast and the sense of purpose and identity discussed in this chapter need to be consistently revisited and reinforced. When new talent joins a group, they must quickly buy in to the culture. The wrong person can do insurmountable damage to an existing culture, regardless of their individual abilities and talents.

Creating and subsequently sustaining a culture within a sporting environment is no mean feat, as summarised by Sean Dyche. 'The culture is massive for me. The culture and the environment are two key things. It is easy to say but not so easy to do. People say, "Oh well, they have got a good culture," or, "They are going to put in a new culture" – it doesn't just take a week, it takes time.' Creating the 'right' culture for a specific team is imperative but by no means easy, especially if you take into account the existing norms and values of an organisation. While social media does a rather neat job of conveying culture to the masses, the real substance of a culture lies in what we cannot see: the interactions, conversations and behaviours that go on behind closed doors – not in the glare of the media.

As Dyche highlights, when a team enjoys a period of success, a significant part of the achievement is often attributed to the abstract presence of a culture. However, a strong culture, Dyche adds, is present regardless of victory and defeat and helps a group to mitigate the inevitable ups and downs. Dyche continues, 'Let's not kid each other, it helps when you are successful! The madness is that a culture helps regardless, but let's face it, when you are successful it doesn't half glue it all together and everyone thinks, "We will have a bit of that." Yet ironically it shouldn't matter. A good culture is a good culture whether you are successful or not. But of course, we are only human and the more you win and the more success you get, the more everyone believes it, so that does help of course.'

In high-performance cultures, people align under shared beliefs and values, galvanised by a sense of purpose and direction, and start to put the success and needs of the team ahead of their own individual achievements. This is crucially reinforced by the day-to-day behaviours that allow human beings to build trust, develop as people, form relationships and drive progress and performance.

Admittedly this all sounds great on paper. In reality, however, the nature of professional sport and the need for short-term results often dictates that the sense of belonging and protection that such a culture brings is regularly tested. Results will invariably fluctuate, and conflict will rear its head, but a strong and authentic culture should remain steadfast in the face of challenges and setbacks.

Sporting organisations make great efforts to create cultures and environments that endure beyond the guidance of one individual. However, despite this ideology, the role of the leader remains a crucial one. You only have to look at the departures of both Sir Alex Ferguson (2013) and José Mourinho (2018) from Manchester United to see the impact, both negative and positive, that one person can have on an organisation at a given moment.

There have been times when leaders across industries, finding themselves under pressure, have sought to preserve their own power and position, thus creating a sense of isolation from their most valuable asset – the people. You may well be able to think back to a manager that you have worked with, or the impact that a change in leadership can have on a group of people, no matter how large or small the organisation.

Contrastingly, effective and authentic leadership can instil a sense of belonging in the team. The leader sets the standard for the group and the expectations of those entering the team dynamic. If the leader protects the people, the people will protect the team and reinforce the sense of culture that all organisations strive for.

As you read the following chapter, you will see that all leaders agreed that developing a high-performance culture is a significant factor in their approach to leadership. In fact, Stuart Lancaster believes it is the priority: 'If you don't have a strong culture then, ultimately, under pressure your team will fall apart, and cracks can become chasms overnight. When you might think you are sailing along in the right direction, suddenly you find it has all fallen apart.'

Gary Kirsten believes you cannot achieve long-term success without the right culture. 'Any team in the world can have quick fixes and short-term results. But sustainable performance requires identity, strong culture, and a shift in behaviours, or a realignment of behaviours based on the values system of the team.'

During my conversations with the leaders, I was keen to explore the multiple aspects that contribute to the creation of a culture. As culture is a relatively ethereal concept, the conversations were wide-ranging, covering a multitude of factors. As a result, this concept has been split across two chapters. The first covers the various concepts of big-picture thinking and how leaders constantly balance these with short-term results. Chapter 4 explores the process leaders go through when assessing a culture and establishing initial buy-in from athletes, before considering specific examples of interventions and cultural shifts, the role of values and behaviours, and the importance of the environment.

Think of culture as the foundations on which a leader builds their house. Without that bedrock in place, the house might appear comfortable and enticing but, under testing conditions, its core substance is weak and exposed.

BIG-PICTURE THINKING (AND SHORT-TERM RESULTS)

A leader's position in elite sport can never, even during the most fruitful periods, truly be described as stable or safe. The nature of the industry dictates that managers and coaches find themselves in a turbulent and precarious profession, operating in a results-based business where those outcomes are on stark display to the watching world. They exist in a constant state of professional vulnerability as, ultimately, it is the leaders rather than the athletes who are held accountable for performance. Of course, we see this in business environments too. It would be understandable for leaders to focus solely on the here and now. However, if you examine the literature exploring leadership and consistently high-performing organisations, you will find that the virtues of purpose, spirit, vision and values are extolled time and again. In fact, it is apparent that big-picture thinking is essential to the creation of a high-performance culture.

One of the earliest books I read in this field was the 'Peak Performance' literature from the Waikato Management School in New Zealand.* Published in 2001, it identifies business lessons from the world's top sporting organisations. It was also incidentally one of the books that pushed me towards a career in performance psychology. Grounded in organisational theory, it details case studies of sporting dynasties (including FC Bayern Munich, the New Zealand All Blacks, the Chicago Bulls, the San Francisco 49ers and the New

---

* Gilson, C., Pratt, M., Roberts, K. and Weymes, E. (2001). *Peak Performance. Business lessons from the world's top sports organizations.* London: Harper Collins.

York Yankees) from an organisational perspective. These dynasties were found to possess common characteristics including purpose, passion, inspirational goals and an acknowledgement of long-term development.

Over fifteen years since it was originally published, the theory the authors present still rings true and is supported by the sustained performance of successful sporting organisations. Of the examples above, the All Blacks, despite enduring a relatively fallow period in the early 2000s, remain a popular cultural reference point here. FC Bayern Munich have also continued their dynasty, both domestically and in Europe. One can also point to the ongoing success of the New England Patriots and San Antonio Spurs. The Patriots' head coach, Bill Belichick, has been in post since 2000 and has led the team to six Super Bowl victories, yet there was a testing barren spell between 2004 and 2014. In San Antonio, Greg Popovich has achieved five NBA titles since starting with the Spurs in the 1996–7 season. He too has endured setbacks and failures, but the long-term approach has ultimately prevailed.

I was fascinated to explore leaders' perceptions in this area. I wanted to know more about how they are able to genuinely commit to the pursuit of concepts such as legacy and purpose, which are actually rather intangible and nebulous ideas, while simultaneously balancing this with the very real need to deliver results in the short term.

Leaders discussed the importance of defining an inspirational purpose for an organisation or team, and described their various approaches to designing effective team strategy. This element of reflection, planning and big-picture thinking appears to be a key component in the creation of a high-performance culture.

PURPOSE

A sense of purpose and meaning is a valuable part of both team and individual success. As human beings we strive to achieve things that are greater than ourselves. At our core, we are compelled to explore accomplishments that give us a deeper meaning; a meaning that crucially goes way beyond outcome, results or extrinsic reward.

The world is full of examples in which people are driven more by a sense of purpose than they are by financial reward. That is why we leave the stability and security of jobs to pursue lifelong ambitions. That is why, when you ask people to reflect on the things that are truly important to them, they very rarely choose to identify material goods. Nurses, as a case in point, probably do not do what they do solely for money; they do it out of a deeper sense of duty to care for others. It would also be reasonable to suggest that the majority of firefighters do not jump into burning buildings simply for the extrinsic rewards – they could get those somewhere safer – they are driven by something more powerful: the chance to save lives.

In his book *Start With Why*, Simon Sinek* outlines the three dimensions of his 'golden circle' of leadership. Critically, successful organisations are led from the model's innermost circle – the 'why'. This aspirational purpose provides the deeper sense of meaning that inspires others to follow. Having communicated the 'why', a leader can then galvanise a group to deliver and execute the two subsequent areas: the 'how' and the 'what'. The 'how' relates to the strategies used to achieve the purpose, and the 'what' depicts the focus of the team. In essence, an effective 'why' means it becomes easier to implement the strategy of 'how'.

---

* Sinek, S. (2009). *Start With Why: How great leaders inspire everyone to take action.* London: Penguin Group.

Sinek relates this to human biology. The 'what' to which he refers corresponds to the neocortex, the part of the brain used for high-level cognitive functions such as rational and analytical thought, language and data. The 'why' relates to the limbic system, the section of the brain that controls our emotions, feelings and instincts. These are the elements of human nature that are difficult to explain yet crucially underpin the decisions and experiences that make us who we are.

Achieving this level of emotional connection can also help to cultivate greater levels of resilience and persistence at both an individual and a team level. The emotional driver becomes more powerful than the challenges a team or individual might encounter during the course of a competitive season, encouraging a wide-ranging commitment to the group's values, standards and behaviours. To illustrate this, consider the individual example of someone looking to change a habit.

Let's say somebody wants to be able to run a marathon but have never even left their front door in their running kit. They have a lifetime of habits or rules to live by (e.g. they watch TV, they eat late at night, they work long hours), and limiting beliefs (e.g. 'I'm not a runner', 'I've never been able to run', 'Our family are rubbish at running') that hold them back, that go against the desire or will to run a marathon. These patterns of thinking and behaviours are deeply ingrained and hardwired. They are effectively 'set plays' for the brain to follow. From a basic neuroscience perspective, habits are pathways in the brain, formed when combinations of neurons fire electricity together to release chemicals and, ultimately, create our behaviours and thoughts.

In order to achieve the goal, the marathon runner will need to display three ingredients of behaviour change. The first two are the ability to persevere towards long-term goals and the resilience to recover from setbacks. The final and most important ingredient is the *why*: a clear and emotive picture that drives them on. Without this component, in most cases willpower alone is simply not enough. The brain will take the easy, pre-programmed route and revert to the established neural networks and deep-rooted patterns of behaviour. However, if the emotional component is deemed powerful enough, it can overpower even the most entrenched of habits, creating new, stronger neural pathways in the brain. Returning to our marathon example, an individual's purpose and driver may come in the form of a charitable cause, a family member, or a critical event that has provided a timely wake-up call.

In May 2018, Andrés Iniesta played his last game for FC Barcelona, the club he played for from the age of twelve. Incidentally Xavi, his long-time midfield partner with whom he tormented opposition players, penned an open letter[*] describing his teammate as a 'quiet and authentic leader'. The opposition on the night, Real Sociedad, gave Iniesta a guard of honour as he stepped on to the turf at the Camp Nou for the final time. The red, yellow and blue of the crowd displayed messages of gratitude. The game itself ended in a routine one-nil victory for Barcelona. Iniesta, as is often the norm for a departing player, was substituted to a standing ovation with ten minutes remaining. He addressed the crowd at the end and was presented with a commemorative shirt. Yet despite all of this furore, the enduring image of that night under the lights is of an empty stadium and one man sat in the centre circle in the early hours of the morning, unable to bring himself to leave for one last time.

Barcelona's motto is '*més que un club*' which translates as 'more than a club'. It was initially used in 1968 by Narcís de Carreras as he

---

[*] 'Xavi's open letter to Andres Iniesta – "The most talented player in the history of Spain"' (2018). espn.co.uk, retrieved 27 January 2020.

became the club's president. Since then, it has become a symbol of the club's purpose. Underpinned by the La Masia academy, where the motto is reinforced to the club's young players on a daily basis, Barcelona's position in Spain and in world football is unique. In the year 1714 the Catalans, in the Siege of Barcelona, lost their independence. The anger and resentment still lingers, more than 300 years on, and is often most apparent during the El Clásico games against arch rivals Real Madrid. As a result, Barcelona the football club has become a symbol of so much more, a symbol that represents the history and defiance of Catalonia. It is this unique and deep-rooted history that provides the backdrop that has enabled guardians of the Camp Nou, such as Guardiola and Cruyff, to build a culture of high performance that endures beyond one individual leader. It is both inescapable and formidable.

Iniesta was not asked to leave Barcelona. He officially had a contract for life. The reason he decided to leave was because of the intense emotional attachment and respect he has towards the club. He was adamant he wanted to finish while still winning titles, actively contributing to the team and respecting the badge. In his eyes, becoming a symbolic squad player was not an option. The emotional impact of the 'why' that Barcelona represents would always trump any of Iniesta's personal motivations.

It must be said that the reality of elite sport dictates that individual performers will all have their own ambitions, goals and motivations – their own personal sense of purpose or 'why'. However, if a leader is able to articulate a captivating group purpose and communicate the congruence between individuals' search for meaning and the 'why' of the team, this is a precursor to the winning of hearts and minds. It acts as a driver for individuals to go beyond their own sense of ego and motivation and buy into a set of beliefs, values, behaviours, and the aspiring pursuit of common goals. A team captivated and inspired by a common purpose will be more likely to go beyond expectations. Purpose, communicated effectively, can be the most powerful resource at a leader's disposal.

Communicating purpose at critical moments
Sport has the unique ability to provide indescribable moments of both joy and despair. It captures the imagination in a way that no other vehicle can. If you look back through the annals of sporting history, you will be able to conjure up examples of key moments when leaders have chosen to communicate an emotional sense of purpose to create a spike in feeling, motivation and performance.

In 2008, Sir Alex Ferguson asked Sir Bobby Charlton to talk to the Manchester United squad about his experience of the 1958 Munich air disaster. By all accounts, you could hear a pin drop in the room. Ferguson wanted his players, including the likes of a young Wayne Rooney and Cristiano Ronaldo, to truly understand the depth of their responsibility, what it means to play for the club, and the enduring spirit that defines it. Before the World Cup in 2018, Gareth Southgate also turned to Charlton to address the England squad at St George's Park. The aim this time was not to heap additional pressure on the group by reminiscing about 1966 and all that, but to genuinely connect the current squad to the history of what and who has gone before them.

I was privileged to be part of the support staff to Thomas Bjørn's European Ryder Cup team. Thomas' approach was not overly heavy on motivational strategies. He believed the team was self-motivating enough, so he kept things light and ensured the players had everything they needed to perform. However, there was one key intervention. On the Thursday night before the match, he gathered the players for a team meeting and showed them a two-minute video. The video, which can now be found on YouTube – just search 'Team

Europe Motivational Video' – and Twitter for public consumption, is made up of iconic and emotional images of matches past and present, overlaid by the words of past captains Brian Huggett, Sam Torrance and José María Olazábal.

In the space of two minutes, this video encapsulated just what it means to represent Team Europe at the Ryder Cup. It connects you to the voices of the past and the sense of opportunity that awaits. 'As you get older, things get taken from you. That is a fact of life. You come to treasure the opportunities you have had, and reflect on those moments that define you, both good and bad.' The video pulls on the heart strings – José Olazábal speaks tenderly of his friend Seve Ballesteros – and makes clear the finality and importance of the result: 'There is a tomorrow where you are a Ryder Cup winner. And there is a tomorrow when you are not.' After seeing that video Tommy Fleetwood, one of the standout performers in his rookie year, texted me to say we didn't need to talk that night. The video was enough – it had done its job.

Gary Kirsten highlights the importance of understanding a team's purpose. 'If you go into a corporation or an environment and you look at the mission statement or the vision that sits on the wall and then you try to feel through the conversations you have, through the relationships that the people have with each other, I think you can quickly understand what the identity of that team is, or what it strives to be.'

He feels there needs to be a clear structure to the process, a 'common purpose, a common vision and that needs to be set out', and is excited by working with a group of individuals and consider-ing, 'How can I take each one from all different walks of life and win them over to commit to a bigger purpose for the team?' Such statements – we can call them visions, missions, whatever you like – are designed to enthuse and ignite. However, they only achieve this objective if people are consulted and genuinely invested in the process. For a leader, telling people what to do or how to change on a behavioural level can actually have the opposite effect.

To give a specific example, Stuart Lancaster's purpose for the England rugby team was 'to become highly respected'; he wanted 'to have a cultural identity running deep through the team that can gravitate through to the rest of the organisation'. Part of Lancaster's decision-making upon taking his subsequent role at Leinster was the fact that the various component pieces of the performance pyramid he was trying to build with England, 'where culture was the bottom layer, then identity, higher purpose, behaviour and standards, owner-ship, and player-led leadership', were very much in place. This triangulated and perhaps even utopian approach, if successfully implemented, allows culture to be woven intricately throughout all levels of an organisation.

Rather than extolling the virtues of such an approach, Lancaster and Kirsten warned of the consequences of *not* having a purpose in place that supersedes performance goals. Gary Kirsten also spoke about what can happen in the absence of 'purpose':

> You have a massively talented bunch of individuals and have some level of success because everyone is on their best behav-iour initially in a new space. But when everyone starts to become a bit more familiar with each other and you haven't brought in a bigger purpose, everyone can operate on their own devices. I have seen more examples of teams blowing out in that space than I have of teams being able to hold that culture and that way for a sustainable period.

Lancaster recalled his experience of spending time in another unnamed sport. 'They said: "Our goal was to become number one in the world," they had achieved it and they almost downed tools and everyone overtook them and quickly they become number five again.'

While he did not name names, I wonder if he is referring to the England cricket team who between 2009 and 2013 rose to become the first and only English side to reach number one in the world rankings. Since my interviews with Stuart, *The Edge*, a brilliant and revealing film documenting this sporting journey, has been released.* In a 2009 team meeting coach Andy Flower, who is described by players as tough, intense, scary, intimidating and as having the ability to 'look into your soul', set out a two-year goal to reach the pinnacle of the sport, the remote destination no other England team had ever reached. The journey was mapped out as a series of steps. Despite some initial scepticism, they forged a ruthless winning machine and achieved their ultimate goal.

Yet after that goal was ticked off, cracks began to emerge, and players' minds and bodies began to break. In Sir Alistair Cook's words, they were suddenly 'miles away' from the side they were at their peak. At the end of the film, Andy Flower looks back on some decisions with a tinge of regret. He acknowledges that, if he had his time again, he would look to spend just as much time focusing on the *people* in the team as he did with the *cricketers*. Speaking only as an observer, maybe the outcome goal was so dominant and the drive so intense, that the sense of purpose and its associated values got lost in the heady mists of victory and world domination.

Identity – 'the badge'

Creating an identity and acknowledging the role of legacy are other ways a leader can establish a sense of purpose in their team.

---

* *The Edge* (2019). Barney Douglas, dir. Noah Media Group, Heavy Soul Films, UK.

Athletes, like all of us, are increasingly likely to buy into something that they deem more significant than the achievement of short-term results.

In his time with England, Stuart Lancaster placed great emphasis on the importance of identifying with the nation and the fans, creating an emotional connection to the shirt. 'You are playing for more than yourself, you are playing for the shirt. By talking about the respect we have for each other as individuals, even though they all play for different club teams, you create that sense of a band of brothers.'

Lancaster consistently put long-term development at the top of his leadership priorities, meaning selection and disciplinary decisions were taken with the culture and values in mind, and perhaps to the detriment of immediate results. This authentic and steadfast commitment to building sustainable success throughout the organisation may have contributed in some way to him losing his job, but many would agree that the RFU have continued to reap the rewards for this approach. Lancaster told me, 'Ultimately, the greatest suppressor of self-interest is fighting for a cause and literally that is the people that do go to [sic] war and are prepared to put their bodies on the line for their country. That is not where we would claim to be, but in a sport like rugby, we do need a deep level of commitment to each other and to the cause.' By talking about the shirt, the red rose, and what it means, Lancaster looked to create a tangible cultural touchpoint that linked the players with the wider rugby community.

Dan Quinn echoes Lancaster's thoughts. One of the Atlanta Falcons' key pillars is 'brotherhood', a concept that has filtered through the organisation via multi-layered communication from 'player to player, player to coach, coach to player and coach to coach', and is a key thread in the cultural shift that has occurred at the

Falcons. A video, released by the Falcons to their fans on Twitter* in the aftermath of their 2017 Super Bowl defeat, communicates that falling short does not break their brotherhood, but instead strengthens it. The full text from the video – which was accompanied by the caption 'the Brotherhood was built to rise again #InBrotherhood' – is below:

Brotherhood is not the product of prosperity. Brotherhood is a bond formed by commitment in times of darkness, hurting. Our effort, our passion, our fight – we give it all. Frustratedly close, but ultimately short. Devastated.

We're now faced with two choices: We stay down and allow this moment to defeat us, or we absorb this pain, we feel every ounce of it, and then we get back up – and we fight harder. Because we did not get what we came for. This moment will not define us – our response will – so we dig deeper. We pick ourselves up, we come back stronger than before and we push those next to us to do the same.

This is the standard our brotherhood demands. Our story. Our dream. We've built the foundation. No, our brotherhood was not lost in the darkness. The darkness just fuses our bond and fuels our destiny.

In brotherhood, we fall. In brotherhood, we trust. In brotherhood, we rise.

The video could quite easily be viewed as another glossy social media output to appease the fans. Perhaps there is an element of that – it does conjure images of those classic Hollywood sports films.

* 'The Brotherhood was built to rise again' (2017). twitter.com/AtlantaFalcons, retrieved 15 November 2019.

However, having spent time with Quinn, it is perfectly clear to me that his belief in the pivotal message of 'brotherhood' goes much deeper, that it speaks to his own personal values and those of the team he leads.

Gary Kirsten referred to role of 'the badge' that players represent. 'If you see that your responsibility is greater than just walking on the field and winning and losing games of cricket, then you have got to live that responsibility out every day and the leaders drive that.'

The concept of playing for something bigger than yourself was a common theme in the interviews. Ashley Giles reflected on how, at times, he felt disappointed in his Lancashire team:

> I want these guys to get a real identity about what it is to play for us, what it means. It is not just turning up to do a job, not really; it is much more than that. I have said a couple of times this year I have been a bit disappointed with the performances. It is a huge privilege to put on that shirt. I will never wear it as a player, [but] you guys do every day, [so] you should respect that hugely and that should underpin what they do on a day-to-day basis.

Elite sport does not allow for coasting and a sense of identity brings with it belonging and, crucially, accountability.

Michael Maguire talks about how, in his sport of rugby league, the value of the jersey is significant. 'It is just a jersey but inside that jersey are all these people, hundreds and hundreds of people, having something that is very special to them.' This sense of purpose runs deep at the Rabbitohs:

> Parents look at that emblem and get that feeling that their son has achieved. The young kids I see coming in to our

sheds now and they just run around with the footie, and it's the rabbit. It's just a symbol, but the value of that symbol is what we create. The values that I hold in the jersey, I want to pass those on to the young kids. If they aspire to being a great Rabbitoh in years to come then they get an idea of what's expected. Their parents, they are proud of their kid. As someone who is trying to drive this organisation, to be able to have that connection with the younger kids, I see value in that.

REPRESENTING THE COMMUNITY

There is a palpable sense of community in South Sydney, as the Rabbitohs make a concerted effort to support the development of the region. This sense of community has also been maximised by Sean Dyche during his time at Burnley. A clever piece of marketing by the in-house PR team – 'Our Town, Our Turf, Our Team' – reveals a key component of Dyche's overhaul of the prevailing culture at Burnley, a one-club town where football is at the beating heart of the community:

> When I came here I spoke a lot about this one-club mentality, and yet again winning galvanises that, but I wanted to know, beyond winning, where is the connection with the community? Where is the connection with the people? Are they aligned with the team? The only thing I ever guaranteed as a manager, when I got here, is that you will have a team that will give everything, and I think we have pretty much done that. Few and far between are times when I feel the team haven't given everything to try to win a game, very few, and I think our fans would vouch for that so that is the underlying feel of that kind

of 'our town, our turf, our team'. It is about the collective mentality, and what it all stands for rather than just a player or just the team. What do the fans stand for? Are they connected? Because it means a lot here. I have learnt that over five and a half years, and I'm not saying other clubs don't, but here it dominates the community.

Dyche's leadership in building a team that identifies with the community that it represents has made Turf Moor a notoriously tricky fixture for visiting teams. The team is tough, gritty and persistent – words you might come to associate with an old mill town in the north-west of England.

Mind you, they are also remarkably resilient. When Burnley lose, there is a prevailing sense that the team will rebound and recover. The town itself is surrounded by rivers, open fields, and wild moorland and to the north is the imposing summit of Lancashire's Pendle Hill. Urban and rural areas converge, and grit and spirit combine with areas of real natural beauty. This blend is replicated in the football team – they can play as well as battle.

In order to communicate an authentic sense of identity, sporting leaders can selectively draw from a team's heritage and background. The raw information is often already there, it just needs communicating in the right way, at the right time. Before the 1999 Champions League final, it was no coincidence that Sir Alex Ferguson wore a replica jersey from 1968, a subtle nod to the last time that Manchester United, led by George Best and Bobby Charlton, had won the coveted trophy. Lancaster, Giles and Maguire all talk about the importance of symbols – the English/ Lancastrian rose and the Rabbitoh – the stories that can be told around such emotive imagery and the bond that can create. Dyche and Maguire look to their communities to provide strong and consistent messaging, intensifying an already unbreakable connection. In the USA, Quinn looks instead to instil a common language of 'brotherhood' in a team of highly paid individuals heralding from all over the USA.

Whatever the source, a team with a clear sense of identity is able to operate with an element of certainty and clarity regarding the direction of the group. While this does not guarantee plain sailing in the tumultuous world of elite sport, it perhaps enables them to be better equipped to react rationally and effectively to the inevitable challenges that they will face.

LEGACY

The term 'legacy' became something of a buzz-word as a result of James Kerr's case study* of the New Zealand All Blacks. In 2010, Kerr spent time embedded in the culture and environment of the team. He was able to interview coaches, support staff and players, as he looked to uncover the secret of their success and the ingredients that give the All Blacks their competitive advantage.

Out of his research came a number of interesting findings. Two central components were 'purpose', as discussed previously, and 'legacy'. In the case of the All Blacks, they linked the idea of legacy to their iconic black jersey and the silver fern. When a player wins their first cap for the All Blacks, they receive a book, filled with images of jerseys from the legendary teams of the past. Following these images are blank spaces, communicating and reinforcing the idea that the legacy of the All Blacks is now in their hands. The players are encouraged to embrace what has gone before, and accept they do not own

* Kerr, J. (2013). *Legacy: What the All Blacks can teach us about the business of life.* London: Constable and Robinson.

their shirt, they are simply borrowing it before leaving it in a better place for those that follow.

Some leaders bought directly into the specific concept of 'legacy', as popularised by the All Blacks, more than others. Ashley Giles articulated his opinion, which, since he has now joined the ECB as director of cricket, is revealing:

> It is getting guys to buy into the fact that they are part of some-thing that is far bigger than just now. We will all be here for differing amounts of time. This is the start of what I would call our legacy; some might be here for six months but they are still part of this and have a chance of influencing it. So, it is about influencing the environment, always getting better, to the bigger picture which is to be the best and then it becomes something to be very proud of. So, when we win, the oppos-ition don't think, 'What a bunch of tossers,' they go, 'You know what, they play the best cricket, they've got the best players.' That is all I want. That is in touch with your legacy, it is not just about winning.

The juxtaposition of these comments and the earlier observation of English cricket under the leadership of Andy Flower is revealing. To Giles, culture and specifically legacy are the priority. Sporting careers vary in length, and time spent in possession of 'the shirt' can be fleeting or long-lasting. If a pursuit of legacy is in place, those years or months will hopefully be meaningful to both the team and the individual.

'Legacy' was already a common phrase at Leinster when Stuart Lancaster arrived in Ireland and he was quick to explore the concept with the group. Isa Nacewa, Leinster's captain during Lancaster's first season in Ireland, told me how the former England coach delivered a presentation to the group that focused on winning the European Championship. However, crucially he was not just focused on their next win, the fourth star on the jersey, but the fifth and the creation of an enduring legacy. Lancaster's focus on the future achievement tacitly instils a long-lasting cultural outlook, while dangling the tantalising opportunity to make history.

SHARING STORIES

Storytelling can be an effective component in engaging people with a greater purpose and cultivating a close team environment. Gareth Southgate, in leading England to their first World Cup semi-final in almost thirty years, worked with psychologist Pippa Grange to encourage his players to share their own personal stories. This willingness to be vulnerable can increase the cohesion of a group. There is something empowering about sharing experiences, influences and old wounds with our peers. Only with vulnerability can trust really begin to permeate throughout a culture.

Michael Maguire places great emphasis on the story of South Sydney's Grand Final-winning team of 2014 and what that leaves behind long after they are gone:

> I do buy into it a hell of a lot. Our rabbit is a symbol. But what's inside that is the people. While we have our time, if I think I'm going to do this forever and an end, you know I'd like to but reality shows that time . . . we're going to get old at some stage. But in the time that we are here, the value of that rabbit, the group of people that are there, we get to dictate what our legacy or our story is. The story that we have forged now – I've got a group of seventeen men who have taken the field and beaten history. Those people will be remembered forever.

Every single fan will remember that team that won that final. I always talk to my players, in twenty years' time, if we were to get together . . . you don't need to say anything – we all know. You don't need to talk or spruce, it's just that all the hard work that we achieved, at that time, we are able to tell our story. I guess I am big on that. I think the values that we get to talk about in years to come are the things that I hold dear, because our kids get to enjoy those stories . . .

Stories and the way they are told offer a clear hook on which to hang concepts such as legacy and purpose. Clear and emotive narratives are powerful as they speak directly to the human brain. A leader cannot just order people to do things a certain way, but you can point the way with a good story. The poet, writer and civil rights activist Maya Angelou, herself an amazing storyteller, said, 'People will forget what you said, people will forget what you did, but people will never forget how you made them feel.'

Effective leaders are able to use words to paint vivid pictures, and these pictures impact us at a deeper, emotional level. The brain works on these same three levels – words, pictures, emotions. We remember more vividly those moments that give rise to searing emotions (positive or negative). That is why, long after an event, our recollection conjures those same emotions as if we were experiencing that moment all over again. This knowledge is not useful only for those in a position of traditional leadership. You might just want to convey a message in a different style. Don't hold back from using symbols, emblems and storytelling to drive the feeling you want to create within your teams.

You will note that some of these terms – such as purpose, identity, legacy – are somewhat interchangeable and open to personal interpretation. What they do have in common is an appreciation for the bigger picture of both team and organisational success. They are not boxes to be ticked in a two-hour group workshop, but rather concepts that must constantly be discussed, acknowledged and reinforced by action. Whichever term you use, these concepts form the emotional and psychological foundations that drive a culture of high performance.

These foundations provide a guiding philosophy that underpins the values and culture of an organisation. When performance decreases or a group faces a critical moment, leaders and teams can refer back and check their alignment to a mutually agreed purpose. Consider purpose the compass of the group, helping to answer the recurring question, 'Are we going in the right direction?'

There is no standard approach to creating this purpose, no perfect formula, as each team environment brings its own nuances and contexts. Leaders must be acutely aware of the unique history of their organisation, allowing an appreciation for (but not a reliance on) the past, while creating a palpable excitement for the future.

A RESULTS BUSINESS

While the concepts of legacy and purpose are important and admirable pursuits, all of the leaders were acutely aware of the need to balance the big picture with a more immediate focus on the unavoidable requirement of elite sport: achieving results. Stuart Lancaster prophetically acknowledged that 'people won't give a stuff about the legacy or anything else beyond the World Cup – if I don't do well then someone else will be coaching this team'.

He described the 'interesting moral dilemma' he faced when supporting the policy not to select foreign-based players for England duty. 'When you are desperate to carry on in the role, when you know you are on the cusp of developing a great team, but you also know you might lose your opportunity because of results and if someone could come in and enhance results, would you pick them?'

At the end of that sentence, he shrugged his shoulders, an indication of the genuine conflict he faced in that scenario. He knows that, on the outside, his job is simply to 'win rugby games' but in his own mind 'it is winning in the short term but keeping one eye on the future to win in the long term as well. A lot of my decisions are based around what is going to be good for us in the long term as well as the short term.' Lancaster's comments may lead you to think he is stubborn or idealistic in his approach. Alternatively, you might see a selflessness and a desire to do what is best for the team, despite the potential ramifications for him as the leader.

Ashley Giles spoke about a key learning experience in this area. As part of his academic qualification in sports directorship, he attended a presentation given by a senior police officer. The speaker recalled his experience of working under extreme pressure in the emergency services and highlighted the need to simultaneously keep a watchful eye on both the long- and short-term results. Giles recalls that the police officer showed a picture of the penny-farthing, an old bicycle with one big wheel and one smaller wheel, to the group and initially Giles wondered what on earth the message could be.

> At first I was thinking, 'What is all this about?', but it was brilliant. It hit home for me, these two wheels. The big wheel was the long-term plan, [it] moves much slower, but at the same time you have got this little wheel spinning quickly and that is about action now, delivering, winning tomorrow.

Putting this into a specific sporting context, Giles went on to discuss the impact this can have on team selection. 'Although one player might be a player for the future, for the next game I need another bloke to play. "Sorry mate, you might just have to miss out." It will give me more time and therefore give you more time, all part of our legacy.'

The image of the penny-farthing used by the police officer is compelling in illustrating the duality of leadership. The contrasting forces of results versus purpose represent a never-ending balancing act for the leader. In the example above, Giles' awareness of this push and pull allows him to make a decision that, in his own mind at least, maintains this balance.

Gary Kirsten talks about his approach to achieving a balance between long-term and short-term success, searching for steady wins to keep the 'wolf from the door':

> There is always going to be that focus on results. So, for me the key is twofold. One is to manage upwards so you need to build good relationships with your owners. The other is you need to continue to have small wins along the way. You need to stay in the mix. You need to be performing. You might not be performing to the level that you want but you have got to get those little wins along the way to keep the wolf from the door.

He reflects on his situation at the time of our interview, as head coach of the IPL franchise the Delhi Daredevils, and reiterates his commitment to achieving that sense of purpose:

> Obviously, the results become important in the end because that is where, for many, your credibility sits. I have got that now. We have tried to introduce a new system and a new way of doing things in terms of our identity and our culture which

we are only building now and trying to establish but we haven't backed it up with a massive amount of results, so there are always question marks. You are always trying to re-establish and realign and re-evaluate and bring in new resource into that bigger purpose space. It can be incredibly difficult to manage it, so again it's buying time as much as you can, it's quick wins, it's managing upwards.

You might have short term-success, but it is not going to be sustainable because people will start, once they've had a little bit of success, taking advantage and start using the system for their own purpose. But if they are constantly under the vision of a bigger purpose, greater than their own individual glory, then I think you can hold people for longer. You can have a hugely talented bunch of individuals, but if you think you can take shortcuts because they're talented and they're going to win games . . . they might do it for a while but it's not sustainable.

Building an enduring culture or legacy in a competitive, results-based environment is definitely not easy, but the benefit of this approach can be the rare and revered levels of stability, trust and long-term success.

As is the case with his on-field philosophy, Roberto Martínez is steadfast in his approach to building a football club:

I have been able to work in a way that doesn't rely too much on winning or losing. I rely on the standards that we set daily, rather than being a manger that, depending if you win or lose at the weekend, your group works in a different manner. I want to believe that I work as a manager that builds a football club, rather than having to win every weekend. If I am just going to be guided by winning at the weekend to keep my job then I cannot put time aside to develop youngsters, to do things that the club is going to benefit from two or three years down the line. Working to a vision and a philosophy, it gives me the strength and the confidence to do things that I hope the club will benefit from in the long term.

Since our initial interview, Martínez has taken on the challenge of international football, leading the highly talented Belgium side to third place at the 2018 World Cup, gallantly losing to eventual winners France in the semi-final. The demands of that role are far removed from leading a club side on a daily basis. Now, he does not have the time to build a 'club', and must instead galvanise a group of players, many playing for competing clubs across Europe, to come together to maximise their vast potential.

This is a different leadership scenario altogether, yet these players know each other well, many of them having played in the same youth teams growing up. Martínez's awareness of both the demands and limitations of the situation allows him to adapt his style. He works hard to get to know his players, their backgrounds and personalities, and listens to staff members who have worked in the Belgium set-up longer than he has. He does all this while staying true to his football philosophy and building on the cultural norms he has inherited.

SETTING THE DIRECTION

It is widely accepted that successful organisations have a clear purpose and vision of what success means to them. What remains unknown is *how* that is achieved within specific environments. Here, the term 'direction' refers to the guidance a leader gives to an organisation so as to ensure they continue to strive for their overall and collective objectives. This can come in the form of specific and planned interventions, team meetings or simply informal corridor conversations with key personnel. Consider this part of a leader's role as keeping a safe hand on the tiller, in order to navigate their teams through both calm and stormy conditions. At times they will need to make a concerted effort to set or realign the direction in which they are heading and, at others, make subtle adjustments and reinforcements as and when required.

Sean Dyche sees setting the overall direction of the group as a key part of his role. He acknowledges that he needs results – 'the next game is the most important, that is my job and that's fine' – but strives to build an enduring environment that focuses on much more than the outcome of the weekend's fixture:

It is winning but it's *how* you are going to win, and I don't mean style of play, I mean the mentality towards winning. What are you going to give? Because it takes massive sacrifice to really win, then if you are winning, how are you winning and on what level? Are you winning through work ethic, respect, professionalism, dedication or are you winning by chance? Some teams win just because they have more skill than the next team, then it implodes quickly.

We talk about real winning, what are you building? Are you actually a real team? Are you a real team of people who are going to win by design or are you going to win by default? A lucky season or a one-off season, all the stuff like that. So it is that thinking: winning a game or winning by achieving in the longer term. Not just to win a game, are we achieving over a longer period of time? Are you as an individual achieving what you want to achieve? Is the team achieving?

And is the club achieving? Bigger picture, rather than can we win the next game and 'hurrah' if we do and 'oh no' if we don't, so keeping it to longer-term thinking. Are you winning on a deeper level than just a league table? Of course that is my job but is there something underneath that? I love seeing players moving forward as we discussed earlier. I have to see the bigger picture, players have to focus on their bigger picture.

Here, Dyche reflects on a key, invaluable approach to culture. As a leader, he steps back from events and applies a genuine cultural philosophy to the events (the 'what') that have happened, reinterpreting them to represent a more impactful 'why'. He is balancing the need for results with the team's development on a deeper level. It is powerful and captures legacy and culture in one.

GOALS

A significant part of the leaders' perceived implementation of their vision was the setting of goals, a much-discussed concept that is widely recognised to be of significant benefit to teams and individuals.

Ashley Giles discussed the importance of setting challenging team goals among individual agendas and links that process to his vision for the organisation. Effectively set goals can channel individual plans towards the wider mission:

Teams who have a lot of fear and insecurity don't set goals because they are scared of failure. You need to reassure teams that it is good to set these goals and that they are not always instantly attainable, but they should be big goals. What is the point of having medium goals? If you know where you want to go, you've got a chance of getting there. It is like having a satnav, otherwise you haven't got a clue, you are just aimlessly heading into the distance. Even if you have that massive goal and you get 70 per cent towards it, you are doing all right. But if you don't know you have got no chance, you are just cruising. Now, in terms of that vision and that goal, well, it needs to be something that joins everyone, to be a big team vision, because I am also a believer that there will be a lot of agendas, individual agendas, and that is fine.

It is even more important to reset and refresh goals after a period of success. Michael Maguire, who, in his own words, 'can be a bit cutthroat if people get in the way of where I want to go', described how he realigned his team's goals after a historic season and gives an indication of his own personal drive:

Everyone is on a blank sheet of paper. What we achieved the year before is gone. For me, back-to-back talk and those sorts of things are completely irrelevant because we are all starting over. People talk about things; people are going to come after us and all those sorts of things. Well, we are playing for something bigger, it is the prize at the other end. So, your focus is that, not about what teams might do to you because, if you are not performing, you're not going to get there anyway. I am here to win Premierships. That is why I do the job. Every coach wants to win a Premiership – it's easy to say that. But I would give it away if it was easy.

An illustration of an individual's goal-setting process comes from golfer Justin Thomas who, in the 2017 season, secured his first major and topped the US PGA Tour money list, claiming top spot in the Official World Rankings in the process. Following his victory he took great satisfaction in sharing the targets he had set himself ahead of the season. Crucially, they were a combination of the outcome goals (winning the Tour Championship, winning a Major Championship) he desired, and more measurable and statistic-based process goals (achieving a scoring average of under 70, having +.25 strokes gained* putting) that will nudge him closer to achieving a career goal. The field of psychology is peppered with instructions and formulas for setting goals. I wouldn't necessarily recommend Thomas' approach, but it is a clear example of an individual's process, and in this case breaking down goals into different areas. In fairness to Thomas, he also shared his goals the following season, when he didn't achieve as many of his objectives.

Of course, golf is arguably the most individual of sports and the goal-setting process should be somewhat smoother or at least simpler. With that in mind, consider the convoluted process of effective goal setting in sporting team environments with a multitude of players. In the case of an NFL team, final regular season rosters are made up of more than fifty players. A collection of individual athletes, at varying stages of their careers and contracts, playing different roles within the group, each with their own ambitions and goals, must all buy in to a common goal.

At the Atlanta Falcons, Quinn, his back-room staff and the players look to set goals relating to specific 'things that they can control that affect winning'. Ahead of the 2018 NFL season, those goals were to statistically be the best attacking team, to have the best turnover margin, to be the most poised team at the end of quarters, halves

---

* A golf statistic measuring how many strokes a player gains or loses on the putting greens during a round.

and games, and to display the right mindset in all situations they encounter. You will note these are not simply outcome goals, for example, to win the Super Bowl. Of course that is a target (or *the* target for the Falcons), but it is the step-by-step goals, goals that can be constantly measured and evaluated throughout a season, on which Quinn focuses his attention. It is these goals that will provide the team with the best chance of achieving their greatest challenge, the coveted and thus-far elusive Super Bowl title. Quinn's approach shares some elements with that of Dyche: it prioritises psychological responses to events in order to maintain a cultural focus.

Big-picture concepts are emotional, aspirational and empowering. Playing for a collective purpose rather than a paycheck may well appeal to modern-day 'millennial' athletes. However, these same athletes also possess a driven and focused sense of their own career ambitions. The big picture, as discussed previously, must be finely balanced with an awareness of short-term performance. As individuals, our levels of drive and energy will naturally fluctuate over a set period of time. In this respect, elite athletes are no different. It requires significant reserves of personal resilience to continue to pursue an outcome or goal that is seemingly out of reach. As a result, all leaders must find a way to combine an inspirational purpose with a clear strategy and a sense of constant momentum, challenging athletes to hit targets at both an individual and collective level throughout a season, all building towards the team's ultimate common goal.

CHAPTER 3: LEADERSHIP LESSONS

- Ensure you have a clear purpose, both individually and as part of a team. Why do you do what you do?
- The ultimate human motivation is to be part of something bigger than ourselves. A group of people galvanised by a common purpose is the most powerful and effective resource.
- Always look to balance the exciting big-picture thinking with short-term wins and the need for results. Remember the police officer's penny-farthing.
- Ensure you and your team have a clear sense of direction and common goals. Crucially, the goal alone is not enough. Day-to-day actions and habits are required to back them up.
- Take the time to understand the individual drivers of others and try to align those goals with that of the team.
- A well-written purpose is great, but it can also be meaningless 'words on a wall' if it is not reinforced by behaviours and interactions.
- Corridor conversations are important; check in on those around you and remember most of culture is what people don't see.
- Focus on the 'why' of your message, rather than telling people 'what' to do and 'how' to do it.
- Consider how you communicate. Emails? PowerPoint slides? Use symbols and storytelling to evoke emotion and action in the people around you.
- It starts with the leader. If you can't be vulnerable, how can your teams be?

Building a High-Performance Culture

....

ASSESSING CULTURE: HISTORY AND TRADITION

Elite sport teams are often steeped in history and tradition, making the process of achieving a cultural shift ever more challenging. While there is the rare occasion when a new team or franchise is formed, each organisation has its own symbols, stories, rituals and language. These must be understood and respected by any new leader who arrives into the environment.

Cricket as a sport is steeped in tradition, both in England and across the Commonwealth. My conversation with Ashley Giles takes place on a summer evening overlooking the playing surface at Lancashire's home ground, Old Trafford. Historical images, individual records and memorabilia look down from all angles, a reminder of the sense of tradition that surrounds the players every day.

Giles, referencing his time at Lancashire, says, 'You have to respect that they know what it is to win a championship, respect what happened there before and learn from it.' Gary Kirsten sounds a similar warning: 'You have got to tread carefully. You have got to respect the history of that team or that group of individuals. You have got to respect what they stand for and what they've done. And then just slowly start to introduce new behaviours.' However pressing the need for cultural shifts, leadership requires tact and delicacy at certain times.

Michael Maguire uses the history of an organisation to his advantage by simply choosing to 'use the good years because that is what really holds the club together'. Recalling his time at Wigan Warriors, who have a long and illustrious honours list, he was able to utilise 'a lot of the people that were around the club, because they are winners, they are used to winning'. When we met, he talked about taking the same approach during his time with the South Sydney Rabbitohs:

> There was a time when we were winning and winning and winning. There were a lot of guys that were involved and I brought them back into the club because that's all they knew as players so why not get that feeling around the place of what winning is all about. I guess I use the history of the winning parts of the club . . . I want to know the stories about why that club, at that time, was winning, because that is what I constantly aspire to do.

Maguire's natural drive is to lead and move forward, but his lack of ego allows him to pull symbols of past successes back into the environment, taking inspiration from the past in order to push the team forward.

Despite the positives that come from being able to draw upon a rich history, leaders also warned of the need to sometimes take a different direction. Stuart Lancaster, for instance, does not believe that history should 'define where you go in the future', adding that 'history can provide a sense of identity but, when you are trying to reshape your culture, sometimes you have to make some pretty bold and very difficult decisions and have almost a sudden change of direction'. The skill in leadership, therefore, is to know which approach will work for your team: make a statement, embrace the past, or a mix of the two.

I am sure you can think of a club or business that you might describe as reluctant to change or as being 'stuck in the past'. These organisations, especially those with low staff turnover, may struggle to progress as the past becomes a weight holding them down, preventing them from achieving high performance. Limiting beliefs, expectations and existing group norms can stall a team's progress, irrespective of the level of talent at their disposal.

Michael Maguire spoke about how a club's past can hold back a process of culture change. Here, the mindset of the people throughout the organisation is vital. He looks to avoid a club's 'lean years, eradicating the old news, because it means nothing' to both Maguire and the current group of players. 'We weren't here at those times,' he tells me, 'so why should it hold us back?' For Maguire, the process at the Rabbitohs was about 'changing people's mindsets in a lot of ways. We got caught in talking about the fact we had not won for however long. I had nothing to do with that and neither did the players that hadn't been there for the last forty years!' Maguire is selective in his approach – using the allure of past success while dispelling lingering doubt from years in the wilderness. The past is a powerful force and a leader must tread carefully in the footsteps of history.

ASSESSING CULTURE: CURRENT ENVIRONMENT

As well as understanding what has gone before, leaders must spend time assessing the existing personnel, environment and behaviours of an organisation. This crucial process takes time and focus. Only fools rush in, as they say. Roberto Martínez tells me that there needs to be 'an intense period of understanding the organisation' and where it is at that specific moment in time. Stuart Lancaster provided an insight into the issues that he encountered upon taking over as England's head coach:

> There was a sense of entitlement from the players. There was no real joined-up leadership group at the top from the players. There was a disconnect between the senior players and the senior management and the top leaders in the group all had a different set of values that left the group in the middle and the younger players with no barometer of where to go.

The process of assessing a culture was described by Ashley Giles as something that invariably takes time. 'You can't rush because you will miss something or look past something seemingly insignificant that is the cause. It is generally not what you see in front of you but something underneath that.' This was supported further by fellow cricketer Gary Kirsten, who warned about this potential 'red flag' area for any new coach. A leader must be mindful not 'to come in and straight away feel like you can impose a new way of doing things on to a group of people, many of whom might have been here for a significant period before you. It takes time to establish some trust and create an environment where people say, "OK, we are ready for change and we are ready to look at things slightly differently."'

A newly appointed leader, inheriting a group of athletes, must display a blend of interest, appreciation, respect and humility. They will need to ask questions and genuinely listen to the answers, even when their natural style is to jump in and take control. Athletes are switched-on people, typically at the top of their profession. They are not easily fooled. Actions, just as much as words, are keenly observed and duly noted.

CLUB VERSUS COUNTRY

Those leaders with experience of a range of cultures highlighted the differences they had encountered between international and domestic sport. Ashley Giles observed the demands of international sport, which is 'much more transactional', and referred to the intense scrutiny that comes with representing an entire nation: 'If you don't win you are going to get it in the neck.' Giles compared this with domestic sport, where the coach has 'much more time, as you should do. You are working with them all the time. You have the opportunity to try to mould them and improve them.' A leader will always need to face the facts and respond to the cultural demands of a situation.

Roberto Martínez's biggest challenge when taking his role as head coach of the Belgium national side was the same lack of time with the players that Giles refers to. Whilst the nature of the role did not come as a surprise, it is still in stark contrast to the day-to-day approach that Martínez has been able to apply consistently throughout his career at club level. This has led him to utilise a more 'common-sense approach' where he feels the need to prioritise a lot more. He tells me that 'international football is about finding the priority that is needed in a specific camp and working with real clarity towards it'. With limited time on the field and with the players, a clear and streamlined approach communicates confidence and a sense of control to a squad bursting with talent.

During our discussions, Gary Kirsten drew on his contrasting experiences across the cricketing world. He describes leading a team in the affluent Indian Premier League (IPL), an intense, franchise-based, domestic competition, where the coach works with players from a cross-section of cultures in an environment where 'there is less pressure externally but you have a massive responsibility to the owners who are investing huge sums of money'. He compares this with coaching international sides, where you find 'there are greater stakeholders and bigger responsibilities, but there is a stability because you work with people for a long time'.

Specific scenarios will invariably throw up shifting priorities, but leaders, as demonstrated here by Roberto and Gary, possess an active level of self-awareness that allows them to flex their styles accordingly.

Stuart Lancaster describes the challenges of achieving cultural change at international level, as players who are used to competing against each other on the domestic stage come together to play for their country. 'That sense of mates playing together is quite hard to achieve when everyone is fighting to be number one. Selection is a big factor in the dynamic. They all come from different clubs where often they are playing in big games against each other. So, people think at international level it's easy, you pull on a shirt and it bonds you. It isn't. Not at all. It takes a while to build together and experiences of good and bad times have a huge impact.'

Ultimately, elite rugby is a hugely physical, competitive and collision-based sport. The presence of intense club rivalries within an international camp dictates that conflict (physical and otherwise) is inevitable. The leader has to manage this process, so that such conflict actually contributes to a healthy and competitive culture rather than detracts from it.

Achieving a cultural shift in a club environment, Lancaster continues, often occurs at a faster rate due to the fact that 'you are working day in day out, week in week out, you are doing it for thirty-five weeks of the year and there is a real performance development impact you can make on individuals. If it's young players, senior players, you name it, it is a player development and player performance role.'

He compares this with the nature of international coaching. 'You have long periods of not coaching and nothingness because you've got no games, so you are waiting for the next games to come along. Then when you get the players, you're organising them, you are taking the best players and organising them in a very short space of time. It is less about player development and more about delivering on a single day, and can be an unbelievable high, but the unbelievable lows when you lose as an international coach, you know, are tough to take.'

Lancaster's words emphasise the emotional extremes of international sport, which are heightened due to the absence of a 'next game' mentality and the intense national profile. Often a team must linger on a single performance for a sustained period, harbouring emotions and thoughts without an immediate outlet, before having the chance to respond. This time period provides outside voices with a window of opportunity to scrutinise and debate the team's performance and the leader's decision-making, often to the frustration of the team. This combination of factors means that a leader's own grit and resilience are tested in a unique way.

CULTURAL ARCHITECTS (THE INFLUENCERS)

During their assessment process – which makes it sound more formal than it perhaps should – leaders are often looking to identify the key individuals within the group. These people, who could be athletes or staff members, have the crucial ability to influence the group. They might be the team captain, but are just as likely to be an 'informal' leader, who is culturally influential regardless of job title. Another term for these individuals, first used by Norwegian psychologist Professor Willi Railo, is 'cultural architects'.* In an interview with the *Guardian*

---

* Railo, W. (1986). *Willing to win*. Utrecht: Amas.

Railo, who worked with former England football manager Sven-Goran Eriksson throughout his career, described cultural architects as 'people who are able to change the mindset of others . . . they are self-confident and able to transfer self-confidence to other players'.[*] According to Railo, David Beckham grew into such a role with England.

Utilising the 'cultural architect' concept can be an effective strategy for a leader. These influential individuals are seen as representative of the desired culture and, from their respected position among their peers, can create direction, set examples and initiate action in others. In my applied experience, I have seen cultural architects hold such influence via traditional leadership, stand-out performances, social status or time with the team.[†] Whilst they will predominantly be players, I can also recall numerous examples of staff members who fill these roles. These staff members can come from all corners of an organisation – from the kit manager to the masseuse, and from the assistant manager to the chef, they all have the ability to set the tone on a daily basis.

Ashley Giles highlighted the role that human nature plays in a team setting, and described the need to understand the particular dynamics of a group: 'You need to look at what you have got and where you might have gaps, who are the big influences on the environment . . . there is a lot of human nature in that stuff. Ultimately, when you strip them down, sport and business are both deeply human endeavours, dealing predominantly with people.'

Gary Kirsten described his approach of assessing a culture as 'asking relevant questions and having the right conversations' with

[*] White, J. (2001). 'An interview with Willi Railo.' theguardian.com, retrieved 6 December 2019.
[†] Price, M. S. and Weiss, M. R. (2011). 'Peer leadership in sport: Relationships among personal characteristics, leader behaviours, and team outcomes.' *Journal of Applied Sport Psychology*, 23, 49–64.

the right people. The ability to build relationships and 'connections with prominent and influential people in the space you have inherited' allows the leader to then ask pertinent questions and get honest responses. Kirsten provides examples of the information he is looking to find: 'What are they not happy about? What went wrong down this particular road? Or what went right? You might have moved into a space that has had incredible success.' Relatively open questions such as these can reveal powerful and sometimes unexpected insights into the cultural journey a group has been on. Knowing how to probe for the relevant information can provide the leader with a deeper and quicker understanding of a team's mindset, helping to identify areas for immediate improvement and quick wins, and aiding the quest for a group's 'buy in'.

QUIZ-MASTER

Not every team member will be willing to partake in such conversations. Athletes are all at different points in their own careers, with contracts, finances, and role stability all potential concerns. Speaking up can, depending on what they have experienced before, be seen as a risky strategy. Some players may be guarded and suspicious towards a new leader, preferring instead to take time to see how things unfold. Aside from this scepticism that sometimes infiltrates elite sport, the nature of human behaviour and personality means that it is often the same dominant and influential voices that will speak up, leaving the more analytical or junior members of a team in the background.

Sean Dyche employed a different approach when he took the reins at Burnley to allow for this and to allay any such fears. Dyche reached out to all of the players with a questionnaire:

I gave the players a questionnaire with complete anonymity. I said, 'I am not interested in who wrote what and if you want to mess around with it you can just scribble on it if you like. But you have now got a chance to tell me what you think. If you decide you don't want that chance and you want to draw a stupid picture on it, that is up to you, but then don't come back to me in a week. You have a chance to tell me everything you need to tell me and with complete anonymity.' I said, 'You can do it now, you can take it home with you, you don't have to do it, you can choose not to do it, that's fine, you can send it in, you can type it if you want. I am not interested in who says what, but I am interested in what you are thinking.' Once we got that, we had a look at it, showed the players what came up and then reflected on it and said, 'Right, this is what we are going to have to change.'

Dyche's approach achieved three key objectives that helped him achieve a feeling of trust within the group. Firstly, he created a safe space allowing players to share their honest feedback and doing this anonymously should they wish. Secondly, he encouraged a more considered approach by asking them to take the questionnaires away with them. And thirdly, he acknowledged that any group will have a wide range of personality and learning styles, encouraging all members of the group to have an opinion. The process also allows the leader some time to consolidate the information and identify priority areas for immediate action, which helps to establish buy-in.

One criticism of such an approach may that be it appears slightly reductive, asking individuals to fill in a structured questionnaire and not allowing for the more flexible and dynamic elements that emerge only from conversations. However, the more dominant characters within a group dynamic will always seek out the opportunity to elaborate on their opinion and, simultaneously, the information on the questionnaire will, if the player waves their anonymity, give Dyche an insight into each individual's mindset, thus allowing him to have more targeted conversations with the players. The questionnaire does not replace conversations; it guides them towards a more constructive and informed interaction.

CONSIDERING THE FANS

Roberto Martínez described his 'two-aspect' approach to assessing an organisation. He strives, like all of our leaders, to initially gain a picture of the dynamics and characteristics of the group. 'If you have got older players, young players, players who have been successful, players who have been damaged previously, what is the situation? And then work with those players straight away.' The second element of Martínez's approach is to consider the views of the supporters, asking himself, 'If I was a fan of the club, what would I want my leader to be? That informs the way of playing: is winning more important than playing well or is playing well more important than winning? I try to recognise where we are from a fan's point of view, and quickly engage with what that fan wants.'

Martínez is the only leader to talk specifically about the viewpoint of the fans, but fan culture can be significant. Let's take Everton Football Club as an example. As one of the founding members of the Football League, they have a long and illustrious history that looms over any manager. Situated in the beating heart of Liverpool, the club is an integral part of a city that itself is deeply embedded in our culture, be that through music, art, architecture or industry.

Everton share a tumultuous and intense rivalry with their neighbours, Liverpool FC. The two teams are permanently locked in a fierce sporting struggle, and the Merseyside derby is one of the most anticipated fixtures in world football. The clubs are inextricably linked through geography and history, and the two always come together when the city demands. Despite the fierce sporting battle, there is also a continuous undercurrent of respect and, dare I say it, love that goes beyond sport. Of course, Everton do not want to see Liverpool lifting the Champions League or the Premier League trophy. Anyone but them. Yet love, at times, is not a million miles away from hate. The two clubs love to hate one another. Many families are divided into red and blue, but when it matters most, as in the aftermath of the Hillsborough disaster, Liverpool unites.

Cultural symbols are plentiful, ranging from the club motto *Nil Satis Nisi Optimum*, meaning 'nothing but the best is good enough', to the playing of the same song* before every home game. Reminders of past success are never far away. A statue of the legendary centre forward, Dixie Dean, running with ball in hand, lies outside Goodison Park. Just up the road, against the backdrop of the terraced houses that surround the stadium, there is another statue of the 'Holy Trinity' of Alan Ball, Colin Harvey and Howard Kendall – a permanent reminder of the success of the 1970s.

On the football side, Everton have evolved over the years, leading to some confusion over their identity. Known at different times as 'the dogs of war', 'the school of science' and 'the people's club', these contrasting characteristics still collide today. It is

---

* Known as the theme tune to the sixties television show *Z Cars*, the song actually has its origins in a traditional Liverpool 1890 folk song – 'Johnny Todd' – which depicts a sailor being betrayed by his lover while away at sea.

reasonable to assume that supporters want a team that represents the community, combining the non-negotiable levels of effort, grit and determination, mixed with technical ability, skill and attacking football.

In Martínez's first season, Everton achieved their best ever Premier League points total (72 points) and finished fifth. Over the following seasons, despite a dip in league form, they reached the latter stages of domestic and European Cup competitions. However, despite Martínez's commitment to attractive football, he was sacked in 2016; such is the demand of the Goodison Park faithful.

SWAPPING DIGITS

At the Atlanta Falcons, Dan Quinn puts a significant emphasis on creating a standout culture equipped to deal with the demands of elite sport:

> The culture from the players' side of things, that has been a fun piece for us because we really pushed to get our culture here. We are trying to push to have one of the most remarkable cultures in professional sport. What a huge undertaking that would be – not just in the NFL – but to say, 'These players and coaches regard one another so well, push each other so hard, develop each other' that there would be a standard set that sets us apart.

Quinn's office is a hive of activity. The room itself is spacious and modern, with large windows enabling him to oversee the vast number of training pitches that sweep across the facility. High-resolution black-and-white framed images represent the 'competitiveness and toughness' qualities that he demands from his teams, yet one image stands out as different. Gifted to Quinn by the Falcons' owner, Arthur Blank, it is an old picture showing a young boy serving as a bat-boy for the Chicago Cubs baseball team. The year is 1945 and the boy in the picture is Quinn's father, Jim. Jim died in June 2016 and did not live to see his son lead the Falcons to the Super Bowl. Quinn, however, carried his father's picture with him to the final game of the season.

Quinn provides an example of things a leader might identify that indicate the nature of a culture they inherit. He describes witnessing two players swapping contact details at the end of a long season. It became apparent that this only happened as a result of one of the players being released by the team, highlighting a key observation for Quinn as the leader of the organisation:

> So our first year here was 2015. I can distinctly remember, after the season had finished, we had released a player. I went down the stairs maybe twenty feet behind him. He was talking to another guy and I heard him say, 'Hey man, I heard you got released,' and he said, 'Yeah, let's keep up,' and he asked for the other player's number. It was like a dagger to the heart because we were trying to really promote a brotherhood . . . and that told me we were a long, long way away from where we needed to be. So at that point we knew some things had to change because how can you spend close to six months together and all they knew about each other was work?

Quinn's detailed recollection of a specific conversation between two players illustrates how cultural cues can be found everywhere. They are not just to be found in formal presentations or scheduled performance reviews. A culture often reveals itself in the moments that are not designed to be observed. Considering his emphasis on 'brotherhood', Quinn was taken aback by this observation, but it was a key lesson for him in terms of confronting where the Falcons were at the time and where they needed to be.

ESTABLISHING BUY-IN

SOCIAL IDENTITY

As well as assessing the existing culture, leaders must overcome arguably their most challenging task – to achieve buy-in from the people. An authentically engaged workforce is more productive, irrespective of the sector you are in. It was fascinating to hear not just how important this is, but how leaders go about achieving 'buy-in' within a sporting environment.

The social identity approach to leadership outlines the importance of a shared connection between the leader and the group as the key foundation to effective leadership. During a lifetime, we constantly define ourselves as both individuals ('I') and group members ('us'). Group membership relates to our social identity, or the extent to which we feel part of a group, thus impacting our thoughts and actions.

Social identity theory contends that leaders can build this connection with the players in a number of different ways. Firstly, they must authentically represent the group's values and be prototypical of the collective through their own behaviour. The leader must exemplify the values on a daily basis. If they don't, this sends the message that the athletes don't need to either. Secondly, they need to be seen as champions of the group, to be deemed as acting for the benefit of the team rather than for their own individual gain. From an external perspective, this is most evident in the language used during media interviews. The third element is for the leader to be proactive in constructing and reinforcing group values to ensure behaviours and standards are impacted. Finally, the group must see evidence that the leader is embedding the identity and progressing towards the agreed vision – proof that the big picture is becoming a reality.*

Gary Kirsten emphasised just how imperative this process is to high performance: 'If you don't have the changing room [and the people in it] as a leader, then you have nothing,' while Stuart Lancaster refers to a leader being able to display the 'art of influence, of getting people to buy in to what you believe'.

As well as being sufficiently captivated by a vision of future success, athletes must engage with the leader on a human level. Kirsten has experienced a range of cultures in his time as head coach of South Africa, India and the IPL franchise the Delhi Daredevils. He provided an in-depth insight into his approach and experiences in achieving this level of engagement. He described how the Indian team 'needed to buy into what I was as a human being, my way, and that my way fitted in to what they were trying to achieve'. Crucially, this isn't something that can be achieved with a lone presentation or speech: 'It doesn't happen overnight, it takes a bit of time to build and some guys buy in quicker than others.'

In Kirsten's experience, this process of getting 'everyone to buy into that values system' is the 'biggest challenge for a leader because you are dealing with individuals who are so uniquely different' but this challenge also brings with it the greatest potential rewards: 'If you can get the majority of people to buy in, then I think you have got something very special. If you've got a team that is blessed with some talent and skill then you can move mountains, you can do anything with that team.'

* Slater et al. (2014), supra.

Kirsten recalled a particular instance with India when, by his own admission, he got it wrong, taking what he now believes was a naïve approach:

> My first connection with the team, I tried to present a vision to them in terms of how I saw our cricket going forwards based on my experiences having played against them. It was naive in many ways to think that was going to make a difference. I realised very quickly from that moment on that I was going to actually have to build trust within this environment, as one of their new leaders. I knew one thing that would stand me in good stead . . . if I worked like an absolute dog as a coach, in the nets, and threw to guys non-stop and was just physically there for them all the time to help them on their games, then that would be a quick win for me.

Kirsten became an example for the team, not in the sense of cricketing ability, but in terms of the behaviours and values he displayed as a person. He wanted to connect with the players, gaining their trust, before looking to influence them as a team. On a daily basis, he exemplified the values he expected in them. If he wanted them to improve their timekeeping he made sure that, every time, he was early. He did the dirty work, like carrying bags from the team coach, and treated all support staff with respect. In this example, Kirsten realised that physical demonstration of work ethic and being present with the team would be more impactful than a pre-prepared presentation of a vision. This demonstration helped Kirsten build trust and infuse the team, via stealth, with his vision for the future – one day at a time.

DIGITAL AGE

Sport, like business, has been influenced by the changing landscape of the modern world. Young people and athletes now have a greater understanding of their performances and access to an ever-expanding library of information, which can make them more challenging to lead in some respects.

Kirsten reflected how today's sporting cultures 'are so different... there is such a sense of the individual in the world we live in', describing how 'access to increased knowledge and understanding [means] young people are challenging ideas like never before. They are not just going to arrive in a space and buy into everything, you are going to have to win them over.'

The prevalence of technology and the internet allows athletes to be armed with data and statistics to reinforce opinions about performance, analysis and financial rewards. The leader of today must contend with this somewhat noisy third party that sits in our pockets all day every day, providing immediate access to masses of information.

ATHLETE ROLE STABILITY

There is a pragmatic side to understanding athletes' individual motivation. Athletes may be reluctant to engage if their personal financial situation and employment status is unclear. Ashley Giles, in his time with Warwickshire, Lancashire and England, acknowledged the importance of understanding each player's personal and contractual situation. 'There is uncertainty and worry. This year [at Lancashire] is a good example. I've got nine guys on one-year contracts so as much as I can say, "Come on, play with freedom, I'll back you", they might be saying, "Hang on a minute, I've only got one month left on my contract." Whatever the hierarchy of an organisation, a leader must be up to speed with each individual's situation. This allows for authentic conversations to take place. A leader can appear dishonest and even deluded if they misjudge an athlete's personal situation.

RELATIONSHIPS ARE KEY

The nature of the affluent and high-profile Premier League means that leaders' relationships with individuals are key. Both Sean Dyche and Roberto Martínez, in their own unique styles, look to engage with their players on an individual level.

Dyche looks to align his players, making clear the connection between their role and the direction he sets for the team. In order to achieve this alignment, he regularly communicates with players about their own progress, starting with the individual and linking that back to the bigger team picture:

> We talk to them a lot, we offer them a lot of thoughts, about the fact that what is good for them is also good for the team. There is a combination there. I don't necessarily think we've had anyone here who has not bought in, we have had a few who couldn't quite grasp it but not in a negative way, they just couldn't quite fathom it out. I start with the player and help them understand what is good for them and then if we can connect that with the team, it's good for all of us.

Roberto Martínez consistently emphasises the importance of rela-tionships and the role of engaging with players on a personal level. He works to find commonality and identify how he can help the person be successful in their specific situation:

If it is an older player, it might be about how he can start think-ing about the game a bit more. How can he have a bigger influence on the other players? If it is a young player, how can he become an important player to the team? You normally look for where the player is in his career and how you can help him to make that step up. That step up is very different and sometimes you find it easier to engage with players that are similar in the beliefs that you have. But that is very much a one-to-one relationship, you need to develop that, you need to engage. Sometimes it's a player that is out of contract around the corner, another is not a regular, another one is regular but is not an important player because of the style, or it could be that they are at the end of their careers but they have got a strong affiliation because of what they've done for the club and you need to be respectful of that. They are millionaires and successful. In football, it's for two reasons: one, because they love the game; and two, because they are elite footballers. It is very easy to engage with these people in terms of aspiring to achieve. They want to win and they are good at it – otherwise they would never be in the situation.

The current group of Belgian footballers, including the likes of Eden Hazard, Kevin De Bruyne and Romelu Lukaku, have been dubbed the 'Golden Generation'. I asked Roberto how he got the buy-in of such a star-studded group. After all, he is not Belgian, so how can he convey what it really means to play for Belgium? He could not draw on national pride – he is Spanish and the players would see through that. Instead, he looked to create a natural and enjoyable environ-ment with clear roles and responsibilities

He describes the approach he took, with a group of players who have, in many ways, grown up together, as being one of 'common sense', preferring to 'naturally allow the group to get together and make the decision of wanting to work very hard for each other' as opposed to any dramatic and forced intervention. He said, 'In any team you need to have role clarity, but then you also need to have people enjoying each other's company and enjoying being part of a team.'

SENIOR PLAYERS

Having worked in several 'dressing room' environments, Gary Kirsten identifies the successful engagement of senior or influential characters within a team dynamic as a factor that can make an undoubtedly challenging process that much easier:

> You are typically going to have the more senior players within that group who are going to probably question your thinking, question your ways and you've got to be very clever in your management of people in that space, rather than just coming in with a blanket, one-size-fits-all approach. That might work well with youngsters because younger players tend to be more open to change and to looking at things differently for several reasons. One, they don't have a voice, or they have less of a voice; and two, I think younger generations are more open to change than older generations.

Kirsten advocates an approach based on traditional hierarchy, emphasising the role of older players. If this process is managed well, the senior or influential people within a team can drive a process of culture change. If they fail to engage, they can become a source of scepticism and negativity at the core of the group dynamic. Kirsten continues, 'It comes from the top down, not the bottom up because the players at the bottom are not influential enough within the team context to drive culture. So, for me, what was critical with India is that I won the senior players over. You actually only need to work with the top group and the senior players do the rest for you.'

Stuart Lancaster referred to an international camp, scheduled shortly after taking over as England head coach, that was pivotal in forging a strong relationship with his people. Whatever prior relationships exist, new team members will need to have their buy-in 'earned' by the leader:

> It was a combination because there was a group of players that I had worked with before, so they were probably halfway there anyway, and a group of players that I needed to sell the vision to. Then, we needed to set up and run a productive camp that had a big difference on the mindset of a player. By the end of that week, they had to feel it was a different team to when they walked through the door at the start of the week and I think they all did that. As such, the credibility we have as a coaching group rose, and the commitment rose on the back of the credibility.

EXAMPLES OF CULTURAL SHIFTS

During the course of our conversations, it became apparent that 'quick wins' are a key component of any cultural shift. Such small victories reinforce to athletes that they are heading in the right direction and that the leader can help them achieve their own ambitions and potential.

Roberto Martínez, unwavering in his philosophy, describes his experience at Everton of inheriting 'a very experienced group who knew how to win football matches' and the role of specific achievements in starting a process of culture change. He referred specifically to winning at Old Trafford, something that had not been done since 1968, and 'out-possessing' (having more of the ball) Arsenal. He went on to say that, 'To achieve two things that the players looked on as taboo, that gave us incredible engagement. You get credibility and can push on.' Martínez was able to offer on-field evidence to encourage buy-in.

Stuart Lancaster described his much discussed and high-impact approach to achieving a cultural 'reboot' within England Rugby: 'I think you can slowly change a culture from within as well but we needed to take a bit more of a dramatic approach and eventually we turned the ship in a completely different direction.' This fast-paced approach was partly down to the nature of international rugby. 'Ideally you gradually layer on depth to your culture in a systematic way but by that time, three years has gone past. It takes longer at international level because you are not in camp very often. You have got a lot of club relationships and they can be bitter rivals, so it takes a while to build it and bring it together.'

He involved guest speakers and the media, holding open training sessions and using them to 'correct some of the perceptions around the group and communicate with them about where we were trying to go'. Lancaster also wanted to re-engage with a frustrated set of England supporters:

> I was sat watching at my local rugby club and a lot of fans were getting turned off by the frustration of watching a team under-perform on the field but, more importantly, not seeming to give their all and apparently be more interested in socialising than they were in winning. I think that cut quite deep with a lot of people and we lost a lot of goodwill and support from the fans and we needed to get that back. I think by the way you

behave, the way you conduct yourself, it definitely has an impact on people and it can change in a positive way if you do things right.

All of it, he tells me, 'was designed to reboot and recalibrate the culture of the team'. His overall aim was to 'reset the culture and point it in a completely different direction', something he thinks was achieved. This was no small undertaking and Lancaster's integrated approach was designed to reach all stakeholders: players, staff, media and supporters.

Michael Maguire described his approach of overhauling a culture of underachievement, describing a combination of shifting mind-sets, redefining expectations, and making key personnel changes:

> I moved a few players. I developed a few players. Those younger players that were coming up, they had nothing to do with the previous results. I just said, 'We are going to win,' and in building that winning mentality, a lot of people don't feel comfortable saying, 'We're gonna win,' but that's why we are there, so why not win? Once you alleviate that from a lot of people and they start recognising that 'I now have someone who is looking down a different pathway', their thought patterns change, and then suddenly it starts evolving and changing and they see where the organisation is going. Then they decide they want to jump on board.

Culture change invariably involves making personnel decisions and shifting the team dynamics. Significant (and at times controversial) decisions must be made. For all of Stuart Lancaster's interventions, he admitted 'changing fifteen players helped along the way'. Maguire gives people a choice: 'You can jump on board now or you can leave.

I never hold anyone to having to stay and they are more than welcome to leave.' Reflecting on his time in Sydney, he tells me that such a process takes time and is not an easy task: 'There were players there that didn't hold the same values as what I wanted to achieve and unfortunately you have to move them on. It doesn't make them bad people but they just didn't want to drive in the same direction. If you don't have everyone driving in the same direction, then you are not going to make it.'

An enduring image of the South Sydney Rabbitohs' Grand Final win in 2014 is that of Sam Burgess playing almost the entire match with a fractured cheekbone. Burgess sustained the injury in the opening tackle of the game. I asked Maguire about that and he acknowledged that Burgess is 'a pretty unique human being' and 'one of the most mentally tough players' he has ever dealt with. The fact Burgess played on didn't surprise Maguire, saying, 'That's Sam, that is what he does.' However, despite the character of the player, Maguire believes that this show of bravery was partly down to what 'the club had embedded in him' and because of 'all the training and the commitment that he put into what we wanted to achieve . . . it put him into that mental state to go through that situation'.

This bravery is also found in Maguire, who was not afraid to reshuffle the pack and reorganise the team based on the culture he wanted to create.

INTERVENTIONS

Several leaders provided specific examples of interventions they have used to contribute to the creation of a high-performance culture.

Stuart Lancaster partnered with performance coach Owen Eastwood to design 'a video about what it means to be part of the team, the players that have gone before and the history and heritage'.

The video formed part of an informal induction process to integrate new players. Players also spoke in front of their teammates about what it meant to them to be playing for their country – an effective way of 'getting them to understand how much it means' – and, by all accounts, these were 'very emotive and emotional occasions'.

Lancaster uses these speeches and videos as a galvanising tool in place of the more traditional or old-school team initiations. Referred to as 'hazing', usually taking the form of an initiation that intentionally causes embarrassment or ridicule, this process is now becoming less prevalent in elite sport. Lancaster tells how such events are now less common because they can actually 'become more nerve-wracking for the player than the game itself, which is ridiculous'. Debutant players might still sing for their teammates, but that is *usually* as far as it goes.

Gary Kirsten recalled the 'special' Indian team who achieved victory in the 2011 World Cup. Stepping into a new culture, he took a more informal approach than usual which complemented the nation's 'way of doing things'. 'We were not just completely blasé and open, but there wasn't a heaviness in the air about our approach to anything. We kept the environment as light as possible because we knew that the external environment and expectation was intense.' He knew that 'to throw a whole load of structure into that team space and a whole lot of formality would have been a perilous task'. This approach goes against Kirsten's desire for structure and process but illustrates the importance of a leader's ability to adapt to a team's cultural needs.

They did bring in some 'external motivators', a space in which Kirsten is extremely selective. One such speaker was one of the top adventurers in the world and he recounted his experiences of extreme environments. Before the final, Kirsten describes how 'he spoke about an experience where he actually failed. He got bad frostbite and had to make the decision to turn around; I think it just pumped the guys up. I think that type of intervention, it just freed them up from worrying about and thinking about the final too much, it just freed that space up.'

Like Lancaster, Kirsten also tried to reconnect the team with the nation's public, seeking to understand 'how the Indian people historically operated in a combat situation'. He summed up the more congenial approach by saying, 'We messed around with stuff. I would say that we largely tried to create that greater sense of purpose, we tried to do that mainly informally.'

A leader's experience and beliefs will drive their preferences in terms of external contributors to a culture. Sport is perhaps moving away from the motivational speaker and towards a more relationship-based model. As a player, Kirsten was sceptical of people in that space and this has influenced his approach as a leader: 'I'm just not a big believer in the kind of "rah-rah" kind of intervention that is supposed to get people up to play for their country, they need to feel it and they need to live it out.'

In order to shift the culture at the Atlanta Falcons, Dan Quinn implemented a number of significant adjustments. The first was environmental, as he altered the layout of the players' locker room to encourage more interaction: 'It was just how it was designed, it was a smaller locker room, so you had to fit a lot of lockers in. So we made the lockers smaller and put them just around the corner so the players could talk to each other.'

Quinn also took the Falcons for a pre-season camp with the Navy SEALs, an organisation Quinn holds in high esteem: 'We added some military operations into our off-season programme. In the United States, the Navy SEALs have a very connected, historical model of teamwork, and so our aim was "We basically want what you have".'

Quinn points over his head to a log mounted on the wall of his spacious office:

> You see the log . . . we did log training and the log by itself is only about two hundred and fifty pounds, so it's not really heavy because you split it over six or seven guys about thirty or forty pounds apiece, but if you're not holding up your end of it, it gets real heavy. We all did this, coaches too. We learnt a lot. We knew we wanted to become a mentally tougher team, become more resilient, more accountable to each other and all the things you are looking for in a team sport.

These moments are the things that, when a team is successful, are often lauded as the secret ingredient for success. In reality they are just a small part of the group's achievements. The key is that the intervention must be relevant to the team, and utilised as an addition to an existing culture, as opposed to something that is seen as a shortcut or miracle cure to creating a high-performance culture. A shift in culture is not something that can be faked. Taking that approach will usually mean that a leader focuses only on what behaviours need to change, meaning they are often 'found out' fairly quickly by their people. Genuine shifts in culture can be accelerated by more choreographed interventions, but are built by targeting people's hearts and minds, or their thoughts, emotions and belief systems.

VALUES AND BEHAVIOURS

It is widely acknowledged that the establishment of values and behaviours is key to creating and sustaining a high-performance environment. My aim in this part of the interviews was to examine the practical processes involved in agreeing these and how they are then governed and monitored by the group to ensure they do not simply become 'words on a wall', and instead turn into the principles and standards that form a building block of the group's culture.

Ashley Giles described the approach he took in leading a group meeting with the players at Lancashire County Cricket to establish their cultural standards. Note the active involvement of the players, increasing their feeling of ownership and responsibility:

> We started by talking about winning cultures – so belief, honesty, accountability, professionalism and consistency. But what we did from there, because often groups of people in any organisation throw out these words and they stay on the wall and nothing happens. Originally we'd thrown out about fifty words and everyone's saying, "Oh we should have this and this." So, we broke them down and defined them. So, what does it mean to us? We got them to do it, not us. We got them to define what each of these meant. So, for us, 'belief' is defined as 'being positive in all situations, particularly in adversity, never doubting or questioning that consistency that will bring success'. We had them printed on the wall as a reminder of the standards we hold each other to. So, if a player is in doubt, you would go to say 'honesty' – defined as 'separating friendship and professionalism', so if your team is not doing it, sort that behaviour, you're doing nothing about it, talk about it and confront each other. I like this one, 'accountability – personal responsibility for what we think, feel, say and do'. So, you are accountable. If you talk shit, it's your fault.

At the Atlanta Falcons, Dan Quinn and his coaching staff have sought to create and sustain 'three rules, three pillars and a style of play'. The three simple rules are 'protect the team', 'no complaining/ no excuses' and 'be early'. These rules are then connected to the three pillars which evolved over a two-year period:

> The first pillar is 'Ball' – the word ball, and in our sport the turnover margin is a huge one, so we were going to make that a central theme in the way that we wanted to play. The second part is 'Brotherhood', that part was a communication piece, it was player to player, player to coach, coach to player, and coach to coach, so how do all of those things keep going? How does that communication keep going to make sure that players here know we are really going to be committed to their development. And to say, whether you are here ten months or ten years, you are going to get it all from us as coaches, and I would say that doesn't happen overnight. The third piece was 'Battle' – and that is the way that you really fight for it, the strain and the preparation, all the things that go into getting ready, so those are the three pillars.

As you travel along the corridors of the Falcons' training facility in Flowery Branch, Georgia, there are constant references to the rules and pillars of the team. As well as the usual slogans and images, which are refreshed each season, there are also multiple American footballs attached to the walls by brackets. The balls are at perfect height to touch, grab or punch as you go by, a constant reminder to the players and staff of a key pillar of the team's culture. Quinn combines subtle moves like this with more big-ticket interventions such as 'the log' and redesigning the changing rooms to encourage interaction and promote buy-in.

The final element of Quinn's method is the style in which he wants his team to play. 'You have got to be clear on the style and we do not waiver from it.' Quinn is acutely aware that sport has a way of defining and measuring performances solely on individual production and statistics. He asks me what sport I played (football or 'soccer' is my answer), my position (central midfield) and what I was measured on (goals and assists, I reply). 'You probably played some really good games when you didn't have either a goal or an assist and you probably had a few games where you had a goal or an assist, but you didn't play that well,' he tells me, before asking, 'How do we measure things that don't show up on the stat line?'

Away from the traditional metrics, Quinn looks to measure his team on his non-negotiables of 'competitiveness and toughness'. He does this by giving his players a numerical grade on both counts. 'It is different to your production,' he tells me, and is another way he reinforces the qualities and values he wants from his players on the field. In today's data-rich sporting environments, it is refreshing to see a coach such as Quinn acknowledge the limitations of statistics, looking to combine traditional measures with a genuine appreciation of the behaviours required at the Falcons.

A COMMON LANGUAGE

Gary Kirsten strives for his teams to 'have an identity and to play a certain way' and for players to 'give 100 per cent to their values system and to be uncompromising regardless of whether it brings winning or losing'. If they do that then 'the way they play represents the team's values', and Kirsten is satisfied. Describing the process that underpins this style of play, Kirsten highlights the importance of a shared language: 'You need to create a common language and that can be done in a formal way. You might run a workshop to do that, but you need to bring in a language to that group of people that you can use every day for the rest of your time together.' He gives two examples:

If we have made a commitment as a group of people that we are going to commit to excellence in our training, then that is the language we have set out for ourselves. That is the language I am going to use, as the leader of these people, every single day while I am on this job. If you are not committing to the training, then I am going to call you out on that.

If we have decided in our values system that we are going to respect each other's individualism within the team environment . . . in other words, encourage flair and an individual way of doing things . . . we have to be true to that. If we then have a team strategy session and an individual does something which is completely instinctive but goes against your team strategy, you can't come at him for that because that is the language and expectation that you as a group have set out – that you want guys to play freely and express themselves – so you have to back it up with your actions."

In this example, Kirsten looks to utilise a clear cultural framework, built on player buy-in, to protect his players.

NON-NEGOTIABLES

At Burnley, Sean Dyche is now in a position where the 'key core values are in place' and the group revisit these values to 'layer them up and add detail'. However, when he first took the job he took a gradual approach of consistently reinforcing his key messages:

What are the key common values that you follow beyond everything else? We do a lot on that . . . or we did. Obviously now it is quite set so it is easier. You start with a framework to offer the players, this is what we are going to look to do, this is what we stand for, this is what we are about. Then you reinforce it, constant reinforcement, through everything that you do, from the way the players warm up, the way they conduct themselves, the way they dress. They are guidelines really. Certain things are non-negotiable, but I have a lot of negotiables, so my non-negotiables are far outweighed by negotiables. Eventually the players go, 'OK, I'll have bit of that.' Some players drive it, some accept it, not many don't accept it, there's been a few who questioned it but, once they get the hang of it, they go with it.

The standards and non-negotiables are important to Dyche who gives the hypothetical example of a young player who, when asked his occupation, replies 'professional footballer'. He goes on to describe how 'everyone wants the "footballer" part but not everyone wants the "professional" bit. You have to have a certain level of respect for yourself and for the game and for the team, that's the professional bit. So I try to guide the players towards a professional edge. Now private lives, that's completely different – I don't judge players' private lives. I don't tell them they have to do this or that or whatever because that is not fair. They have a private life, everyone does, but when you are on club business, when you are in the team environment of what the team needs, then we all buy into it together and I think that has been an important process.' In team environments, there will be players who enjoy a structured approach – each day mapped out – but there are others who enjoy a sense of freedom. In this example, Dyche demonstrates the need to balance structure and expectations with an element of trust and independence.

Stuart Lancaster's approach to developing collective values begins with 'the management team initially, then the leadership group, and then the values and behaviours are sold to the whole team'. Ashley Giles took a more formal approach with Lancashire, outlining his expectations for 'a gold standard; doing the little things really well and being committed to the simple disciplines'. You know the players are on board with the leader when they take the responsibility for reinforcing and protecting those standards:

> I gave a short presentation before the season started. I know from experience that one of my bad habits is sarcasm so sometimes if I see consistently poor behaviours I get sarcastic with it. Like, if someone is late, I say, 'Oh what time is it?', that sort of thing, and that's not particularly good from a leader. So, I said to the group – rather than letting me get like that and you not knowing, these are some of the basic standards I expect. And we just went through it and I said that's it, it's not much to ask for. Some of it is simple, I expect you to work hard for each other. One of my things would be not wearing caps at the dinner table. Just don't – it shows a lack of respect for your club and to your teammates. So, if someone is sat with their cap on I've gone in recently and said, 'What's going on?' But then some of the other players will go, 'Take your cap off.' You need to develop that so it becomes a non-negotiable.

For some, these behaviours are written down, while for others it is a more informal process. Lancaster does not create a code of conduct, except a guiding principle of 'doing the right thing'. Lancaster expects players to realise that being a player for club or country is twenty-four hours a day, seven days a week. This is echoed by Kirsten who talks about off-field behaviour and conduct: 'I just love the concept of the twenty-four-seven athlete.'

The twenty-four-hour standard is one that many athletes around the world now embrace as the norm. I work with individual athletes who, in the absence of a traditional team structure, must set their own schedule and standards. In team sport, the time spent at the training ground and together on match days is usually taken care of. It is when the players leave that bubble of elite preparation that they choose whether to take on extra responsibility. It is not uncommon for players to personally employ practitioners including nutritionists, chefs, psychologists and fitness coaches, all to maintain their edge. Cristiano Ronaldo is now entering the twilight of his career, although you would not know to look at him. Throughout his career he has always taken responsibility for his own development, be that gaining muscle in the gym in Manchester, learning about optimal sleep patterns, installing a cryotherapy chamber at his home, or his ongoing work with a personal dietician.

Former England rugby player and World Cup-winner Jonny Wilkinson had his own method of evaluating his relentless pursuit of excellence. A self-confessed perfectionist to the extreme, Wilkinson battled mental challenges throughout his illustrious career. Coaching expert Steve Black played the role of mentor to the English fly-half and, talking in the *Guardian* after Wilkinson's retirement from the game, Black recalls the unique analogy they used to frame their conversations:

From day one we had little standards we set. We always said do things that would make the people who loved you feel proud of you. And one of the ways I tried to explain that to him is if you have a twenty-four hour camera following you about. At the end of the twenty hours could you sign the bottom of the resulting movie and say: 'Yes, I am happy with that. That truly represents who I am to the world.' Jonny has lived by that code and the imaginary video camera ensures it is a very high moral code. It's been habitual through the years because we've spoken about it on a daily basis.*

A leader can strive to guide players' behaviours within a controlled team environment. However, it is the level of buy-in and trust they provoke among the group that, together with an athlete's professionalism and attitude, dictates what they do behind closed doors. The work you do in the darkness makes you shine in the spotlight.

THE STANDARD

Referring again to the Navy SEALs, Dan Quinn described the process the group went through when creating their own internal document, which summarises the expectations that come with being a Falcon. Called 'The Standard', Quinn reads it out loud to me in his office but asks me not to print it in the book. 'We do not publish it out to people,' he tells me sternly. '[The] living, breathing document [symbolises] a commitment to one another' and, with the assistance of the SEALs, was written by the players themselves. This constitutional approach has provided a constant point of reference for a large and multidisciplinary team.

They started writing stuff on the board, almost like word-smithing, you know, these are the things that are important to us. It helped us, because we kind of had a little bit of a guiding

* McRae, D. (2014). 'Jonny Wilkinson: "the most famous, most talented, most grounded". theguardian.com, retrieved 30 January 2020.

light, because I could say to him [pointing at his Offensive Co-ordinator Steve Sarkisian] 'Hey man, is that The Standard?' If he wasn't performing up to the ability, I had a way to talk to him about that. A framework. We say we are going to demand everybody's best and be accountable to each other so having that alone helped. Now, it is one thing to do it. We felt that was our job to keep putting that in front of them and promoting that. Now [with] Jesse [Ackerman, the Falcons' head of strength and conditioning] downstairs in the gym, they will read that before they train with him, so that is a way to keep it alive across our organisation, so it doesn't go away.

As Quinn points out, maintaining the values requires a consistency and clarity in communication. Now at Leinster, Stuart Lancaster works alongside Head Coach Leo Cullen to ensure the club's core values are reinforced throughout the season. At critical moments, a big game or an important week, videos and presentations are used to reaffirm these key concepts.

Michael Maguire, when returning to the UK with South Sydney (to play St Helens in the World Club Challenge), visited his former colleagues at Wigan Warriors. He sees values, embedded effectively into an organisation, as something that can endure after a leader departs:

I was just there two days ago and you still see the same values embedded in the organisation. Which, you know, you sort of sit back and see that and it was actually really pleasing. You could still see how they play, how they went about their training, it was probably very 'my style' I suppose and I obviously had Waney [former assistant and then the Warriors' head coach, Shaun Wane] there who supported me and did great things for me while I was there.

PLAYER-LED CULTURES

All teams will have values and behaviours, but high-performance cultures are often led, to an extent, by their athletes. Player-led leadership, the idea of ownership transferring from the coaches to the athletes, is 'the ultimate goal', according to Stuart Lancaster, who refers to it as 'shared leadership'. Gary Kirsten believes that in a high-performance environment the players 'have to drive culture, they become your marketing tool and sell the concepts to everyone else'. In this respect, the players begin to embody the principles instilled by the leader.

One of Lancaster's mantras is 'You should always have an opinion', and Isa Nacewa, former captain at Leinster, describes how the newly appointed senior coach challenged the group to be their own leaders, 'never wanting players to be in the meeting room and just sit there and listen'.

Nacewa, who Lancaster cites as the best on-field leader he has worked with, clearly recalls one particular team meeting that took place in Dublin after the British Lions had played the All Blacks in New Zealand in 2017. Lancaster wanted to know what the Leinster players thought of the game, what they had noticed, what they had learnt. It was a relatively junior group, as many of the senior players were in the Lions' squad. Only two more senior players offered their thoughts. Noting this, Lancaster's response was to inform the players that 'from now on, you come to meetings with a point of view and an opinion'. This approach keeps the players thinking, learning and developing. In Nacewa's words, 'He got everyone upskilling themselves over that twelve-month period.' Lancaster, as demonstrated by his willingness to openly share his musings on culture and leadership on online platforms such as LinkedIn, aims to develop both the person and the player, the mind and body.

Michael Maguire looks to his senior players to instil the behaviours in the generations that follow. 'The values that I have in those senior players are the same values I want them teaching the younger boys. My senior guys are like middle management. They are the role models that are coming through under me.'

Gary Kirsten reiterated the need for senior players to be on board. 'I need ears and eyes on the ground. I don't think it needs to be many guys, but three or four incredibly influential guys in your team. Senior players drive behaviours and they drive cultures. If those senior players aren't living it out, then you've got nothing.'

He gives two examples of on- and off-field behaviours that can indicate the mentality of a senior pro:

> If the team is on a night out and a senior player is out there and he sees one of the younger players getting completely out of hand and not being the twenty-four-seven athlete, representing the badge, then he can pull him in and say, 'Hey, let's go home, we've done our bit here,' rather than let a guy self-destruct and then ultimately betray the values system of what the team stands for.
>
> If you see a player not diving to stop a ball on the boundary where he knows he's not going to get recognised for it and he just lets it go by because he doesn't want to hit the ground and save the four, that is a behaviour that is indicative of what the value system is.

Ashley Giles, while acknowledging the role of player responsibility, warns against letting an environment 'drift'. 'There have got to be some team rules and behaviours and that process should involve the team. So what is acceptable and isn't acceptable for this team. And then strong discipline; by that I mean bloody hard work but also discipline in the sense that if people are out of line then I step in. Otherwise, if you let an environment drift or someone, one person, drifts out of it, then you are in trouble.'

While Giles remains acutely aware of the leader's role, he also continues to invest in the players as influential voices. He prefers the players to deliver the inductions, to inform any new arrivals that 'this is how we do things' or develop a player's handbook to communicate 'some of the basics and non-negotiables'. In so doing, he hopes that 'the environment is controlled by the group', not by him.

Dan Quinn highlights the more dominant role of the coach in American Football.

> Here, it often comes from the coaches because we make a lot of the decisions. It is different in a sport like rugby where the manager might be up in the box and the captain makes a lot of the decisions on the field. So, in ours, we make a lot of the calls for the players, but their execution of that has to be rock-solid. So you better be really accountable to what you do and have your shit together, because hey man, we are counting on you to get this part done.

With this in mind, Quinn identifies 'The Standard' document as a 'really significant way to push leadership to come from the players and really be player-led in a lot of ways and take that ownership'. The 'unwavering and non-compromising' three rules and three pillars described earlier come from Quinn, but The Standard, he reminds me, comes from the players. 'It has their DNA in,' he says, 'they wrote it,' doing so with his unwavering support:

I fully agreed with it, because I believe in it too, but it is a way for us to determine when we onboard new players, they each get a book that has 'The Standard' inside it, to say, 'Hey man, welcome, I want you to read this, tell me what you think, and let's talk about some questions you might have.'

I get the impression that for all the players' involvement, in order for this approach to hold water in the NFL, the coach must act as the immovable focal point, Quinn-style.

IT'S ONLY A GAME . . . OF SPINS

Sean Dyche believes that once 'players take ownership, you are a long way to creating an effective culture because they start policing it'. He reveals how, on certain occasions, players will call out their teammates: 'We have had that, on one issue where the players have gone, "No, no, no, that is not acceptable," to another player. That has been built over a long time.'

At Burnley, they also have a rather unique way of ensuring that the players own their environment. They use a game format called 'Spins', which Dyche borrowed from rugby. The large circular board conjures images of the old gameshow, *Wheel of Fortune*. Chuckling and shaking his head, Dyche describes how the players regularly convene on Fridays for a game of what they call 'Spins':

Where it comes from . . . part of the culture is professionalism, and footballers are renowned for being sloppy, because a lot of people do a lot of things for footballers in the working environment. So we had this idea of a fining system and it went a bit loose and the professionalism went a little bit too. Now we could go stampeding all over players every day, army fashion, but that's not right, so we spoke to the players and said, 'We want you to start this and understand where it lives in your profession': simple stuff, pick your clothes up, pick your gear up, be respectful, help the kit-man out, the people who work in the kitchens, surely it is not beyond you to pick your plate up and put it on a stand, those sort of things, little things.

It got a bit soft, so we brought in this spin wheel, with varying things on it, your squad number and the letters of the alphabet. The letters are a forfeit of some kind, some positive, some negative and the numbers obviously correlate with whoever is getting the spin. It built into this cultural thing where every Friday we go, 'Right, what's happening, are there any spins?' And you just see the honesty of people calling each other out on it. It's gone up and down, good spells, bad spells, when the lads aren't really on it, and every summer we've said to the lads, 'Right, do you want to keep the spins? Or do you want to get rid of it?' But if you get rid of it, we still need the culture to be the culture, it still needs to be set. We don't want to be going around saying, 'You've not done that, have you done that?' Every year they've said they want to keep it and we just change it. Forfeits can be . . . I pay for you and your wife or partner to dine out, you can get your car valeted, or you can win fifty quid back if the white joker comes up, you can win a saved forfeit so you have a free one the next time, you can pay that forfeit forward, you can have two-times forfeit where you have to get it and double it. We have a buyout, we have three buyouts in a season but they're quite harsh, about £200 . . . But if you buy out of it three times, after that you are doing whatever forfeit you get. It's just to keep a little bit of order but in a friendly way, a bit of banter, we've had some classics, absolutely hilarious things. People rolling laughing, so a bit of camaraderie as well.

To the players, 'Spins' means fun, banter, and the chance to rib a teammate for something they perhaps thought had been missed. However, underneath the light-hearted exterior, there is a wider significance to the game that encapsulates Dyche's own approach to leadership. It is a combination of non-negotiables, humour, leeway, common sense, second chances and, most crucially, ownership.

THE ENVIRONMENT

During the process of writing this book and in my academic and applied work, I have been fortunate to visit training and match-day facilities for a number of sporting organisations. Everton's Finch Farm training complex is one of the best in the Premier League, while Burnley FC have left no stone unturned in designing their site at the leafy Gawthorpe Hall in Lancashire. In Atlanta, the sheer size of the Falcons' headquarters at Flowery Branch is the first thing to hit you when you arrive on site, greeted by numerous staff along the way. Within these walls you will often find the latest technology, data analysis and gadgets, all designed to give a team the edge against their opposition.

I was keen to explore how the leaders felt the 'environment' could impact on a culture. Here, I am referring to the physical environment (e.g. training grounds, changing rooms, offices), sports science provision, data analysis and the technology available.

MARGINAL GAINS

An area popularised in no small part in the UK by the wild success of British Cycling and Team Sky is the aggregation of marginal gains. The concept can be defined as the continuous search for the 1 per cent margin of improvement in all relevant areas, with the aim that if every area can be improved by just 1 per cent, those small gains combine to give rise to significant improvement. There is, however, an argument from experienced sports science practitioners that this is exactly what they have been doing for years, just with a new name.

The leaders all appreciated the benefits of marginal gains, to a point. Gary Kirsten looks to find them in 'the process, in your preparation rather than in your performance'. He sees each 'gain' as a 'little tick on the fly wheel, something slightly different in our behaviours compared to what we have done in the past. So, if a guy says, "Well I'm going to commit to hitting a thousand balls a week"–, "Well, OK, are you doing it?". "OK yes, I am," and that is one tick on the fly wheel. That is going to help our performance by 3 per cent or whatever. If you've made a commitment to get fitter and stronger, "Well are you doing it?", "Yes I am," then that is another tick on the fly wheel and if you can have these little gains, and I suppose that is the right word, then ultimately it will end, if you've got a talented group of individuals, it will end in increased performance because of them. I don't think that is just in your physical endeavours, I think it is also in your mental endeavours and in your values system.'

Stuart Lancaster believes that such areas are the 'icing on the cake stuff' but thinks that in the past, 'we have been guilty of going for the icing on the cake without getting the cake in place. That is the best way I can describe it. You can forget about your marginal gains if you haven't got a good culture and good people and good character and good coaches.' In Lancaster's mind, it can become 'a bit of a distraction' and is something that can be overplayed, giving 'the players a crutch to think, "Right, we're going to win because we've done this fancy thing," but actually the fundamentals we have not done well enough.'

Ashley Giles echoes this viewpoint – 'There is no point worrying about the 1 per cent if you haven't got 10 per cent' – and thinks marginal gains only become important after a point. 'All these things, cultural development, environment, vision, legacy, they are all by-products of doing the hard yards and doing the basics incredibly well. One of the army guys who spoke to us said the SAS will do the simple things better than anybody else, that they train so hard that they warm to it when it gets harder because that is how they train. And they have to get those first things right before marginal gains.'

The comments of both Lancaster and Giles acknowledge the potential benefits of marginal gains, but only once the fundamental bedrock of culture has been established. It can be tempting for a leader to look for subtle improvements in technology, data and equipment and hold them up as an example of a forward-thinking organisation. As consumers and fans, we might only hear of the latest innovation, but the pursuit of marginal gains is more than simply finding the 1 per cent. It is a mindset and an overall approach which has its origins in the way people think, converse and operate – in other words, culture.

PHYSICAL ENVIRONMENT

As I drive down the tree-tunnelled path to Burnley's brand-new training facility in the grounds of Gawthorpe Hall, I pass a much smaller building, hardly giving it a second thought. However, the first season Burnley got promoted, Sean Dyche tells me, it was that 'little tiny building' that served as their training ground – 'So the environment isn't everything,' he adds with a wry smile. In fact, those environments have their cultural advantages, as Dyche describes: 'That building gave us an inner connection – the staff, the players bumping into each other all the time in this little environment, it is all very controllable.'

It is indicative of the family and community feeling of the club that some employees were 'a little bit stressed and worried' when they moved in to the new premises partway through a season, not wanting to get in the way of the players. Dyche insisted on everyone moving in when the building was 'nearly finished and structurally ready'. He didn't go in with all the images and messaging already complete, as he wanted 'to evolve over time'. Some staff expressed a desire to wait until the summer and make a clean start in pre-season but Dyche was adamant. 'I said, "Absolutely not, we have been waiting for that, don't start all that hoodoo nonsense." Look at this facility, how could you not thrive off a facility like this?'

The facility brings the first team, development squad and youth team players on to a single site for the first time. Additional pitches, an indoor area and a floodlit pitch, together with the spacious buildings, make it an impressive site. 'It has been a massive step forward for the club,' Dyche adds.

During Burnley's first foray into the Premier League, Dyche's 'positive realities' stirred into action as he managed the looming prospect of relegation. However, in a move indicative of the long-term approach the club have committed to, their moderate financial expenditure on the playing squad allowed them to invest substantially in the new training ground. In Dyche's words, they 'jumped on the grenade because the training ground was important for the longevity of the club'. This kept squad funds low but, as he describes, 'the rest is history because, the second time we've been promoted, the club is in a better place ready to go and take on what it means to be in the Premier League and we are still doing that at the moment'.

It is commonplace to walk into a place of work and see slogans and catchphrases adorning the walls. In some cases, these illustrate an organisation's journey, offering a glimpse into their past. In a sporting context, you might find inspirational photos or shirts from iconic players of yesteryear. A lot of time and money is spent in developing these seemingly inspirational environments. For example, teams will 'brand' a dressing room at an away fixture of a cup final, but how impactful is this? Does it serve to motivate? Or could it perhaps push some athletes over the edge in terms of the pressure they experience? The answer to these questions can be found in the authenticity of what lies beneath the surface – the cultural foundations of the organisation.

Without question, a psychologically informed physical environ-ment can help to communicate and reinforce an existing culture. The key thing here is to ensure such things are relevant and specific to the group, as opposed to generic statements thrown on a wall as a 'sticking plaster' approach with the aim of motivating elite athletes. Ashley Giles talks about the Lancashire dressing room having 'all these quotes up but, if you ask the players, most of them won't be able to repeat them, won't know any one of them. They are not the sort of stuff I am into. I'm into good quotes from great leaders in the past about real situations rather than this bullshit that's just made up. You know, like "run away from tiredness" and all these things in the gym . . . bullshit. You are better off just putting a mirror on the wall. Can you look in here every day? If you can, you are doing all right.'

Stuart Lancaster reflected on what he implemented during his time with England, believing the creation of an elite training environment was an important part of creating a wider high-performance culture:

> I wouldn't have started with the physical environment because I wanted to get the cultural environment right. But the physical environment soon followed because it gave the players a perception and a feeling, an accurate feeling, that this is a high-performance environment and you have got a quality pitch and quality facilities to train in. As a consequence, they feel you have invested in them to make them better and they want to repay you in return for the investment you've put in. So, there is a sense of "We owe it to these guys because they have gone out of their way to make it as professional as it can be", so I think it does have a knock-on effect.

He referred to his 'one of us' concept, which is a physical cultural cue, found in a player's individual cubicle, to remind them about 'the people that have worn the shirt before them'. The aim here is for the players to think, 'Christ, there have been some good players to wear this shirt and to sit in this cubicle, who have sat in this spot' – a physical cue designed to emphasise the feeling of identity within the team.

Michael Maguire believes a professional working environment, in the intense environment of rugby league, only has an impact if you get the right people:

> I have worked with some of the financially poorest of teams and won, and you walk down the street and look at other organisations who have everything who haven't achieved. It comes back to the people. But if you add the people and quality of people to a good, strong facility then that adds value to where you are going.

He uses imagery of the current players to create a sense of belonging and responsibility at the training ground. 'It is their home. I utilise pictures of the players, so they physically see some sense of belonging to the organisation. By putting the photograph up there, it gives you that sense of belonging. When you are in your own home, you look after everything, you respect it and you work hard at it.' Once the right characters are in place, the use of imagery can communicate to a player that they have a place here and that they are valued as part of the fabric of the club.

Gary Kirsten thinks that a 'physical environment certainly can enhance the quality of your preparation and the experience the players will have outside of match time' but would not allow players to moan about the training environments they frequent. He gives an example of a team arriving at a rundown facility, again highlighting the importance of a shared language:

> We would arrive at facilities where the nets were in shocking condition, we didn't have a home base, and you are on the road the whole time. We just inculcated that into our language right from the outset. Regardless of what facilities we have, regardless of what conditions we play in, we will accept all the challenges that come our way. I would just set the language out straight away and just say, 'Guys, just to remind you, one of our discussion points in terms of our culture and identity was we are going to make the most of the facilities we've got and the conditions we've got, so get out there and let's go and do the work,' and I wouldn't have a problem!

While he would maximise the sessions, Kirsten would always try to 'manage upwards, to my bosses to make sure I had the best for the players. I wanted my players to have the best of everything.' Despite this, he believes that if a strong culture is in place, irrespective of the physical environment, 'people won't moan, they'll just get on with what is confronting them'. A high-performance culture should be strong enough not only to endure an element of adversity, but to thrive during that experience. Teams can actually bond more in those times, and come to enjoy a change in environment. That is why pre-season often involves a trip to a military camp in a remote area. In the example Kirsten provides above, players may well appreciate what they have that little bit more, or think back to the times they fell in love with the game, when the quality of the facilities was the last thing on their mind. They just wanted to play.

DATA

The analysis of data and the use of technology is an ever-expanding industry within elite sport and business as organisations search for the extra '1 per cent' that can provide an edge in terms of performance. Video analysis, performance statistics, GPS data, sleep analysis and cognitive monitoring are all being utilised. In a world where information is accessible at the click of a button, the use of data analytics and sport science is an area I was keen to explore with the leaders, who gave a balanced view.

Ashley Giles spoke strongly about his belief that 'stats, information and sports science should be there as an addition and not as a crutch'. He recalled how, when video analysis was first introduced in cricket, players, having been bowled out, began to immediately turn to the video for objective evidence and data, rather than conveying their own thoughts and opinions, an approach that can negate the athlete's own perspective.

Gary Kirsten believes that 'if managed properly, sports science plays a massive role' but he has experienced issues with its implementation in the past. 'Often it becomes an end to itself,' he says, 'so it kind of serves the purpose of the sports scientist and doesn't serve the purpose of the team. That drives me mad, when people come in and come up with an innovation or new design and they are using your team to sell what they are doing.' The sports scientists, like the players, must be an integrated part of the group. They 'must feel the badge'. He does not want them 'to be an outsourcing arrangement and they just come in and do their work, because then sports science is an end to itself'.

In Kirsten's mind, the key to effective sports science is when it drives performance and has a 'direct link with how a player is going to behave on a sports field and the actions they are going to do on a sports field, I have no problem with that'. Kirsten's objection lies in science becoming 'an end to its own and science being used in a way that drives more science'.

Sean Dyche highlights the role of the media in emphasising the importance of data and statistics in elite sport. He believes football has followed the lead of American sports, where 'they have stats for everything' and Dyche is careful 'to not go too far to the point where it almost dehumanises it'. He is mindful not to 'forget the score, the score is the most important stat, if we score and they don't, that's an important stat'. He points to the randomness of the game, recalling how Burnley beat Liverpool at Anfield with a record low of 21 per cent possession, and only five efforts on goal compared to Liverpool's thirty. What those stats don't highlight is that almost all of Liverpool's shots came from outside the penalty box, a place which Dyche proudly tells me is 'statistically very difficult to score from'.

He does, however, identify the practical application of data analysis: 'There is good practice, there are good processes, and good detail in a lot of different parts of the game, both in the training for performance and the game. We are trying to pick the best bits out of it and then mix it into the culture to make it work for everybody.'

Stuart Lancaster describes himself as 'quite old school' and believes that data should support but not drive a leader's decision-making. He describes how coaches can often find themselves 'at logger heads with the sports scientists who are trying to dictate how many kilometres players can run in a training session'. Lancaster acknowledges the growing role data plays in 'supporting decision-making and the physical development and management of players,' but also believes that, in rugby, the players are not 'too over-reliant on it' and that they 'recognise that playing rugby is still a sport, not a science. He continues, 'I think the players get that. They know there is some science behind it but, you know, you can have the greatest athlete in the world playing rugby but it doesn't mean he's going to be in the team.'

Michael Maguire, speaking in his own direct style, thinks that 'sometimes the science is a load of garbage' but does, at times, 'utilise it to understand the people that I'm working with'. He believes in his instincts and how there will be 'times when you have to push through the data and break every rule'. In Maguire's opinion, 'Being able to utilise that information and take what you need is part of the art of coaching.'

What becomes clear, in listening to these comments, is the importance of maintaining a sense of perspective. Data is *part* of the culture, it is not *the* culture. The key to data is how it is interpreted and applied – constantly asking ourselves, 'What does it mean?'. I have seen this executed to great effect in sport and dovetailed with data analysts in both golf and football. A great example from golf is when data informs how a player can prepare for a specific event, or plan their schedule around courses that suit their skill set. Athletes are often creatures of habit and routine; data can offer 'proof' and challenge the way a player thinks and how they do things. At the Ryder Cup in 2018 the data, alongside an appreciation for different personalities, informed some of the selection decisions from captain Thomas Bjørn. Within leadership, data has a clear and obvious value. However, the 'hard' numbers must be combined with the less tangible 'people' skills.

Ashley Giles concluded by making an interesting point. Today's athletes are often maligned for being unable to make independent decisions in the heat of competition, at critical moments. However, conversely, we are 'giving players as much support as possible to take away some of that noise or interference of having to do it themselves' while at the same time, claiming to try to 'breed responsible, professional, independent people. If everything is done for them how are they going to do that?' It is an interesting question, and there is certainly a balance to be struck.

CHAPTER 4: LEADERSHIP LESSONS

- Respect the past of an organisation, but do not let it dictate the future.
- Take your time to assess the situation. Step back. Resist the urge to jump in.
- Identify the cultural architects. Focus on their engagement and buy-in, as they are powerful whether they are with you or against you. The rest will follow.
- Do not underestimate the importance of short-term interventions, as long as they are underpinned by genuine and demonstrable values and behaviours.
- Encourage people to take accountability for the values and the culture that they help to create.
- If you want others to lead, you must allow them the chance to thrive on responsibility.
- Consider your winning and losing behaviours. Both are equally important, but a single losing behaviour can cause irreparable damage.
- The physical environment can impact performance, if the cultural foundation is solid.
- Embrace the use of data but keep it in check. Let it inform, but not dominate your thinking.

Leading and Managing Others

....

The distinction between 'leadership' and 'management' can be traced back to the exact origins of both words. To manage is derived from the Latin *'manus'*, meaning 'the hand', and is associated with the ability to assert 'control'. In comparison, to lead has its origins in the old English term *'laedan'*, meaning to 'go before as a guide' or 'accompany and show the way'. This exploration of origin offers a remarkable insight into the differences between the two terms that is still relevant today.

A management-focused individual might be more likely to take a short-term view to achieve targets, apply existing processes and take control over their employees. Contrastingly, a leader will be more inclined to inspire and guide a team towards a common vision, challenge the status quo, build relationships, and empower others so that they thrive collectively and individually. Both roles bring with them stressors, responsibilities and, usually, an element of office politics. Central to each focus, however, is the need to truly understand people's motivations and nuances, in order to get the best out of them.

In any organisation, sporting or otherwise, some individuals will possess the rare skill set to effectively take on both roles. Some might have an affinity with leadership yet struggle with the detail needed for acute management. Others, perhaps promoted from within due to displaying effective management skills, will fail to have the expected impact as a leader of an organisation or team. In elite sport and business, leaders have to adapt across both interchangeable roles, switching between the two skill sets in response to day-to-day events. A morning might involve taking a coaching session, while the afternoon is spent with commercial partners.

It is important once again to highlight the varying and specific demands associated with different roles and sports. As performance director of Lancashire County Cricket, Ashley Giles was responsible for the long-term success of the entire organisation and he is now in place as director of cricket at the ECB. His current remit is different to that of a traditional 'head coach', a role that is more commonly found in sports like football and rugby, and which usually involves responsibility for team performance, whereas a director role focuses on the direction of the organisation as a whole.

As Stuart Lancaster has pointed out, there are vast differences between the demands of leadership in club environments, where you are working day-to-day with the same group, and international sport, which requires a group of individuals to unite behind a common goal in a relatively short space of time. For instance, Roberto Martínez, when leading the Belgian national team to third place at the 2018 World Cup, will have been focused on maximising performance and getting results for that specific campaign. By contrast, Sean Dyche has taken a sustainable approach to Burnley's Premier League journey, building upon stability, individual and collective growth, a willingness to confront the facts of a situation, and a clear knowledge that there will be obstacles along the way.

MANAGING THE INDIVIDUAL

PEOPLE FIRST, ATHLETES SECOND

While a strong culture and its associated values are undoubtedly key facets to achieving high performance, the nature of elite sport dictates that working closely with individuals and enabling them to reach their potential is a crucial part of the leader's role.

During my applied work with clients in business and sport, I often meet those who naturally associate leadership with a command and control philosophy. This is not a criticism of those people, it is reflective of a dominant bias that still remains when it comes to leadership. While each leader has their own style and approach, a common and substantial theme to emerge from my discussions is the consensus that an aptitude for 'influencing people, not just athletes' (Ashley Giles) is an important component of best practice. It was also clear to see that each leader, irrespective of personality, feels a genuine warmth and sense of duty to their athletes.

ALL-ROUND LEARNING

Stuart Lancaster describes his desire for players to 'learn and grow on and off the field', helping them to develop 'their individual characters'. Relating back to his own leadership philosophy, Giles states that an organisation's 'most important asset is the people, the best people'. Trophies offer a helpful 'stepping stone' approach to his true motivation, which is seeing 'people – not cricketers – move from A to B, if I am helping their life and developing them then great', although he begrudgingly acknowledges that you will never 'keep everyone happy, you just won't, you just have to do the best you can'.

By taking this approach, Lancaster and Giles give their players a reason to follow them. They start to build a picture of what is in it for them, the potential growth and associated benefits to their wider life and relationships – not just the execution of on-field performance. A genuine drive to develop each individual – whether that is the superstar, the captain or a fringe player – communicates a sense of trust and care in people that cannot be fabricated. This way of thinking offers a sense of empathy and understanding towards players' lifestyle issues. Issues that the leader themselves, who has typically played in a different era, may struggle to naturally appreciate.

Michael Maguire highlights the importance of athletes living their lives in the right way. 'How they live their lives is how everyone looks at us and how we go about things. In sport, you have got sponsorship and all sorts of different moving parts. Your players are your people and that is what everyone looks at. How they are as people, how they talk, how they go about their behaviours, it all plays a big part in where the organisation is going.'

This perspective allows Maguire to establish himself as a key component of a player's wider support structure. He will undoubtedly communicate this in his own direct manner, but underneath the stern exterior lies a real desire to help players navigate the turbulent nature of elite sport and the associated media interest.

Stuart Lancaster concurs. 'Players are role models both on and off the field. Ultimately, I want the players to leave the set-up and be good role models once they finish playing, and to be successful in life. I probably spend as much time talking to players about the off-field stuff as I do the on-field stuff.' Just as we highlighted earlier, Lancaster does not feel that his role stops at the edge of the pitch; the character of the people he helps forge is a key driver.

A GENUINE LIFE IMPACT

To seek to promote a genuine impact on an individual's development is not a gushing ideology, either. Often success in this area coincides with success on the sports field, where players are more purposeful and confident in their own identity. This is upheld by Gary Kirsten.

Kirsten's priority, grounded in his strong sense of faith, is to 'make a significant difference to people's lives'. He tells me he is 'more pumped up by people saying, "Thanks for the influence you have had in my life," rather than, "We won a trophy."' For Kirsten, that is the most important aspect of a leadership role, but he points out that this can go on to influence sporting performance too: 'Quality people drive your identity and culture and they usually make better decisions under pressure.' Kirsten believes in 'trying to educate a mind so they have the ability to make quality decisions on and off the field'.

It makes sense – help to develop an individual's maturity, quick thinking and self-awareness, and those qualities are highly likely to permeate an athlete's life, therefore encouraging more rational and considered reactions to the critical moments, sporting or otherwise.

Similarly, spending time in the local area and getting to know the communities and supporters that a team represents can build character within the team, while also helping to shape an awareness of the club's ethos and create new fans.

To develop as people, Michael Maguire encourages his players to 'do a lot of work in the community and also develop a pathway for life after sport'. This, he tells me, 'is educating them that there is a lot of life to live after sport', something his own early retirement forced him to acknowledge:

Do not be defined by a relatively short period of your career. It might be that they are buying houses or shares or whatever. In sport you get to an age when you are having kids and the wages suddenly aren't the same any more. It is all that knowledge that you are always imparting on these young men and the days when a lot of sportsmen used to blow a lot of their money, that is not something I want in our organisation. I want to see longevity and players utilising their time.

Upon retirement (early or otherwise) many athletes can struggle with a loss of identity. The main aspect of their life is taken from them, and with it goes their sense of value and recognition. Maguire encourages his people to consider the bigger picture and plan for life after sport. This does not mean that athletes won't find this career transition challenging – they most certainly will – but they will be better equipped to deal with the challenges and opportunities that present themselves.

In taking this approach, Maguire impacts his players on a broader and deeper level, going far beyond results on the rugby field. This sense of identity and investment in the individual can only inspire genuine and trusting relationships between coach and player.

Giles spoke with a genuine passion about nurturing players as individuals and understanding their unique personalities. To get to know them and their families, thus bringing out the best in them, is a true priority for him. Understanding the individual is key to his approach:

You have got a lot of people all at different stages of their careers, worries, doubts, debts, marriages and I know I'm a deep thinker at times and I worry about things and they all are as well. The bigger picture is always helping them to get the most out of themselves because if they do it is bloody rewarding.

BUILDING RELATIONSHIPS

THE COACH-ATHLETE RELATIONSHIP

Effective relationships can often be found at the beating heart of sporting performance, mental well-being and personal development. When attributing reasons for their success, athletes, managers and coaches all identify the significance of those bonds, forged by time, training, emotions and experiences.

The coach-athlete relationship has been broadly defined by psychologist Sophia Jowett of Loughborough University as a unique and dynamic social situation that is 'continuously shaped by the interpersonal thoughts, feelings and behaviours of the coach and the athlete'.[*] Jowett's work goes further, explaining that both parties are 'mutually interdependent' and that the thoughts and feelings of one will affect the other, and vice versa. Her research cites the partnership between record-breaking swimmer and Olympian Michael Phelps and his long-term coach, Bob Bowman, as an example of an effective and successful coach-athlete relationship.[†] However, 'effective' and 'successful' do not automatically mean easy and harmonious. Their relationship, like many others, has been fraught with tension and tested to the limits.

Michael Phelps and Bob Bowman
Bob Bowman first coached an eleven-year-old Michael Phelps at the North Baltimore Aquatic Club, laying the foundation of a fiery

---

[*] Jowett, S. (2017). 'Coaching effectiveness: the coach-athlete relationship at its heart.' *Current Opinion in Psychology*, 16, 154–158.
[†] Jowett, S. and Poczwardowski, A. (2007). 'Understanding the coach-athlete relationship.' In *Social Psychology in Sport*, eds S. Jowett, and D. Lavallee. Champaign, IL: Human Kinetics, 3–14.

partnership that would go on to become arguably the greatest coach-athlete relationship of all time. Some may point to the Super Bowl-winning tandem of Bill Belichick and Tom Brady at the New England Patriots, but twenty-eight Olympic medals, ruthlessly gathered from all corners of the globe, from Athens, Beijing, London and Rio, are difficult to contest.

The relationship between the pair can be categorised by two predominant characteristics: tension and trust. Dogged and determined, both men would constantly push one another, with neither willing to back down. Arguments were frequent and disagreements often led to spectacular losses of temper. Yet beneath the testosterone and aggression, there is a deep, interwoven sense of trust between coach and athlete. Phelps, diagnosed at the age of nine with ADHD, 'can be stubborn, hard-headed, isolated, unforgiving and ruthless',[*] characteristics that set him on the path to moments of greatness and to periods of personal anguish. Phelps had a complex relationship with his father, while Bowman represented a stabilising, consistent and paternal figure. And so, eighteen years after their first meeting in Baltimore, when Phelps made the decision to come out of retirement in 2014, he called Bowman. Struggling to hit his own exceptionally high standards, Phelps recalls,[†] 'I just had to trust Bob. I've trusted him since I was eleven years old. I had to keep trusting him. I knew he wouldn't let me down.'

Tommy Fleetwood and Alan Thompson
Trust is also a word I would use to personify another coach-athlete relationship, and one that I have witnessed first-hand, between

---

* Drehs, W. (2016). 'Michael Phelps' Final Turn.' espn.com, retrieved 18 March 2020.

† Forde, P. (2016). 'The complicated relationship that moulded Michael Phelps into the greatest.' uk.sports.yahoo.com, retrieved 18 March 2020.

golfer Tommy Fleetwood and his swing coach, Alan Thompson. Knowing them as I do, I would suggest the personalities of Fleetwood and Thompson are polar opposites from their American counterparts. However, like Bowman and Phelps, the two first worked together at an early stage, in this case when Fleetwood was aged just thirteen, and a far cry from the Ryder Cup player now easily distinguishable by his flowing locks. In elite golf, it is commonplace for players to move coaches so, unlike Phelps and Bowman, their working relationship has been inconsistent. However, when Fleetwood was struggling with his swing in 2016, under the calm advice of his dad Pete he called 'Thommo' for help. Having fallen as low as 188th in the world rankings, in less than three years he climbed into the top ten, winning the European Tour's Race to Dubai in 2017 and playing a starring role in Team Europe's victory at the Ryder Cup in Paris, 2018. The resurgence was, on the surface at least, meteoric. Yet at the core of this sporting success, alongside the toil, emotion and challenge, lies the trust and relationship between the coach and the athlete.

Thompson and Bowman have both coached a range of other athletes in their careers, needing to adapt their styles accordingly. With another swimmer, Bowman might not have been able to push so hard for a reaction. Another golfer might not have had the humility to ask his childhood coach for help, never mind make him godfather to his young son.

While these examples are taken from individual sports, where coaches typically focus their attention on smaller cohorts of players, the context and colour of the bonds themselves remain valid. Relationships are a cornerstone of effective leadership. Leaders themselves cannot operate in isolation, and their role remains one of human interaction, engagement and collaboration. These relationships represent the ability to truly consider the thoughts and feelings of others. The challenge for leaders in team environments is to find a way to build relationships with a large number of individual characters, all playing under the same team identity, united by the opportunity for collective achievement.

ONE SIZE DOES NOT FIT ALL

When encountering any team dynamic, it is crucial to acknowledge the individual characters within a group, rather than taking a one-size-fits-all approach to leadership. The history of sport is full of tales of players who were treated differently as individuals. Eric Cantona is a prime example. The same rules just did not apply to the Frenchman, because Sir Alex Ferguson knew how to get the best out of his star player when it mattered. Interestingly, the other players accepted it because he delivered when it mattered the most. While this example comes from a maverick individual, the wider learning can be applied across the board. To get the most from one player will often demand a different approach to another.

At the Ryder Cup in 2018, Thomas Bjørn and his team of vice-captains were acutely aware of how to communicate with the different characters within the twelve-man team dynamic. Some personalities were by nature louder, more dominant and extrovert, while others needed a more structured and detailed approach. The same can be said for the Belgian national football team and, without talking about specific players, each individual, superstar or unsung hero requires the same level of understanding. Being able to do this, either intuitively or with support, helps unite individuals behind a common purpose.

THE ROUGH WITH THE SMOOTH

It would be simple to categorise Michael Maguire as a tough, demanding and assertive taskmaster and, dare I say it, there would be some elements of those adjectives that ring true. Upon first meeting Maguire, you can see why people might find him intimidating. He certainly doesn't take any prisoners. Yet Maguire acknowledges that 'everyone is different internally . . . some are self-taught, some aren't, some need a bit of a shake, some don't really like those sorts of behaviours, so as a leader you are dealing with those things all the time'. He describes himself as a leader that 'will praise when required and also give a kick up the backside'. All Maguire is doing is selecting the most appropriate form of leadership for the individual and that is driven by the fact that underneath the tough Australian exterior is a genuine warmth and desire to see his players develop:

> I always want to get the best out of them and that is what I really enjoy about the coaching, seeing that growth in the player and knowing that I can sit down and go, 'You know what, they've done everything possible to achieve what they can get out of themselves.' Now they might not be the greatest of players, but I have seen some of the lesser-talented players become superstars because of what they have put into it and that is, really, what I try to do with the players.

Maguire's personality is competitive and with that comes a natural emphasis on achievement and results. At times leaders need to switch their focus from wanting to lead for the sake of results, towards leading with the aim of development. As Maguire exemplifies, the two are not mutually exclusive and the latter can naturally lead to the former.

Like many of our leaders, Maguire has a strong sense of family, stemming from his own tight-knit upbringing. He certainly brings this into his leadership philosophy, offering a model that shares striking similarities with a family unit. In contrast to his relentless focus on winning, he offers a glimpse into this lesser-seen side of his leadership style, identifying the importance of the family-like relationships he builds with his players:

'A lot of coaching is about being a father or a friend or a relationship that they value. They are human beings and we are all different. I understand that. We all come from so many different backgrounds, but to understand their family values and bring them and incorporate them into our values inside our club, I think that's a pretty special time. The family go through everything that the athlete is going through so for them to understand the ups and downs, we all go through it.'

An awareness of a player's family environment can provide the leader with crucial information to be used to maximise the performance of each individual. This knowledge can help to identify potential challenges or red flags, enabling the organisation to take a proactive approach to supporting their asset. Family is often the ultimate source of a player's purpose and motivation, deeply woven into the reason they play the game in the first place. This can be vital information that a leader can use to tap into the psyche of the athlete in critical moments.

Invariably a leader will form closer relationships and greater trust with some athletes than with others. The same can be said for family units. Nevertheless, each relationship is important and contributes to a leader's overall impact.

RELATIONSHIPS OVER STRATEGY

The realities and rhythm of both sport and business mean that the somewhat softer value of 'getting to know your team' is never going to be measured and evaluated in the same way as economic success or points on the board. In many sporting cultures, despite all the best intentions, the bottom line still rules.

The fluctuating pressure levels of a professional environment also dictate that a leader does not always have time to get to know each and every team member to the same level of depth. This is especially true in business as, while a sporting leader can focus on building relationships with a relatively small group of senior players, a CEO in a Fortune 500 company cannot reasonably be expected to know everyone in their organisation at a personal level. At times, leaders must look to their support staff to impart the same values and play a crucial part in developing the relationship between the player and the wider organisation.

In the United States the NFL, like rugby, is a sport associated with big collisions, confrontation and extreme competitiveness. Underneath the on-field performances, Dan Quinn talks about the fulfilment he takes from building relationships with his players, something that is not easy to achieve when you are working with upwards of fifty players across the various offensive, defensive and special teams. The NFL is unique in our sample in that it is a clearly structured and siloed team sport. These sub-teams will regularly practice and train in their own units, developing specific skills, so the various 'co-ordinators' (offensive, defensive, special teams) will have a significant impact in terms of relationships and leadership.

Since his early coaching days, Quinn has focused on the defensive side of the game. He was defensive co-ordinator as the Seattle

Seahawks' defence (nicknamed the 'Legion of Boom') powered them to two consecutive Super Bowls, winning Super Bowl XLVIII in 2014. In early 2019, Quinn made the bullish decision to take on the role of defensive co-ordinator at the Falcons alongside his head coach responsibilities, ultimately shifting his game-day focus from macro to micro. In November 2019 he reversed this decision, relinquishing the defensive role and looking instead to work collaboratively with the other coaches, while still remaining across all of the on-field calls. This brief snapshot gives us an insight into Quinn's leadership style. His relentless energy level and personal drive gave him the bandwidth to take on the demands of dual roles, while his self-awareness told him it was time to step back again. Initially this could be seen as an example of a leader taking on too much, due to their desire to be across the detail and a belief that only they can fulfil the role to the required standard. It is a strength, however, to then have the humility to realise that they too need to lean on others to get the job done.

Quinn's players regularly talk in the media about his energy, how he keeps team meetings honest but entertaining and, crucially, that despite his tough physical appearance, he *cares*. Earlier in the book (p.10–11) we used a quote from former Falcons linebacker Brooks Reed and it is worth revisiting here:

When you first see him, you're like, 'Oh man, this guy looks tough.' You might be intimidated. But the second you start talking to him, he's all about you. He cares about people, cares about his players first and foremost. You can see that in the way he talks about us and treats us.[*]

---

[*] 'Why is Dan Quinn the NFL's most unique coach?', supra.

To convey a sense of caring and empathy to a crowd of NFL players, an environment brimming with ego, testosterone and the trappings of success, is an impressive achievement. Individuals are impacted by how a leader makes them feel, and Quinn applies this knowledge to take a people-based method into the chaos of elite sport. This enables him to add substance to an environment that can sometimes be overly driven by data and systems. At its core, sport remains a human endeavour of performance.

For Coach Quinn it is the relationships he forms with players, in a highly pressured environment, that bring the game to life. 'I enjoy the relationships with the players. I think that overrides strategy to a certain extent because so often, in our sport anyway, there are plenty of really talented, good coaches who have a fantastic strategy model, not just a few, but a lot, but I think the relationships that you make are really important. That is what makes the whole game come to life, we're not robots.'

RESPECT

From Atlanta to Burnley, and my conversation with Sean Dyche. Here is another leader who on first impression could easily be perceived as aggressive, but the Burnley boss places great emphasis on the establishment of respect in building relationships with his players:

> I think about it like this. You are a human and so am I. How would I wish to be treated? Then pretty much treat you like I would wish to be treated. Which usually is [to be] spoken to with a bit of respect, and hopefully with a helpful edge, and usually positive. That is not a bad start. I tend to try to park all the other noise as I call it, get all that out of my system and go,

'Right, what do you need? What can I do to help you get that?'
That is usually how I would start to approach it.

Against the dramatic and unforgiving backdrop of elite sport, Dyche takes a refreshing empathy-based approach. One of his golden rules which exemplifies a deep sense of respect is that he never calls players by derogatory nicknames because, as a player, he 'used to get called all sorts' and would think, 'Why is the manager calling me that?' Dyche realises that his players are all 'trying to improve, trying to learn' and wants to focus on giving them something to help them do that.

Dyche's approach is laden with the human elements of leadership, terms like respect, development and growth. To some this might seem to be a real contrast from more aggressive management styles of days gone by. However, Sir Alex Ferguson, known for his dressing-room rants and 'hairdryer' treatment of the likes of Beckham and Giggs, also cared deeply about his players as people. Let's not kid ourselves here. Sean Dyche – and this can be said of any of our leaders – is still more than capable of calling people out for sub-par performances. He may even overstep the mark at times. However – and this is the crucial point – when this is done against a backdrop of trust and care built over time, the message is usually received by the player in question from a more rational perspective. Even in times of conflict, understanding the person is a golden route to effective leadership.

For Ashley Giles communicating this same sense of 'respect', regardless of individual styles, is a key attribute of his leadership style. 'One coach said to me that every dressing room has the same eleven characters, just with different names. You have all these different people, some are a bit more precious, some are your rock-solid individuals who just get on with it, some need a bit more careful management . . . but certainly there always has to be respect.'

Giles knows that he cannot take a one-size-fits-all approach to his people. An understanding of behaviour underpins an understanding of leadership. It is this knowledge that enables leaders to build relationships over time, allowing players, according to Ashley Giles, to see that the leader's 'intentions are very strong and clear, and that there are no hidden agendas'. This process builds trust which, in turn, leads to the ability to have honest conversations, cultivating a sense of accountability and ownership within a team dynamic, as Giles explains:

> I might one minute go, 'You're late again, you've not got the right kit,' and I could just walk away from that and go in my office. Now I can do that and then half an hour later I can go, 'Come here, I want to show you something,' a technical skill and that's good. You've built up a bit more trust, and actually it is easier to manage because they realise that you are only doing or saying that because it needed to be said, but you're not holding a grudge, there's nothing in it. That is my personal way, that's my method really.

Office politics and the realities of modern life can sometimes hinder our ability to stop and be mindful of respecting an individual. We might rush past somebody, eager to get to our next appointment, or ignore a subtle plea for help. Conditions dictate that we do not always react to situations in the most competent and impactful way – human beings are not perfect – and the leader's mindset can itself be affected by other factors at home or at work. In Giles' example here, he describes how a direct and somewhat blunt approach can be neatly juxtaposed with a more caring touch all in the context of a single working day or training session. This element of leadership is not a quest for perfection, but more an awareness of our impact on others and a willingness to correct something that may have been wide of the mark.

Roberto Martínez believes that the ability to build relationships is a crucial component of his leadership. 'Unless the player feels on top of the world, he won't be able to perform in the manner that I want them to so it is very demanding, in a way that you feel a player would never let you down. He trusts what I am doing and what I am saying to him but in the same way, it is a personal relationship that we are working together in order to achieve something, so if he doesn't work well enough, he is going to let me down and let himself down.' For Martínez, this relationship is built by finding 'mutual inspiration or mutual aspiration' with an athlete. Ideally he wants players 'to be free, to enjoy, to express themselves' and he works with 'the individual to achieve something together'; for example, 'That could be to achieve a certain amount of games or certain individual prizes, or winning titles together.' While a mutual goal certainly strengthens the connection between the leader and the player, there may be a point where failure to achieve such a shared endeavour, in which both parties are heavily emotionally invested, can cause a breakdown in the very trust that fuels the relationship.

TIME AND AUTHENTICITY

Stuart Lancaster, talking in this instance about his time with England, makes sure he spends time with all players on an individual basis. 'I would always meet players at the start of every camp. Just to connect with them really, find out what is going on, find out how the club has been, how the motivation is. It is sometimes a good time for me to give them certain messages and sow a seed about what we're think-ing about [in terms of] selection further down the line, so it doesn't come as a shock.' He spends his time building and maintaining relationships with all the players, whether they have made his team or not. Each player is 'equally important' and has an impact on the overall team dynamic. Arriving at Leinster, one of the first things Lancaster did was to spend forty minutes with each player to go through their backgrounds and interests in order to get to know the human being behind the rugby player. Across both international and domestic environments, Lancaster's desire to spend time with the individual remains steadfast. It is the *amount* of time that is the key differentiator here. I imagine his meetings at Leinster are flexible and dynamic affairs, covering a number of areas relevant to both sporting performance and personal development, and continuing over the course of a season and beyond. With England, these meetings will invariably feel more transactional, at least at first, as he seeks to ensure performance for that camp or tournament. The decisive factor is how impactful these interactions are and how those people feel as a result. Time is a precious commodity and the leader needs to weigh this up against the need for results. In reality, both are vital to a leader's success.

The leaders I interviewed felt it was important to be honest and 'as authentic as you possibly can be' (Giles) when managing athletes. Giles gives a specific recent example. 'I sat two players down and got tough with them. I told them that I have high expectations because I think they are good enough. If I didn't, they wouldn't be here. So, from a professional standpoint, that is what I am asking for and maybe I get frustrated because I'm not seeing them put in the hard yards to get there. So the message was, "Come on, let's work together to get you there, then we won't be having any more of these conversations."' Tough messages can be delivered more effectively with a tone of authentic concern, especially if you are committed to a people-based philosophy, and Giles conveys this via his belief that the players are 'good enough'.

However, the somewhat ideological concept of authenticity is not always as clear as it first seems. When authenticity is wavering or there is a need to compromise on the amount of information shared, a leader cannot afford to also question their moral stance.

In a nod to this reality of leadership, Martínez believes 'you need to be honest; I don't believe in lying to your people' but also makes it clear that 'that doesn't mean you have to tell them everything all the time. That helps them, because it is a competitive environment and sometimes you need to get them to fight for a dream.' Giles provided a caveat to his previous statement: 'Of course it is important to have the honesty, the trust and the loyalty. But we all have to tell white lies occasionally, because,' he chuckles, 'some people can't handle the truth.'

I regularly work with organisations navigating change processes against a backdrop of uncertainty. In such situations a leader cannot, in reality, share everything with everyone at all times. In some scenarios the stipulation that a leader cannot be altogether open causes them to shut off completely and not share *any* information with their people, which can potentially have a damaging and long-lasting impact on the morale of their teams. In these situations, it is imperative that the information a leader *can* share is communicated in the most impactful way, with regularity, empathy and care.

Michael Maguire recalled a specific situation, where he decided to change the captain of the Rabbitohs due to a well-publicised and clear breach of the club's values and behaviours. Due to the relationship Maguire had built with the player over time, the two were able to continue working together. He communicated the decision in an open forum, leaving the team in no doubt as to the decision and the facts and rationale behind it. While the outcome may not have been universally popular, the way it was discussed once again reinforces a culture of trust and authentic communication:

We communicated about it. I just put them all in a room and we spoke like grown men. I let them know how I felt, obviously, the position we were in as a club, what we had to do, and the fact that they either accept it or they don't. Fortunately for him, he accepted it and he put his hand up straight away. He knows that we care for him immensely. We haven't changed the way we are, our relationship, I still hold him in high esteem but if I didn't show some value-change in who we are as a team I wouldn't be doing my job. It was incorrect behaviour for someone in our organisation, so it needed to be changed. He and I, we are different in personality but we worked extremely hard to create what we have and he understands that. If you show honesty towards the situation and you go about it in the right manner, I think, well, at the end of the day, yes it was wrong but we get on with it.

Sean Dyche believes there is always more you can elicit from high-achieving individuals. In order to identify the areas for improvement, a leader must tap into the athlete's intrinsic motivation and understand how to drive that human being. This inner drive is something that he believes is either present or not: 'There has to be a will and desire to continue to want to be successful and that is undefinable. If people can show signs of it, I always say if the fire is burning inside, we can make it burn brighter, but if the fire isn't there, we can't make you have it.' In certain situations, leaders must reluctantly accept the reality that an athlete does not have the fire to go further, and take appropriate action to remedy it. These decisions can have huge ramifications on group dynamics, presenting a critical moment for the leader at which they must trust their philosophy and judgement implicitly.

RELATIONSHIP-BUILDING MOMENTS

Relationships are not formed in a structured and uniform manner. To take such an approach would likely be perceived as forced and contrived. Some of the most impactful conversations take place informally, in passing around a training facility, or after a particular performance. The most effective leaders are able to influence people at an emotional level. Asking an athlete about their family, giving them a quick technical pointer or a pat on the back can build towards a boost in motivation. These moments are difficult for us, as outsiders, to observe. But we can try; next time you sit down to watch a fixture on the TV, keep an eye on what the leader does *after* the final whistle. You will often see them walk on to the pitch and communicate with the players. Compare approaches and consider how the best managers might flex their style, pace and body language depending on the player they are approaching.

When I consider critical relationship-building moments, I will often cite an example from the NBA's Golden State Warriors, and specifically an in-game interaction between coach Steve Kerr and global superstar Steph Curry. The clip can easily be found on YouTube or social media and was also cited by Daniel Coyle, best-selling author of *The Culture Code*, on his personal blog.* Now, I don't know Curry's personality, but Kerr clearly does. The relationship-building flashpoint occurs during a game, at what Coyle refers to as a 'moment of tension', when Curry is out of the game having just attempted a rather ambitious shot from sixty feet. The Warriors' star man is not hitting his own high standards in terms of points

* 'Steve Kerr's 30-Second Master Class on Building Relationships.' danielcoyle. com, retrieved 5 January 2020.

contribution. Kerr focuses on behaviours and Curry's significant impact on the *team* regardless of individual stats:

> That's your shooting totals . . . and that's your plus/minus.*
> All right? So, it's not always tied together. You're doing great
> stuff out there. The tempo is so different when you're in the
> game. Everything you generate is so positive. You're doing
> great. Carry on, my son.

Writing on his blog, Coyle raises the suggestion that all of this might appear 'at first glance . . . a little bit over the top. Curry already knows he's good. Shouldn't Kerr be challenging him?' However, in this moment, 'Kerr isn't coaching, he's building a bond.'

There is a special moment during the clip where you just know the message has landed, as Curry responds with a broad grin as Kerr says, 'I would love to feel whatever the hell you're feeling right now. Just once in my life. For me, if I went five for six and made four threes, that was the best I ever did. Love it.' Coyle refers to this as 'one of the most powerful signals a leader can deliver; a burst of pure delight'.

Kerr shows vulnerability, acknowledging that Curry is a better player than he ever was. He uses words like 'son' and 'love', communicating the depth of the relationship. The feedback is timely, personal and delivered specifically to the player for this moment in time:

> One of the things I love about you is you're two for eleven, and
> you have no hesitation about shooting a sixty footer . . . nobody
> in the league does that . . . You have so much confidence in

---

* This is how many points better the team are when Curry is in the game.

yourself, and within games like this, you turn it on like that. That's awesome. Amazing. I wish I had your confidence.

Kerr repeats his message, conveying confidence and reinforcing his faith in the player. This, according to Coyle, shows that the leader 'knows it's not enough to say these things once' and presume the message will get through. He sends the message 'over and over and over – because that is how bonds are sustained'.

Coyle concludes his article by outlining the key ingredient for impacting people at this level:

> And here's the cool thing: None of this is complex, or dependent on technical knowledge of any kind. It requires only an alertness for the opportunity, and the ability to deliver simple signals – we are connected. I see you. I care.

There it is again, that word 'care'.

Relationships are dynamic and changing. They can also be irreparably damaged by one poorly communicated decision. Think of them as a bank account, but instead of money the account is used to safely store trust, respect and commonality built up between individuals. This bank account must be deposited into on a regular basis in order to maintain a healthy balance of credit. Relationships are everywhere and hold the key to a leader's impact.

MANAGING THE GROUP

Leaders must balance their focus on individual relationships with the creation and maintenance of the overall team dynamic. By default, human beings and the teams they form are dysfunctional. Within any group there will be an element of both demographic (age, gender, nationality, etc.) and cognitive (modes of thinking and perspective) diversity. Teams are a unique collection of individuals, thrown together and characterised by a particular combination of backgrounds, biases, assumptions, characters, egos and beliefs. It is this unique combination that differentiates one collective from another, and an appreciation of this will ultimately impact the mindset and direction of the team. As a consequence, teamwork – a fundamental attribute of high performance – is both critical and difficult to attain. As we will see over the coming pages, it does not necessarily need mutual admiration between all parties, but it does require effort and it does require trust.

Patrick Lencioni's popular fable, *The Five Dysfunctions of a Team*,* outlines the pivotal role trust plays in creating high-performance environments. Trust forms the base layer of Lencioni's Trust Pyramid, providing the foundation that allows teams to engage in constructive conflict, commit to decisions, hold each other accountable and prioritise team goals over individual objectives. By contrast, a lack of trust and the associated invulnerability is likely to lead to a fear of conflict (and an artificial sense of harmony), a lack of commitment (ambiguity), an avoidance of accountability (therefore lower overall standards) and an unhealthy focus on status and ego.

Trust is a term that you will see repeated frequently throughout the pages of this book. That is because it lies at the very core of two of the pillars of high-performance cultures – relationships (see previous section) and teamwork. Developing trust is a challenging process because individuals instinctively want to protect their own interests. A precursor of trust is the willingness to show vulnerability and it is here that the leader must take the first step. By

* Lencioni, P. (2002). *The Five Dysfunctions of a Team: A Leadership Fable.* San Francisco: Jossey-Bass.

acknowledging weaknesses and sharing experiences at the top, we communicate a sense of psychological safety and embolden others to do the same. In the pyramid, trust forms the bottom layer on which the team is built. For our leaders, it must start at the top of the organisation.

RECRUITMENT AND SELECTION

On transfer deadline day, football teams around the world will scramble to make last-minute signings. Some will have conducted their business early, sit back and rather smugly observe the chaos that ensues. While it is exciting for supporters to follow the speculation and abounding rumours surrounding their team, a signing rooted in desperation can have a long-lasting impact on a team environment. A team dynamic is a living, breathing and multilayered environment. As such, when an individual joins a team or an organisation, they can alter, positively or negatively, the make-up of that group.

When bringing someone into an environment under his leadership, Gary Kirsten is keen to explore the individual's values and passion for their sport. He wants to know whether 'they can articulate what the cricket ball means to them'. He wants to know that it is not about financial gain, but rather what they 'do with that ball every day of their life and how they care about it and how they pay attention to it'.

This raises the question of whether passion for the game is more powerful than financial incentive. Not every athlete plays for the shirt; the reality is that for some it is a job and for others it may become a job as a result of more challenging times. If we refer back to the concept of 'purpose', it tells us that those with a deeper motivation will be more engaged, productive and resilient, and this is what Kirsten is looking for. He wants people that 'show courage, character, resilience, and show that cricket means something to them, that they have a love affair with the game'.

He refers to one player who was brought into an international team culture as a result of impressive domestic form. 'He came in and we picked him. In his first game he broke a record. He was then touted as the next best thing and he was going the distance. But that was literally the last performance we got from him.' He blamed the recruitment process: 'If we'd had a more diligent process, we would have spotted massive issues in a whole lot of different areas that needed to be addressed and weren't. Unfortunately, they were exposed at the highest levels of the game.' Even at the highest of elite levels, the same recruitment frailties occur.

The recruitment process is a crucial one, and something that must be understood within the context of individual sports. In Premier League football, the financial investment can be colossal and with that comes a great deal of analysis and due diligence on potential recruits. When considering a new signing, Sean Dyche utilises 'stats, scouting, a lot of facts, feedback, and background checks' but acknowledges that recruitment is 'a really tough thing, because as a leader you don't have the crystal ball'.

Businesses will often use behavioural profiling during their recruitment process and, vitally, before a final selection decision is made. However, from a psychological perspective in sport, legal and personal data constraints often mean a club cannot conduct psychometrics until after a player has signed. Even then, a behavioural profile completed at a high-pressure moment does not always tell the full story. In reality, until the player walks through the door on their first day and starts to operate within the environment, it is difficult to gauge their potential impact on a culture. Leaders take recruitment decisions as a combination of data, due diligence and the intangible aspect of leadership – instinct.

At Burnley, the club has regularly signed players from the Championship, the tier directly beneath the Premier League, due to their budget restraints. One benefit of this approach is the hunger to play at a higher level that you would expect a Championship player to possess. 'If you have got someone coming into the Premier League that really wants it, and really thinks, "Right, I am in the Premiership, I've got a chance to make a name for myself," then that is a great fuel to have.' However, Dyche makes it clear that this 'is only part of the thinking' as he strives to create a mix within the group, 'so it is not a given that we just want a hungry player out of the Championship, it can be a hungry player who knows the Premier League'. He looks to grasp the specific mentality of a recruitment situation, with the aim that 'if you throw them into the right culture with the right coaching then that's a great chance for them to thrive'.

Here Dyche is searching for a partnership between individual and club that will be mutually beneficial to both parties. First, he considers the demands and realities of the role that the club is looking to fill. What are they missing? Is the recruitment being made for the short or long term? Should it be based on experience, know-how, impact or toughness? He then looks to match these attributes with what he knows (or thinks he knows) about the individual in question. A good match should, all things considered, make for an effective and fruitful alliance.

CASE STUDY: JOEY BARTON

One of the players that Dyche recruited to Burnley is Joey Barton, an individual who carries unavoidable baggage due to a storied past. Consequently, the media were quick to question the decision and its potential impact on the harmony of the group. The rationale behind the decision was to provide the team with 'an edge, a competitive edge, competitive spirit'. Dyche felt Barton's image had been some-what misrepresented in the past, although both player and manager acknowledged that this was sometimes brought on by the player's actions. A meeting between the two left Dyche confident that Barton would prove a cultural 'fit' to the group. 'I told him what we would offer, he told me what to expect, we both agreed on certain ways of working. I found you could speak to him very openly and honestly. You can be brutal if you need to. He doesn't cry or worry, he goes, "Right, OK."'

From Dyche's account, it seems that the 'win-win' aspect for all parties was communicated and committed to in a very direct and simple manner, resulting in a successful working relationship. Despite Barton's reputation, the leader backed his own judgement and was able to separate the individual he encountered face-to-face from the image of the player that was persistently portrayed in the media.

The contractual agreement between the two parties was concluded swiftly: 'I made the offer and if he chooses to buy into that, fantastic, if he doesn't then he'll go and he just went, "Right, OK, that's the deal." So we did the deal pretty quick and it worked. It worked for him by the way, first, and he had a great time here and we got the benefit of him having a great time, because he was absolutely terrific for us.'

In the subsequent weeks, Dyche was repeatedly asked, 'How are you going to manage Joey Barton?' His response was illustrative of his approach to leadership, grounded in common sense and an apti-tude for building relationships with different characters. He said, 'I am not going to manage him in the way that you think. Do you know why? Because he's a man, he's not a boy.' Dyche acknowledged that the Barton sat before him at Burnley was an altogether different leadership challenge than the younger versions he would have encountered at Manchester City or Newcastle: 'People forget that we had him at thirty-two, thirty-three, he's worldly wise, he's football worldly wise and a little bit life worldly wise, more than a little bit in fact!'

It is through experience that we ultimately learn, evolve and develop. Leaders are in a position to provide opportunities for players to prove doubters wrong, and to find strengths where others see only shortcomings. In this example, Dyche consciously considered and challenged the preconceptions that surrounded Barton. He also needed to reflect and ensure he wasn't doing this as an ego-based challenge, to be the manager that was seen to 'tame' such a combustive character. For his part, Barton echoes this sentiment and rates Dyche highly as a manager. In his autobiography *No Nonsense,*[*] Barton describes Dyche as a welcome antithesis to professional football, an industry he perceives to be 'infected by fear and restricted by a lack of emotional intelligence'. Dyche's readiness to accept Barton, rather than professing a desire to 'fix' or 'change' the player, was key to him signing for the club:

> I joined Burnley because of Sean Dyche. We sat in his kitchen and made mutual promises that were more than fulfilled. He accepted me as the finished article, the older, wiser person I have always wanted to be in a dressing room. I responded to him, as one of the few managers I felt was a friend.

Barton references the polarising characteristics of Dyche's leadership style; on one hand you have the aggression, but on the other, the genuine emotional intelligence. 'He might slip down a couple of points if he started banging cups of tea at half time, but they would

---

[*] Barton, J. (2017). *No Nonsense*. London: Simon & Schuster.

soon be recovered because of the intelligence of his strategy and the depth of his character.'

Dyche describes their working relationship as 'healthy', in part due to the honest and open approach he takes with all of his players. 'Joey enjoyed it here. He enjoyed what we were about. He enjoyed the staff. I told him the truth and we backed up the truth and I think he enjoyed that and thought, "OK, you are actually backing it up. I see it every day. You are backing up what you told me," and I think that was an important part of that.' By treating him with respect and honesty, Dyche was able to maximise Barton's on-field output and witness the player having a positive impact on the team dynamic.

PERSONAL GROWTH

When recruiting a player into the group, Michael Maguire, in a further indication of the importance of relationships, looks to instil a sense of personal growth: 'I embrace how they are going to grow really. I give them an opportunity, to show them that this is where I want to take them. It's not just about the sport. It is about you as a person, you becoming someone and developing yourself on and off the field.'

In the process of securing a signing, he spends time with the individual. He wants to understand the person, but also for them to understand his style and approach of leadership:

I think, at the end of the day, they're going to be attracted by the person that they are going to have to play under. I need them to understand who I am and what I want them to have long term. At the end of the day, I want them to have success. It is part and parcel of what we all want as people. Through that, it's about working hard to win Grand Finals and having those times because they don't come very often in your life. It is about those players, the marquee player, understanding that I am going to spend time with him so I can try to get him to achieve.

Dan Quinn is a ball of boundless energy and he acknowledges that his style is not a natural fit for every footballer that possesses the technical ability to play for his team. His intense and relentless approach can simply be too forceful for those who do not have the required capacity to respond. To that end, Quinn has to be mindful before bringing a player into the group:

> We want to make sure the fit is right, that we have the right connection, the right relationship to say, "'This would be a good fit for both sides'" because not every player fits every system. Here, you better like being around a lot of energy, and being around a beat and a fast-moving pace because that is really how we live our lives professionally. That doesn't mean the guy wouldn't be a successful player elsewhere, he certainly could – sometimes it's just not the right fit.

It is imperative that recruitment is not seen simply as a one-way, power-driven assessment of a 'candidate'. Quinn identifies the importance of a leader being clear in their philosophy and approach in order to congruently convey who they are and how they operate. Only when both sides are equally considered can a more informed decision be made.

In recruitment situations, a leader may need to take a risk and trust their instincts, built over time, to make some tough decisions. To pass on a talented player because they do not fit the culture is not without risk, and is sure to be questioned by supporters, the media and other players should the on-field results fail to measure up. The most important asset an organisation possesses is not something material. It is the people: a unique, living, breathing combination of human beliefs, thoughts and emotions. The recruitment process is key to building, maintaining and, at times, shifting a high-performance environment.

TALENT AND CHARACTER

GLORY DAYS

If you are a fan of Bruce Springsteen, you may well be familiar with the song 'Glory Days',* which tells the tale of a high-school baseball player who failed to maximise his on-field ability. Years later, the player sits in a bar wistfully reminiscing about the best days of his life – the 'glory days' that will, he warns, 'pass you by'.

We all have that friend who utters the immortal line, 'I could have played professionally, but *insert excuse here*'. Sport is littered with examples of athletes who failed to fulfil their vast potential and, contrastingly, those with less natural ability but a strength of character that led them to have highly successful careers. The former almost become mythical anti-hero figures. The ones who didn't 'make it' – who the public would not recognise – but their youth-team peers, now superstars in their own right, recall with wide-eyed tales of prodigious adolescent brilliance.

There are those sought-after individuals who possess both ability and character in equal measure; a rare commodity in the raging war for talent. However, it is becoming increasingly common to hear commentators or pundits bemoan the lack of 'character' within

---

* Springsteen, B. (1985). 'Glory Days.' Columbia Records.

teams. It is easy and somewhat reductive to throw the word around as a nebulous term covering anything that isn't related to physical or technical ability, yet the notion of character deserves a deeper level of understanding.

CHARACTER, GROWTH MINDSET AND GRIT

Professor Martin Seligman (University of Pennsylvania) and Professor Christopher Peterson (University of Michigan) took a meticulous approach to studying 'character', exploring accounts from all major religions and philosophies going back three millennia. The resultant handbook, *Character Strengths and Virtues*, provides a robust empirical framework for the development and components of 'character' across more than 700 pages.*

Seligman and Peterson identified six classes of virtues that are made up of twenty-four individual character strengths. While I cannot do justice to the remarkable depth of this work here, a summary is below:

Virtue	Associated character strengths
Wisdom/knowledge	Creativity, curiosity, judgement, love of learning, perspective
Courage	Bravery, persistence, honesty, zest
Humanity	Love, kindness, social intelligence

* Peterson, C. and Seligman, M. E. P. (2004). *Character Strengths and Virtues: A Handbook and Classification.* New York: Oxford University Press.

Virtue	Associated character strengths
Justice	Teamwork, fairness, leadership
Moderation	Forgiveness, modesty, prudence, self-control
Transcendence	Appreciation of beauty, gratitude, hope, humour, spirituality

Looking at the virtues and strengths that Seligman and Peterson present, two things become apparent. Firstly, 'character' is not an individual ingredient that we either have or have not. Secondly, not everybody's character will be the same. In reality, we are all a unique combination of these strengths – and I am yet to meet somebody who possesses them all in equal measure. You can start to form an idea of your own character strengths by considering which attributes, from the list above, your attention was drawn to. This self-awareness, coupled with an appreciation for the strengths of others, is key to building relationships.

Researchers in this field agree that such virtues can be developed and practised, and the ability to do this is inextricably linked to the celebrated research of Carol Dweck.* Dweck, a Stanford professor, has a particular interest in the field of motivation and she highlights the importance of adapting a growth mindset, rather than a fixed mindset, both of which impact behaviour. The contrast between these two states is similar to the nature versus nurture debate; a fixed mindset considers qualities such as intelligence or sporting talent to be rigid traits that you have little or no

* Dweck, C. (2008). *Mindset: the new psychology of success.* New York: Ballantine Books.

control over. Conversely, if you consciously work to develop a growth mindset, you will likely build a powerful belief that such qualities can improve with time and effort. This distinction might seem simple, yet in reality people often shift between the two mindsets, and it is easy to slip unnoticed into the more debilitative and fixed state.

In schools across the world, teachers devote themselves to cultivating a growth mindset in our children. However, often it is the adults these children look up to who must reflect on their own mindset and the impact it can have on those around them. As with many elements of leadership, it must start from the top.

In order to develop a growth mindset and, therefore, develop our character, we need to pay attention to the way we think, and start to actively practise our desired mindset and beliefs. To do this, we must instruct the most powerful muscle at our disposal – the human brain and, in particular, the prefrontal cortex. Sounding like something from a science-fiction film and situated at the front of the brain, the prefrontal cortex is responsible for what scientists call our executive function, a collection of cognitive processes including attention, memory, planning, decision-making and problem-solving. Think of this area as the CEO of the brain; it is the orchestrator of your thoughts and actions.

The presence of 'character' can also be closely linked to the research of psychologist Angela Duckworth and her colleagues[*] on the quality of 'grit', the relentless passion for long-term goals which we previously referenced in the context of the leaders' personal qualities. Their academic and applied work across educational, sporting

---

[*] Duckworth, A. L., Peterson, C., Matthews, M. D. and Kelly, D. R. (2007). 'Grit: Perseverance and passion for long term goals.' *Journal of Personality and Social Psychology*, 92, 1087–1101.

and military environments, examines the variations in performance (estimated at 75 per cent) that talent (the other 25 per cent – IQ, aptitude, ability) does not account for. For both teams and individuals, it is not always the most talented group or person who wins, as with 'grit' comes motivation and mental toughness, commitment to training, a willingness to do 'extras' and the ability to push through pain thresholds.

Talent alone is not enough, although it certainly helps. To get through the door at an elite sporting organisation talent is a prerequisite. We would be naive to think any differently, but in high-stakes environments it is the interaction between grit, talent and character that critically impacts an individual's development and growth. Michael Jordan's famous quote 'talent wins games, but teamwork and intelligence wins championships' certainly rings true. This is echoed by Bill Belichick of the New England Patriots, who is quoted as saying 'talent sets the floor, character sets the ceiling'.

In an ideal world, the talent available to leaders would strike an appropriate balance with an individual's character and leadership. In reality, this is no easy task and, as Stuart Lancaster describes, 'it really is quite unique, utopia, to find someone who can do it all'. I was keen to explore what the leaders were looking for from their people and their take on the 'talent versus character' debate.

Referring to the group of players he coached at international level with England, Lancaster felt at that point in their development, he had 'some B+ talent and A-grade characters'. 'A-grade', for Lancaster, means top three in the world in a certain position and you could argue that players like Owen Farrell and Maro Itoje are on their way to achieving that. Within that group of players, some 'of the best talent were also some of the best characters' and that is ultimately what a leader is looking for.

The leaders all acknowledged the role that character can play in creating a high-performance environment. Gary Kirsten believes 'you can't put metrics in place to measure character', and looks instead to 'how an individual operates and what makes them tick' to get an idea of their personal qualities. He talks about players who have 'it' (character) and gets 'really excited with the players who exceed their skill levels, who go and perform above themselves' and disappointed 'with those who have a great level of skill but don't match it up with their performances under pressure'. It is important to point out that 'character' isn't a personality trait in the same way as assertiveness or extroversion. Broadly speaking, it is someone's moral compass and the mental attributes that enable them to, as Kirsten describes, deliver when it counts:

> I think the game of cricket is going to move in such a way where your assessment of an individual and what he offers you and the team is going to be more along the lines of . . . yeah he has got skill and got talent but do his character and his personality traits match up to his ability to be able to make big decisions under pressure?

To a certain extent, anybody can learn and develop a specific skill. However, it is the presence and endurance of character that helps us to persevere through the natural ebbs and flows of life. How we respond to situations and inspire others is a true measure of the most human of qualities.

Michael Maguire acknowledges that the notion of character is important on and off the field 'because there is so much more that's involved besides playing now. It is the life away from sport, the brand, all those fancy words that are used now. It is those people who are really focused around what they want to achieve that can take you to the Promised Land, because of how dedicated they are. You have got to have those talented players, those "X factor" players within your organisation, but they have got to have the same self-driven process as the lesser-talented players.'

The 'X-factor' players that Maguire refers to have the ability to impact through their talent, flair, creativity and jaw-dropping ability; think Steph Curry, Kevin De Bruyne, Lionel Messi, Ben Stokes, Kevin Pietersen or Tom Brady. However, a dedication to their craft, and the associated commitment, desire and perseverance must also be present. Let's take Kevin Pietersen as a case in point. When he was on board with the ethos of the group, his unrivalled talent led the England cricket team to glory. Conversely, when he was disengaged and his morale dipped, his form suffered and his presence became a divisive and significant factor in their demise.

When it comes to selection decisions, the character versus talent debate presents the leader with an interesting dilemma. Stuart Lancaster puts a strong emphasis on character and 'if it is a fifty-fifty call and the talent is the same, you go for the guy you trust', while Maguire believes the specific situation dictates his decision:

'Sometimes I will select on character because I see the values that he may be able to develop. From the most talented player, I will assess his character because he is not going to come into the organisation and deteriorate what we have already created. There is a real mix. Whether it's fifty-fifty, I wouldn't say that, I think it is different for every single player but I have a clear idea of the style of person I want.'

He recalled a player who 'couldn't hack it' because they had a perception of his temperament, and the way he goes about things: 'The players that tend to hang around under me are able to handle the intensity of what I bring. Not everyone is made for that.'

A leader has to be clear about the qualities they want to see in the characters of their team. At the same time, they need to be constantly mindful that those characters can change depending on the situation the team finds itself in. Roberto Martínez believes the sporting context of a situation ultimately dictates a decision in this respect:

> It depends who you are fighting against. Let's say, if we are fighting against another team and we are both very equal on talent, maybe the one that has better character will finish on top. But if we are two teams with a similar character, the one with more talent will finish on top. As a manager, you need to make conscious decisions on the short term and in a specific moment, pick which one is most appropriate in order to win the competition at that time. So, if you know you have a very similar character to another group, but you can beat them immensely on talent, you have to concentrate on talent just for that period.

ASSESSING CHARACTER

A great deal of my work as a psychologist within professional sport has focused around team dynamics and working with coaches to ensure an awareness and appreciation of the overall balance of the characters that invariably make up a team environment. This process, using profiling and observation to provide insight into an individual's behavioural style, crucially equips the leader with practical strategies for flexing their approach to coaching and motivating a range of individuals.

The quick profiling process is done online and is a significant departure from the other tests athletes complete during pre-season.

There are no 'good' or 'bad' profiles yet, due to the nature of the task, some clubs and coaches are reluctant to ask players to sit in front of a laptop or tablet and complete such a profile. This might be due to the 'academic' feel of the task, the wider misconceptions of psychology, and concern about how such an activity might be perceived by the players. Others, like Sean Dyche, believe that if communicated effectively, the benefits are significant and easily outweigh the scepticism. Dyche works with Simon Clarkson, a mental skills coach, to ensure he is aware of the individual personalities under his leadership.

> I think the biggest thing for me with the profiling is how subtle it is. I was one of the first to do it. I was like, 'I'll do it,' and how it changes the little details, and how you feel in those moments ... I have been quite impressed with how that works, how fine-tuned it is. I must say mine is bang on.

At Burnley the players update their profiles each season. While personality traits are relatively stable past a certain age, other nuances of human behaviour can fluctuate. For instance, energy and morale naturally ebb and flow with the rigours of life. As we feel more secure within a group environment, we can also become more committed to our style, showing our personality to a greater extent. Finally, depending on our own situation, we can look to flex our styles in different ways – for example, working at a faster pace due to a change in leadership, or increasing assertiveness due to an increased level of responsibility.

Joey Barton, who has recently taken his first steps into management at Fleetwood Town, was part of the group who took part in the process. Barton's reputation inevitably precedes him and one might mistakenly expect him to discard the benefits of such a tool. Dyche recalls how the midfielder, one of the big characters and cultural architects in the Burnley dressing room at the time, embraced the approach, and shared his with the group:

> Joey was amazed by his. He was like, 'That's me, that is unbelievable, how I actually feel and that has told me how I am.' I use it for behavioural styles. I make it clear to the players that I never break the trust of it. If you've got something psychologically that you really need to work on that is private to you, then that remains private to you. We never break that rule, or we ask the player if he is happy to share it with me. The profiling is really about behavioural styles. It is all about how we can enhance our way of working with the players as individuals. And we explain all that to the players and the openness of it. Joey Barton did his and put it up on his locker, he just said, 'Have a read lads, that's me.' I showed the lads mine as I am like that, I am quite open, some choose not to. All we ask is that they allow us the chance to understand them purely on behavioural styles.

Barton's profile, which he shares in his book, tells us he is assertive, driven and goal-oriented. Essentially introvert, he is selective in his social interactions and seeks time to reflect. He is impatient and restless, needing pace and variety on the job, and this is coupled with a real need for perfection. This final combination (fast-paced and perfectionist) may well be the source of the frustration and associated red mist we have seen descend at times during his career. Barton's stressors include a lack of challenge, not having enough time to think, intrusion into private thoughts, failing to achieve targets or meet his own high standards, having no opportunity for spontaneity and being confined for long periods of time.

Armed with Barton's profile, his emotional intelligence and, vitally, the willingness to apply it, Dyche was able to tap into the player's character, as Barton recounts:

> Dyche took my mentality into account when he offered the opportunity to prove myself to him and a tightly knit squad of players. I enjoy working for him more than any other manager I have had, since he is attuned, emotionally and instinctively, to the obsessive nature of those who excel in elite sport. I can accept his authority and still have a two-way relationship with him. I studied the nature of his job and he took time to understand my motivation and mentality. He identifies with the senior pro who is determined to fight for his place in the pecking order. He recognises the integrity of a player who refuses to yield and responds positively to pressure. He puts up with the sound of my voice because he understands I am a compulsive communicator.

This is an example of how a knowledge of behavioural styles can provide the leader with a framework to apply over the course of a season. There is no perfect combination, but an appreciation of the different characters and their preferences, together with his willingness to share his own profile, informs Dyche's emotionally aware and empathic approach.

A profiling tool is designed to enhance, not replace, a leader's instincts and intuition. To Dyche 'it is just another piece of the jigsaw', used with existing players and new signings. He sees it, correctly, as 'a guideline that provides an insight in to how a player will want their information' and he gives the players some time to do that. 'We don't sit there all day looking at them!' he points out.

Dyche does not rely solely on this structured method, therefore avoiding the 'analysis paralysis' that is sometimes associated with a leader's desire to be across the minutiae and specifics of a situation. In fact, the establishment of a clear framework and an increased knowledge of personality traits ultimately enables the leader to develop an instinct towards behavioural styles, meaning their application naturally flows. As with any information, it is only as effective as the people delivering it.

ON-FIELD LEADERS

The presence of leaders within a team is a topic often debated within sport. Owners and managers are constantly searching for those players and athletes capable of making calls in real time, during the critical moments in the heat of competition. There are similar concerns to be found in boardrooms and offices around the world. I have worked with commercial clients who are looking for their people to show more initiative, to take decisions independently and to analyse less, and back themselves more.

The lack of leaders and characters in modern sport is often bemoaned by pundits and commentators, who pine for the culturally revered leaders of years gone by. To some people's minds, our academies and training centres do not do enough to allow such characters to flourish, perhaps preferring a player who does as they are told to one who might voice a differing opinion, and risk being labelled as a troublemaker. Indeed, there is a recurring argument that on-field leaders are becoming harder to find across all sports.

Sam Walker of the *Wall Street Journal* penned an entire book* on the role of the sporting 'captain'. Drawing from examples across the world, he argues that the best teams in history all had the same type

---

* Walker, S. (2017). *The Captain Class: A great leader is not what you think*. London: Ebury Press.

of captain, and believes their importance is equal to or even more impactful than that of the coach. Citing examples such as Richie McCaw (New Zealand All Blacks) and Carlos Puyol (FC Barcelona), these individuals are often not the most talented athletes. They are rarely the provider of the match-winning moments. Rather, they do the dirty work, and get the ball to the others. They are self-sacrificing, giving everything to the team and are not afraid to bend (or rather break) the rules in order to win. They retreat from the glare of the media, preferring others to take the limelight. In contrast to the glamorised image of captains giving roaring speeches to their teammates, Walker found these on-field leaders to be superb one-to-one communicators, spreading their time across peers, initiating brief and focused conversations. You will note there is real synergy between these qualities and the characteristics of effective team leaders.

Like many others, I have played in teams where the real leader, the one that people look to in tough times, is not the one wearing the armband. It follows that on-field leadership is not the exclusive domain of the captain. Instead it is a desired characteristic that infiltrates and flows to all corners of the most successful teams. In their quest to identify and work with their on-field leaders, some leaders take a formal approach and others allow such groups to form organically. It is critical that a leader challenges their own thought process, questioning what type of on-field leader they are looking for, and remembering that not all leadership qualities present themselves in the traditional way.

A KEY DIFFERENTIATOR

According to Gary Kirsten, recruiting individuals with leadership potential and the ability to think independently is a 'massive differentiator in teams, in terms of the quality of the leadership'. Kirsten wants more athletes 'with leadership potential in the mix because they can come up with their own thinking, we can create collaborative leadership environments and they can be solid leaders when the coaches are not in the mix. The more I learn about it the more I realise it is almost becoming a prerequisite to recruit individuals who you feel have leadership potential.'

The elements of talent and character are both considered by leaders when identifying and selecting their on-field leadership teams. Roberto Martínez looks for three main aspects: *emotional stability*, because a leader 'cannot be emotionally unstable from one day to another'; *understanding*, 'because it is a multicultural dressing room [with] different nationalities, different types of people and as a leader you cannot be narrow-minded'; and, finally, 'you need to have really *high standards*'.

Martínez's captain with Belgium is Vincent Kompany, the eminent central defender who spent most of his career at Manchester City, before taking on the dual role of player-manager at his first club, RSC Anderlecht. Kompany, who commands the respect of teammates and has a convenient habit of scoring crucial goals, has struggled with injury over the years, meaning he has not been fit to play as many games as Martínez would like. However, by all accounts he fits the bill perfectly in terms of the human qualities outlined here. Note that the words used by Martínez – emotion, understanding, standards – are a far cry from the stereotypical 'motivational' qualities we may have come to associate with archetypal on-field leadership of the past.

The qualities set out by Martínez and exemplified by Kompany are becoming increasingly sought-after in a business setting too. In industry, there is a growing acknowledgement of the broad spectrum of effective leadership attributes. In my applied work, there appears to be a far-reaching desire to move away from ego-driven leadership and to develop traits such as emotional intelligence, resilience, trust and authenticity.

CLUB AND COUNTRY

Referring to his time in international sport, Stuart Lancaster based his selection on the effectiveness of players' on-field decision-making. He looks for the leaders within the squad to provide feedback to him 'as to how the players feel the camp is going and also for them to inform the group about what is coming up', to act as a conduit between the players and the coaches. Lancaster is able to work closely with this player-leadership unit who then, in turn, are able to mentally prepare the team for 'what is coming around the corner' and the rationale as to why he has made certain decisions.

The role of player leadership will vary depending on the environment. As Lancaster describes the approach he took with England, it is as though he is looking for players to take up more of an ambassadorial role, ensuring messages are conveyed to the team and impacting performance in the short term. It feels, perhaps inevitably, more transactional than Lancaster's natural leadership style would like.

In contrast to this account of leadership in international sport, Lancaster takes a longer-term approach to developing group-wide leadership in the players he works with at club level. At Leinster, where he leads the majority of meetings, he individually asks the players to complete a behavioural profile (similar to that discussed previously by Sean Dyche) in order to gain a deeper understanding of their personality. Nothing out of the ordinary there, but his next step is a little different and perhaps something you would more typically find in an office environment or on a leadership development programme. He arranges meetings for carefully selected pairs of players to sit down and discuss their own qualities and weaknesses. This encourages an element of vulnerability amongst the players, but also crucially the emotional intelligence that kick-starts leadership development at the group level, designed not just to benefit the club in the short term, but for many years to come.

LEADING BY EXAMPLE

Gary Kirsten describes specifically the qualities that he is looking for in his players: 'Someone that generally toughs it out in difficult situations, that is prepared to do the hard yards in training, they do a bit of extra work, show great team qualities, and have a selfless demeanour to them, they add value to other people's lives, they've got great leadership capabilities, make big contributions, they're courageous in their decision-making, and courageous in the way they do things.' Courage, the strength to face challenging situations head on, mentioned twice in quick succession by Kirsten, can manifest itself both on and off the pitch.

Michael Maguire looks for those players who have a 'presence around the team and an influence on it' to effectively take up managerial-style roles. Maguire has already told us he enjoys learning from business and he compares this element of leadership to a commercial setting, describing how 'in an organisation, you have your boss and you have your managers underneath and they become your eyes and your ears of what is going on when you are not there'. Maguire looks to challenge those player-managers in all areas 'which then influences the younger guys', creating a cascade of behaviours and culture throughout the team:

'A young kid coming into the organisation is always looking up and whatever is up above him is what they tend to end up as. So, the behaviour and how the players at that top end, the senior end, tend to go is where the club is going to go.' He allows his leaders to 'have their say . . . it might be heated discussions about what is required but once we make up our mind, we then move on to the next thing and away we go. They accept it.' When selecting a leader within a team, do not be put off by the likelihood of conflict. If built on the right foundations, the opportunity to challenge can prove a vital component of an effective culture. But note Maguire's last words – 'They accept it' – ultimately the decisive call falls to him as the leader.

CHARACTER OVER EXPERIENCE

Ashley Giles described his thought process when selecting his captain at Lancashire, eventually opting for character over experience. In cricket, the captain decides the batting order, the bowlers for each over and where fielders are positioned. This decision-making and understanding of tactics and strategy, in conjunction with the lesser role played by coaches, means the role carries more direct responsibility than in other sports. Giles' successful candidate, Tom Smith, had no real leadership experience but Giles describes him as 'a fantastic character and one of our best players, respected by everyone, and you never heard a bad word said about him. You can bolt skills on to good people. You can't do that without the right ingredients.' While Smith might not have had the practical experience, in the loyal Lancastrian Giles saw the raw human ingredients of the on-field leadership he values. Unfortunately, Smith picked up a serious back injury that ultimately led to early retirement and he was unable to captain the side for most of the season. Despite the lack of contribution on the field, Giles ensured Smith remained a key part of the group, a cultural architect if you like, passing valuable advice to younger players.

The structure and sheer magnitude of an NFL team, together with the American affinity for leadership, dictates that such organisations need to take a more formulaic approach when selecting their on-field leaders. At the Atlanta Falcons the group is affectionately called 'The Chiefs' and is made up of players that are 'elected by the team as leaders'. With such a large and siloed roster, this process is more formal than in other sports, and each team (offence, defence and the special teams) is represented by 'Chiefs' who the others can turn to for leadership. Dan Quinn defines the Chiefs as the 'guys who represent and uphold The Standard [the Falcons' code of conduct, inspired by the Navy SEALs] at the highest level'. A Chief does not necessarily have to be one of the more senior players but 'has to be somebody who has real accountability and the discipline to get it right. So if you have questions, in the first instance you see a Chief.' This has been key in encouraging a player-led culture and, referring to The Standard, Quinn says 'they wrote it, so then they police it'.

I am unsure whether the Falcons actually hold an official and democratic vote, where votes are counted and a set number of Chiefs elected. Indeed, this method is not without obstacles. While being put forward by your peers signifies a significant level of trust and respect, leaders must also look to question the motivation behind votes. Perhaps rather cynically, we might point out that a player's rationale for their voting decision could be based more on loyalty, friendship or favouritism as opposed to the optimal outcome for the group. There is also the likelihood that, in an election scenario, the more dominant characters will take control and the charismatic influencers will launch their charm offensive to achieve the desired result. The danger here is that the result becomes a misrepresenta-tion of the group's actual diversity, and reflective of specific, more demonstrable types of leadership. It is in this situation that the leader must draw upon the foundation of a strong culture to ensure a genuine process takes place to ensure the on-field leaders represent not just the biggest of personalities, but all of the divergent characters that combine to form the group.

YOUNG PLAYERS

An individual's talent and character also come into consideration when a leader is faced with the dilemma of when to give a young player their first-team debut. Roberto Martínez believes it is down to the performances he sees first-hand in 'match situations in training . . . when a player makes good decisions with their talent, when they start making decisions that are a bit more proactive with the senior players, rather than reacting to something that is happening, that is when you see a player that is ready'.

As in business, young people will grow into their role and responsibilities, and this can often occur at a gradual pace. A player may show initial glimpses of the decision-making ability that Martínez is looking for, but this can taper off, before they start to display these qualities on a regular basis. For every Wayne Rooney, who by all accounts was seemingly ready-made for the Premier League, there are dozens of players who need to be held back, perhaps loaned and tested before finally being trusted in the ferocity of the big leagues. Patience is a virtue and a leader must hone the ability and instinct to identify the right time for the individual in question. Go too early and you can cause irreparable damage. Go too late and you miss the opportunity. These are critical 'sliding doors' moments which have ramifications at an individual, team and organisational level.

Martínez does not think the eventual decision to blood young talent comes 'down to character alone', because the players have already put themselves in the position to be selected and, in doing so, displayed character. They have already given the leader a decision to make; 'the players that get into the first team young are there because they have the character, they've always been in control'. He looks for 'the moment when you know someone is ready. The character is the same, so that doesn't really change, the talent is probably the same, it is the decisions they make, how they use that talent in a specific football situation and you can start to see that in training.' Given our earlier exploration of the term, I think Martínez quite possibly *is* describing 'character' here, specifically the virtue of 'courage' and the associated individual 'bravery' of a player to back their decision-making and talent amid the fire of elite sport – far away from the safety of the youth team.

Stuart Lancaster and his staff closely observe young athletes in camp environments. They 'use one-to-one conversations to assess personality, do some background work at the club and look to find out what people know about the player, about how they will deal with it'. Crucially for Lancaster, players at international level must 'add something' to the team and 'not just hang in there' because they will 'get found out' – international rugby is not the environment to be taking risks. Initially, Lancaster aims to give young players 'as much exposure to the environment without actually putting them on the field'. He provides an example of one player who 'came into camp during the course of a tournament, and was the twenty-fourth man. So, his experience of what it feels like to play, to be an international player, is greater now, so if we were to pick him somewhere down the line I could be confident he would be ready to play in the game.'

Inside the jamboree, players need to prove they have a cool head and the ability to block out the noise that besieges elite sport. Prior exposure to game day and training camp environments allows the leader a period of observation but also an element of acclimatisation and induction for a young player.

Now in club coaching, Lancaster has overseen a vast increase in young players making the step up to senior rugby at Leinster. Isa Nacewa, who captained Leinster in his final season, describes how there was somewhat of 'an old rugby culture' at the Irish club, where young players would traditionally keep quiet in team meetings. Things have changed and younger players are now encouraged to speak up and nobody 'scoffs under their breath about it'. As well as developing the young players, this simultaneously challenges senior players, sending the message that they 'can't just sit on their reputations' alone. This increasingly regular interchange of opinions and thoughts between generations of players weaves a tighter team fabric and allows young players to evolve into more prominent leadership figures within the dressing room.

Lancaster's person-management is, according to Nacewa, 'up there with the best' and this is demonstrated by his handling of young player Joey Carbery (now with Leinster's domestic rivals, Munster), who was thrust in at the last moment to start a European Cup tie. Lancaster pulled Nacewa to one side and warned him that 'Joey needs to take control of this team, the team needs to see that he is in control'. He also spoke with Carbery directly, prompting him ahead of a team meeting by saying, 'There is going to be a moment here where I think you need to speak up.' By the end of the week, Carbery had a voice and the others had confidence in him. This is subtle management in action. As we know, Lancaster's approach to leadership is dominated by a deep focus on development and growth. In this example, he prepared Carbery for a moment of growth, outlining the opportunity in front of him, rather than putting him on the spot in front of senior professionals. At the same time, he flagged the situation to the captain who was then ready to add senior backing to the player. By doing this Lancaster *shows* rather than *tells* Carbery, allowing the player to seize control of a critical career moment, rather than letting his own ego, and the desire to lead, take control.

Michael Maguire looks at a young player's 'presence around training, how they fit into the team and how the senior players see the younger player and the confidence they have in them. It is just something you gain from experience, I guess. I have had some real senior players playing and I've made a choice that I am going to give this young kid a go because he is diving on a loose ball a bit more than the older player. You do see those sorts of things in training. He is willing to put his body on the line a little more than a senior player now because that senior player knows what it is like to get hurt. Youth brings hunger and that hunger is something we need in order to win games.'

Some managers are more inclined to blood young players than others. One of the reasons for this is the sense of the unknown and therefore risk that comes with young players. It is the leader's responsibility to mould the fearless passion and impulse of youth into something that is of benefit to the group but, until they are given the chance, we just do not know how they are going to react.

Ashley Giles has a reputation for blooding young talent and knows from experience that sometimes 'you go too early or too late' with a young player, but 'until they are in that environment you don't know. At some point you've got to blood them. We have a player at the moment, he won us the game in his first game. It might not be the breakthrough but suddenly you are thinking, "Right, this lad can play," so the evidence is there.' In order for effective decision-making to occur, we need some evidence and sometimes the evidence required can only be found in the cauldron itself.

With that said, Gary Kirsten refers to a leader's intuition and his own decision-making in this situation, which is a mixture of instinct and evidence-based performance. As he puts it, 'Sometimes you take a punt on a player, you're not quite sure what he can do but he has got prestigious skill and talent and he is a young guy and you just take a punt.' Kirsten looks for a consistency in performance at various levels within the sport – 'I like to see guys that can, over a period of time, do it on a consistent basis.' As a former international batsman, big run-scorers get special attention: 'I'm looking for batsmen that know how to score big hundreds.' In the shorter formats of the game, he looks for players who 'can very cleverly go and win a game from a difficult position'. The performance markers are there but there is something to be said about intuition too.

TEAM HARMONY VERSUS GOAL HARMONY

Our leaders clearly commit a great deal of time and energy to building their relationships with individuals, looking to understand the idiosyncrasies that make each player unique. However, a leader must also simultaneously maintain an awareness of the group's overall sense of motivation.

As we have already considered, individuals will ultimately hold different agendas and ambitions, often dictated by their respective levels of talent or desire. As Ashley Giles describes, 'One guy will always play for his county. Another guy will play because he can afford nice cars and whatever. One guy plays because he can play for his country one day and one plays because it's purely money, because it pays the bills and looks after his family. And that's all fine, but as long as when we come together the main goal is that "one" that unites the team.'

It is vital that a leader is aware of such contrasting motivations, as this information provides crucial leadership nuggets that can be tapped into over time. They might decide to challenge a player's thinking and explore the concept of purpose in more depth. However, in these situations a leader must put their own beliefs aside and avoid forcing their personal opinions on to the player. It is quite natural for us to believe that everyone should think like we do. This can be a challenging moment; a leader might not necessarily under-stand or agree with a certain reason or motivation, but the priority is to unite players behind a common group goal.

In American football, Dan Quinn and his team must balance the needs and egos of around sixty individual players (fifty-three who will play and a further ten 'practice' players). At any given time, only eleven players can take to the field, and it therefore follows that many players will not play significant roles (in terms of minutes on the field) during the season. Quinn holds all of his players, starters or not, 'to the same standard. If you have a bigger role, or a supporting role, that's the fun part of being a part of a team, whatever role you have, man embrace it and go after it, so not everybody has a *leading* role but everybody has a role.' Quinn builds his team ethos around a shared endeavour, the aim being to help players go beyond what is in it for them, towards a deeper sense of 'brotherhood'.

Quinn looks to keep this feeling alive by finding ways to celebrate the contribution of the entire group. Each Friday after training, he gives a jersey to the player who has 'really exemplified the levels of practice and preparation' that he looks for. As Quinn describes, 'That player may or may not play in the game but we want to recognise their role during the week and the fact that was really important to help get the team ready. I think small moments like that, to recog-nise those players in front of their peers and highlight that what they are doing is important, are vital.'

This ongoing and vociferous team awareness helps to oversee a key group of players who can rapidly form a clique that detracts from the group, bringing the team down from the inside. Managed effectively however, you might find that the same group forms the foundation of a team's energy level. Across the media and supporters, it is natural for attention to focus on the marquee players, yet an emotionally insightful leader can never afford to let this perspective slide and will often spend a significant amount of time with those who remain in the background.

A relentless focus on the 'one' goal to which Giles refers can be described as 'goal harmony', where, irrespective of differing motivations, all individuals are united behind a common purpose, forming a key component to successful sporting organisations. Crucially, this is different to 'team harmony', the notion that everyone has to get on socially in order to achieve a sustained level of high performance.

Teams that are under consistent, intense pressure to perform can be difficult environments to operate in, home to spiky confrontations and flashes of direct conflict. This comes as no surprise given the undeniable focus on results and the combustible presence of strong personalities. Sporting history is awash with examples of teammates who clashed on a personal level, perhaps competing for starting positions, or simply dressing-room status. Kobe Bryant and Shaquille O'Neal (LA Lakers), Teddy Sheringham and Andy Cole (Manchester United), Sebastian Vettel and Mark Webber (Red Bull), Lewis Hamilton and Nico Rosberg (Mercedes F1), Lothar Matthäus and Stefan Effenberg (Bayern Munich and Germany), and Bradley Wiggins and Chris Froome (Team Sky) all reportedly experienced levels of personal friction during their time together.

However, despite personal differences they still performed consistently at the highest level. Environments with clear goal harmony but without complete team harmony can evidently still thrive. By contrast, the outright absence of conflict and niggle may ultimately mean that one environment lacks the intensity and edge of another. This is professional sport after all; it is not all about skipping off into the sunset as best friends. However, within a true high-performance environment, leaders are able to influence athletes to put aside their egos, respect (though not necessarily like) one another and recognise that, united, they can help each other to fulfil their individual ambitions.

The management of this inevitable conflict is part and parcel of a leader's role. Elite athletes are often headstrong and will invariably challenge each other, criticise a teammate, or speak out in the media. If that action comes from a position of 'goal harmony' and a desire to improve, it is easier for a leader to deal with than the problems that occur when individual agendas start to merge and this harmony goes missing.

In a conflict situation, the core group dynamic can be maintained by the strength and nature of the relationships within the team. Despite the clear emphasis on the sense of 'team', human nature dictates that individuals will also ask, 'What is in it for me?' Therefore, in order to unite a team behind a common goal and create goal harmony, the leader must balance an understanding of personal drivers with an overarching team focus and the knowledge that each individual holds significant value to the group. Every player is equally deserving of a leader's time and focus, yet it is easy to let this slip. Other more pressing priorities take precedence and it is simpler to focus on star players and social architects. Each individual commits substantial personal energy to a group's endeavour and the team becomes greater than the sum of its parts. Our propensity towards forming groups relates to our social identity, or the extent to which we feel part of a group, thus impacting our thoughts and actions within that environment. We define ourselves by both this group membership and our individual sense of self. A high-performing

leader must remain continually aware of these two crucial components of human identity.

CASE STUDY: PROMOTION AND RELEGATION
IN THE PREMIER LEAGUE

Over the last five years, Sean Dyche has led Burnley through an
intense period of growth on and off the field. During that time, the
club and the town have experienced the entire spectrum of experiences and emotions that professional football can bring. In those
five years, they have been promoted, relegated and qualified for
Europe. As part of that journey, there have been multiple shifts in
mindset and approach, and undeniably a significant cultural shift.
Dyche describes the identity and group mindset under which they
achieved their first promotion.

SEASON 2013–14

> The first identity was as a 'surprise package', even to us by the
> way! Not because I didn't believe but it is a tough challenge
> getting out of the Championship. We had a small squad, we
> had sold the main goal-scorer in Charlie Austin. But it started
> to evolve quickly in pre-season. You could smell it in pre-
> season and, as a staff, we thought, 'We are on to something
> here,' but you never know. Then you get to sort of November
> and you go, 'We are still on to something,' then we are flying
> and you're into January thinking, 'We could do it you know,'
> and then you get to March and scaremongers start saying,
> 'Ooo they can't do it, surely they can't do it.' Then we did it –
> that was an amazing year . . . I thoroughly enjoyed it, I learnt
> a lot about myself and a lot about what it entails.

Starting as a 'surprise package', Burnley were able to take something of an underdog mentality into this season. While the pressure builds on other teams, the underdogs, with less expectation on their shoulders, can develop a 'nothing to lose' mentality that creates less anxiety and pressure.

SEASON 2014–15

As an organisation, Burnley went into their maiden Premier League season facing the brutal facts of their situation – 'positive realities' to Dyche. He says it was very much, 'Let's be open-minded and see where we can go, but we know it is going to be tough.' This is an interesting overarching mindset that, in all probability, will have been in sharp contrast with the short-term desire of the players. As above, the underdog mentality applied, allowing the team to play with freedom and experience some unforgettable moments, whilst learning some valuable lessons for the future. This will have presented an interesting leadership dilemma for Dyche, as he balanced an overall awareness of the situation with a desire to maximise the team's development. An alternative view may be that Dyche's realistic viewpoint provided the players with a motivation to prove their leader wrong.

The Clarets were relegated back to the Championship that season but, critically, the club managed their finances and targets, allowing them to start work on the new training ground.

SEASON 2015–16

With proof of success comes confidence and the following season, back in the Championship, was not a surprise. This time, Burnley and Dyche were operating from a position of strength and the mindset had shifted; it was 'by design, it was more businesslike. Now we know what to do. It is just whether we can get the players in and focus them.' That was the year Burnley, looking to add to their team dynamic, recruited big characters like Barton and Andre Gray. The approach of the coaching staff was, 'What have we learnt, what are we going to need to do, what can we put in place to do it? The way we did it was a lot more businesslike and then of course we won the title and it worked.'

SEASON 2016 ONWARDS

Now back in the Premier League, Dyche knew he needed a deeper squad with greater quality, 'and also to have that competitive spirit in training, who is getting the shirt, the in-house competitive spirit' in order to establish the club at the highest level. Ahead of the 2017–18 season, the club had to adapt as they lost key players such as Michael Keane (Everton), Gray (Watford) and Barton (serving a ban for gambling offences). As Dyche puts it, they 'had to remodel again'.

Our interview takes place in early 2018, with Burnley riding high in the league and chasing a European spot, and Dyche outlines the team's targets:

> Our big goal this year was firstly to improve on last season performance-wise, which I think we have done. Secondly, that has to go on the league table, so therefore you need more points, which we have done, that is a massive thing for me, a massive achievement because to keep moving forward year on year on year in football is really difficult. We have also seen players mature and grow and new players come in and players are moving forward and we get the reward of more points on the table, and a nice league table to look at. I think it is a tremendous sign of this continuing shift forward.

In May 2018, Burnley finished seventh in the Premier League, behind only Manchester City, Manchester United, Tottenham Hotspur, Liverpool, Chelsea and Arsenal, and were rewarded with a spot in the Europa League. Throughout this period of collective success and momentum, Dyche has ensured the overall culture and his own intensity, set during his early days at the club, has prevailed:

> I think the original culture and what we stand for, the key core values are still there. I think we just layer it up and it gets more detailed because the players bring detail as well, it's not just us. The core values we set down five years ago are still there, we still make sure they are adhered to, we haven't gone away from them, we certainly haven't lost them. I still keep my edge, I still work hard, I still want it, I still question myself all the time, am I doing this right? Am I doing enough of that? Am I doing enough of this? So I have still got that self-questioning happening. We certainly don't sit back and go, 'Oh well, it's all all right,' which we could do because the club is in a massively improved situation compared to when we got here, but we choose not to and we want the players to choose not to.

FLEXIBILITY AND CONSISTENCY

As Dyche offers a whistle-stop tour of Burnley's journey over the last five seasons, he provides glimpses into his impactful and flexible leadership style. During the first pre-season, he talks about the role of a leader's instinct, describing the 'smell' of opportunity that he sensed within the group. Once in the Premier League, the leader of the league's 'surprise package' opted to 'jump on the grenade' and patiently balance immediate ambition with the need to secure the long-term foundations of the organisation. Here, Dyche is looking once again to maintain an approach of 'authentic optimism', uniting a relentless sense of belief with a willingness to confront the brutal facts. The staff reflected on their subsequent relegation, taking the stark lessons of this first foray into the Premier League and putting steps in place to bounce straight back.

Dyche's words, focusing on the ongoing aim of achieving both sporting performances (process) and results (outcome), and building a genuine sense of personal and collective growth, remind me of Ashley Giles' big wheel, little wheel (short-term/long-term) bicycle. While the personnel have changed and the objectives have shifted, it is clear that Dyche has maintained a consistency in both his own approach to leadership and the culture that fuels the performance.

CASE STUDY: LEADERSHIP IN THE WORLD CUP 2018

When Roberto Martínez took on the role of Belgium's head coach in August 2016, questions were asked about whether he would be able to generate the levels of performance that are now expected of the nation's 'Golden Generation'. After all, the same group of players had been knocked out of the 2016 European Championships at the quarter-final stage by an invigorated Wales.

While my first interview with Roberto took place during his time with Premier League club Everton, I was able to pick up our conversation following Belgium's third-place finish in Russia.

Upon taking the international role, Martínez was technically focused on 'developing a flexible way of adopting different systems and different ways of playing'. He believed that, due to the level of ability in the squad, opposition teams now try to adapt to Belgium's way of playing, meaning they sometimes have to be patient and find a way to break a team down. He described the importance of developing a sense of confidence in 'having the ball and being comfortable having to break teams down'. It was, he tells me, critical that the team was able to 'play without anxiety and to be tactically flexible'.

While a number of the players represent top European clubs, meaning that they will regularly compete against one another for the top domestic and European honours, Martínez also highlighted how the core of the group have evolved through the age-groups together:

A lot of players leave Belgium when they are very young and they leave as good potential players and they come back as big stars. They develop abroad. At the moment we have fifty-two players playing away from Belgium. So when they come back, they are very happy to share time with each other. They are good friends. They developed together from the Olympics. They have good relationships. It is not a case of players who have just met as rivals on the pitch. They are players who met as good friends, who shared the ambition and the dream of becoming a professional footballer, and now they can share what it means to represent Belgium at international level.

In 2008, a young Belgian side containing Vincent Kompany (22), Thomas Vermaelen (22), Jan Vertonghen (21), Marouane Fellaini (20) and Moussa Dembélé (21) finished fourth at the Beijing Olympics. Midfielder Axel Witsel was also part of this group at the Under-21 age group. Competing at the Olympics and living in the village amongst athletes from all over the globe is a vibrant and unique experience. Shared moments of struggle and glory, lived as striving young athletes, provide the emotional bond that lies at the core of this Belgian team. It is no coincidence that, as these players have matured as players and people, they have become the leaders and cultural architects of the group.

As the team gathered to begin their preparation ahead of the World Cup, there was to be no glamorous training camp to the warmer climates of Dubai or the USA. In a bid to maintain normality, a consistent theme throughout the tournament, the team remained at their purpose-built headquarters in Tubize, Belgium:

> We never felt we needed to go abroad, we did not need to take the players out of their normal environment, and I think that worked very well. As much as we could, we had normal days, being able to work, being able to spend time with families. This probably allowed the group to work and get prepared for the World Cup without having the restraint of missing the family environment too much. At club level, players train in the morning, go home, see the family and get prepared for big games. I think at international level you have to be very careful that you don't interrupt that routine and way of working too much.

Belgium progressed comfortably through the group stages, beating England along the way. In the round of sixteen, however, things did not go quite as smoothly. With twenty minutes to go, Japan were leading the 'Red Devils' by two goals to nil. Another early and unexpected tournament exit was looming in the shadows. Martínez, who before the tournament had considered a range of scenarios the team might encounter, made some key tactical changes that helped to change the momentum of the game, as Belgium scored three goals to win in injury time.

Some of you may have noticed at the recent rugby World Cup that some head coaches, including England's Eddie Jones, stopped talking about 'substitutes' and looked instead to refer to these players as 'finishers' who can have a significant impact on a game: a subtle change of language that provides an insight into a team's mindset and culture. Note here how Martínez emphasises the role of his 'finishers' in the same way:

> We knew we could count on the players that we had on the bench. The mentality was very clear. We did not beat Japan just because of the changes we made. We beat Japan because those players were ready to affect the game and become game-changers. When you have the players that we have in our national team, we can variate things, change things, approach it in a different manner. We wanted to attack from an internal position, to have more of a second line of players getting in to the box. We used that well. But I would say that anything you can do tactically depends on the mindset that the players have. Our mindset towards beating that adversity that we were going to face started very early in our preparations back in Belgium.

In the quarter-finals, Belgium faced five-time champions Brazil. Martínez highlighted how easy it can be for players to become fixated on the history and legacy of a team like the South Americans:

> When you play against Brazil, you need to believe that you can beat Brazil. You go to the ground, everything is yellow. Of course, they are the team that has won the World Cup five times. There is a mental barrier. I think our team grew during the competition, after scoring the third goal against Japan. I think mentally we were very confident, very strong, and because of that we could be very aggressive. Tactically, we took a big risk. I think that is needed to try to tactically prepare against a team like Brazil. We tried to allow the players to be able to focus on their tactical roles, rather than the fact they are

facing Brazil. We had a team that was fully focused on what they had to do on the pitch, and clearly that was the way we performed – with a lot of bravery and incredible togetherness throughout those ninety minutes.

Emotion can work both for and against a team. In this situation, Martínez looked to avoid the emotional overload that can come with facing the history, mystique and aura of Brazil (a little bit like the All Blacks in rugby union) by focusing on tactics, mentality and process.

This story is not without despair. As most of you will know, there was to be no fairy-tale ending. Belgium ultimately succumbed to eventual winners France in a closely fought semi-final. The players, one game away from a World Cup final, were understandably distraught. How then do you pick them up for a third-place play-off against England? Does it *really* matter? The chance of a best ever finish at a World Cup remained a sufficient driver.

When you lose a semi-final, probably, in your head, you feel that that is the end of the World Cup. But it is a moment that you can regret further down the line in your career because it is still an opportunity to win the bronze medal. The bronze medal is a huge achievement. For us it was the opportunity of playing seven games and winning six. With the amount of goals that we scored and the way that we arrived into that position, finishing third was essential.

Just like they did before the competition, the approach was to try to keep the feeling in the camp one of normality, while at the same time acknowledging the draining and emotional experience of such a cruel defeat, allowing them some time to heal and process the events of the semi-final:

We tried to give them some normality. We gave them a bit of time to manage the human being, rather than the footballer. We had the opportunity to bring the families in and that time that they shared together allowed them to become a bit more relaxed about the disappointment and made sure that slowly they were getting ready for the opportunity of having the bronze medal, which would be a historic achievement for Belgian football. Looking after the human being gave us the opportunity to prepare for the game just forty-eight hours before the third-place play-off and the players felt mentally quite refreshed.

Belgium ran out two-nil winners against England, claiming the bronze medal with goals from Thomas Meunier and talisman Eden Hazard.

To gain an understanding of how a leader reflects, a subject covered earlier in the book, I asked Roberto what he had learnt about his own approach to leadership during the World Cup. He identified how the need to take a consistent and focused approach becomes even more important during a major tournament. This answer surprised me somewhat, given the aspirational focus of our earlier conversation, and perhaps reflects his own development during the course of this book:

I think the World Cup is the competition that as a young kid you dream about – that is why you are involved in football. What you learn is that the bigger the occasion, the bigger the competition, is when the basics become so essential. Rather than thinking about participating in a World Cup and trying to get far in a World Cup, you need to make sure that you can work on the things that you can affect and the things that can really make the difference. I think getting back to those basics in the culture that we have now, rather than trying to affect little aspects that give you more glamour than real results, has been important.

A major tournament like the World Cup conjures emotion and images of childhood dreams, not just for players, but for leaders too. In the passage above, Roberto acknowledges the importance of 'the basics' for the players, but he could also be advising himself. Given their experiences, our leaders are acutely aware that a World Cup, like the Olympics, only comes around every four years. The fervent sense of desire and opportunity can lure a leader to change their approach or look for the 'glamorous' touches to which Martínez refers. A leader's management of their personal emotions and the ability to calmly trust their approach and preparation is a vital precursor to their impact on the team.

The theme of focused improvement continued when I questioned whether he has overseen a shift in mindset amongst the players. He does not seek to comment on what went before but describes the staff's mindset as being focused on 'trying to help the players improve on a daily basis, and trying to use being together – both players and staff – as a unique opportunity to make history.'

He describes how, at club level, 'you have your own goals and it is great to try to achieve them'. But, he tells me, this does not compare with the responsibility that comes 'when you represent a whole nation. The entire country kicks the ball with you, and you can feel the feelings of happiness and sadness it brings. Our mindset has been very much about making that little bit of improvement in every area that we could and almost enjoying facing adversity as a team, a team that wanted to make history.'

No journey worth going on is without its obstacles and the need to thrive and almost 'enjoy adversity' is a worthy characteristic of any high-performance team. This indicates a level of toughness and grit, an element we do not always associate with Martínez. I often ask people and teams to describe what they are like at their best and it is surprising that they initially think of moments when they are winning comfortably and everything feels easy and enjoyable. In fact upon reflection, our most effective performances regularly occur when we are united by a sense of struggle, and the need to demonstrate real courage in the face of intense challenge. Embracing the moment, striving to win, but accepting the fact that failure is part of sport is fundamental to an athlete's or a team's mindset.

It is popular to assume that a somewhat gung-ho mindset of 'only gold matters' and 'second place is first loser' drives a culture of high performance. 'Show me a good loser and I'll show you a loser', and all that. Of course, the outcome goal is to win and to stand on the top of the podium, but I have spent time with athletes who, at the end of their career, wish they had appreciated the good times that little bit more. Their perfectionist and self-critical nature often dictates that it was always 'on to the next game', constantly asking, 'How do we get better?' rather than embracing the moment. Yet in international sport, the next game is often not one week away. In the case of a World Cup, the next game is four *years* away.

When an athlete looks back on a career, they might look at the medals but they will also remember the moments and emotions they shared with others. Earlier, I referenced *The Edge*, a film about the England cricket team. There is a moment, as the film draws to a close, where former batsman Jonathan Trott is asked what he misses from the game. His answer does not focus on trophies, but revolves around the emotions you share when batting with a teammate: 'I won't miss cricket – the playing, the travelling, the practising. But what I am going to miss the most is batting with Straussy, Cook, Pietersen and Bell.' In tears, he adds, 'And that is basically it.'

Once the disappointment faded, Martínez was keen to acknow-ledge the sense of achievement and joy that came as a result of claiming the bronze medal. To see this, one only has to look at the team photo after the third-place play-off. A best-ever finish. A marker laid down, and the chance to learn, reflect, and go again.

SUPPORT STAFF

Behind the success of any sports team, or individual for that matter, there is a group of passionate, knowledgeable and skilful people working around the clock to ensure the athletes have everything they need in order to perform. Experts in their own specific areas, a support staff will be made up of assistant coaches, scouts, analysts, sports scientists, nutritionists, physiotherapists, masseurs, doctors, conditioners and psychologists. In high-profile sports such as those we are discussing here, the size of this 'team behind the team' is significant. The Atlanta Falcons have twenty members of technical coaching staff, as well as seven physical coaches, four video analysts, four equipment managers and seventeen scouts. Head Coach Dan Quinn believes he 'spends as much time managing the staff' as he does the players. As such, a key role of a leader is identifying, selecting and developing an effective back-room staff, a collection of individuals to complement, challenge and support the leader.

RECRUITMENT

The recruitment process and the scale of involvement from the leader ultimately varies between sporting environments and the demands of a specific role. At the South Sydney Rabbitohs, Michael Maguire prioritised knowledge over sporting experience, pointing to the fact that he does not have any staff 'who have played the game at the highest level or who are big sporting personalities'. He insists on getting 'the best person for the job' and describes his team as 'all very down to earth, with a lot of expertise in their specific areas'. Whether this dynamic is by accident or design is unclear. At Wigan Warriors, before his time with the Rabbitohs, Maguire worked closely with two individuals who played rugby league at the elite level and who enjoy legendary status at the club: General Manager (now Executive Director) Kris Radlinski and Assistant Coach Shaun Wane. Maguire is an assertive character, motivated by the opportunity to lead and dominate others. Having experienced one challenging extreme of personnel in England, perhaps he looked to take a more obvious hierarchical approach in Australia. It is a measure of his leadership that both support teams enjoyed tremendous success.

At the RFU, Stuart Lancaster was involved in all staff recruitment decisions. 'The process was open, honest and transparent. We advertised to the game and we took the best person. It wasn't a head-hunter situation, it was first past the post. And whoever earned it, earned it. But I made sure I was involved from the start to the end of the process.' While Lancaster may not have led the process for the recruitment of each position, he maintained an overall awareness, overseeing the people who were joining the organisation. A leader cannot always control all aspects of recruitment. Appropriate delegation and trust allows others to take on that responsibility, but making the effort to understand the evolving picture of talent within a team is key to a leader's role.

Ashley Giles describes his recruitment of a strength and conditioning coach: 'I sat in the interviews. I didn't make the call but I gave my opinion. The guy we picked was clearly just very authentic and honest, and that is a good start. So, he might not have a CV as long as anyone else's but, to a degree, from the other two, there was a bit of bullshit. I thought, "If I am feeling that now, what will I be feeling in six months?"' In this example, Giles' instincts take precedent over the more impressive résumés.

LOYALTY AND KNOW-HOW

At the 2018 World Cup in Russia, as Belgium fell to France in the semi-final, two of Roberto Martínez's assistants took to the field to console and support the crestfallen players. One, the former Arsenal, Juventus, AS Monaco and Barcelona forward Thierry Henry, has won the World Cup and European Championships as a player. The other was Graeme Jones, whose former clubs include Doncaster Rovers, Wigan Athletic, Bury and Boston United. Jones, along with performance specialist Richard Evans and goalkeeping coach Iñaki Bergara, have worked as a unit with Martínez at Swansea City, Wigan Athletic, Everton and Belgium. The juxtaposition between Henry and Jones illustrates a specific combination of qualities – loyalty and know-how – that Martínez looked to blend in his preparation for one of the biggest tournaments in global sport.

It should perhaps then come as no surprise that Martínez's top priority from his staff is loyalty. 'I think the staff need to be loyal. In football, [it is] always so volatile because you have the results to cope with. It is not a normal business that you can be very consistent in your evaluation of your work because the results make everything great or everything wrong. You need to feel that loyalty in your staff. So, if you get a staff member, you know you can trust him, you can go along and believe that over the course of ten months, he is going to be successful, so that is the most important aspect.' Elite sport can be fickle and unforgiving, so a loyal staff helps to create a sense of calm, that remains steadfast, irrespective of results. The relationships and trust encourage a consistency of method, providing the stability and coherence that Martínez clearly values.

As Martínez enjoys working with a stable group of key lieutenants, I was intrigued to know the rationale behind his decision to
recruit Thierry Henry. I asked him what Henry brought to the group.
His answer was concise and simple – 'know-how'. But what did he
actually mean by this?

> As a technical staff we worked for ten seasons in the British
> game, seven of those consecutively in the Premier League. It is
> a very clear and consistent environment. We were missing the
> know-how of international football. We were missing the know-
> how of dealing with the expectation of a whole country, knowing
> what to do – sharing the emotions on the pitch of a group of
> players representing a nation in a World Cup is the biggest role
> a footballer is going to have. I think Thierry brought that – he
> won the World Cup, he won the European Championship, he
> was part of a very talented generation that started with great
> potential and ended up becoming very successful. When you
> have someone who can relate to the players, for what they are
> going through, and to share experiences with the staff as well.
> In the same way, Thierry was a very good team player that took
> to the group and the way of working really well. He brought the
> know-how of what to expect in a World Cup.

While the opportunity to recruit a superstar former player may seem
like a no-brainer, such a decision can actually generate a level of challenge and threat to a leader's own position and authority. A player
like Henry, having won a plethora of international and club honours
in his career, could quite easily become a figurehead to inadvertently
challenge the status quo. A leader, therefore, must be confident
enough in their own approach to allow such a personality into a
long-established team unit. At a critical moment, Martínez showed

the strength and vulnerability to admit his team was lacking a key ingredient ('know-how'), and then go and recruit someone who possessed this in spades. When Henry left the Belgian Red Devils following the 2018 World Cup to pursue his own leadership ambitions, he was replaced by Shaun Maloney who played in Martínez's team at Wigan Athletic. Having made a key decision to bring in Henry in 2016, Martínez, now established at international level, has reverted to his trusted template of loyalty and consistency.

THE VALUE OF DISSENT

One key characteristic of an effective support staff is a willingness to challenge the status quo, as Michael Maguire attests: 'I want staff that aren't "yes-men". I want them to challenge me and the things we do.' He is happy to have open conversations and for people to tell him he is wrong. 'The last thing you need is a group of people that will just go along with what's going on. I know for a fact that, with so much going on, I can't be spot-on every single time. For my staff to challenge what we do, it makes the environment better and it improves us.' Gary Kirsten agrees and believes that staff 'need to feel comfortable to challenge the leader on certain things' and should feel able to 'really express themselves and bring in ideas that may be slightly different'.

The humility to actively invite dissent from team members is an undoubted characteristic of effective leadership. Within their own teams, global management consultancy McKinsey & Co. look to create an 'unrivalled environment for exceptional people', and a central value of their approach is to constantly 'uphold the obligation to dissent'.*

* McKinsey & Company. *Our Mission and Values*. mckinsey.com, retrieved 2 January 2020.

This culture, established by former managing director and figurehead Marvin Bower, empowers the most junior person to feel able to challenge their most senior colleague.

The same term, 'obligation to dissent', can be applied to the turbulent world of elite sport. It sounds great in theory but, for all the leadership jargon and honourable intentions, it remains arduous and painful to put into practice. Leaders must open themselves up for evaluation at a somewhat personal level, and the staff, operating in a combustible environment, must display the courage to fulfil their own side of the bargain. In reality, this combination is rare and takes time to achieve, yet without this attribute of dissent one could argue that there is no real leadership present at all. Some leaders might start this process with a formal meeting, outlining expectations and processes, while others will take a more informal, conversational approach. Ultimately, only by constantly encouraging those around us to speak their minds, offering this element of positive dissent and challenge, and then responding in an appropriate manner, can we look to establish the combination of creative thinking, cognitive diversity and process that leads to high performance.

According to Dan Quinn, one of the worst things for a leader to have is 'someone who just always agrees with them'. Quinn looks for 'different styles of teaching and people who challenge'. He wants his people to 'have the balls' to give an opinion, as opposed to those 'who say, "Yes, I agree it will be awesome," but behind your back they're saying, "This is a mistake."' Such individuals are often looking to protect themselves and can prove poisonous to a culture. At the Falcons, ultimately it is Quinn who makes the final call – 'At the end of the day, I will make the decision but if you have an opinion on it, you are a valued member of our team and we'd like to know about it.' As is his way with the players, each member of Quinn's support staff knows their value.

Sean Dyche, like Martínez, has trusted assistants Ian Woan and Tony Loughlan with whom he has worked for a long time. These relationships, built on trust and friendship, are crucial in the cut-throat theatre of the Premier League. However, the trio also balance and challenge one another as a result of their differing personalities and approaches:

I don't want the staff to all be the same, that is of no use to anyone. My staff were deliberately picked to be different. As it happens, we have worked together for a while. But when I put them together, you know Woany was a good friend of mine as well, a family friend, but I didn't get him involved because of that. At first people thought I did, but then you realise he is completely different to me as a person and Tony is completely different to both of us. We have got this nice combined unit. The only time it runs out is in stressful situations, you want to deal with it that way, someone wants to deal with it another way, situations like that are the only time when that gap occurs. You get some good thoughts from people who don't think like you. If everyone thinks like you, how can you get the right process? The ideal process is to get the different views and, eventually, as manager, you have to pick the ones that count.

Dyche's close assistants offer different perspectives and his relationship with them, together with his focus on players' behavioural styles, is a big part of his ability to listen and respond to his people. He talks about how this dynamic can be challenged during stressful situations. I wonder how often he changes a decision and instead backs the view of an assistant. It is the leader's role to make the final decision, but to have the humility to justly challenge one's own biases and beliefs is an indicator of genuine and authentic leadership.

Like Quinn, Dyche also expects honest opinions from his staff: 'Honesty is a big one. Because if we have meetings, there is no point in not giving me the truth, you've got to give me the truth and I can take the truth, the brutal truth if it's needed. What are you thinking? What are you feeling? What do you think we ought to do? Tell me the truth, that is a massive, massive thing. They've got to work hard – we take that as a given – be respectful but be honest. They are two things, respect and honesty, that are massively high on my staff thinking.'

While having staff who think differently and are empowered to challenge is a key component of a leader's support staff, it is also important to have people who a leader can truly rely on. Gary Kirsten strives to strike a balance between the two. 'It is good to have some-one you know you can trust, that has got your back and that you can bounce ideas off. I tend to want to have a split support staff, where I have one or two guys that are very close to me and back me in every-thing I do, but also to have some others on the staff specifically to come up with new thinking and new ideas.'

Stuart Lancaster succinctly describes his approach as looking for 'good team players, people who are honest, trustworthy, hard-working, good at what they do, they are effective and efficient and experts in their field'. In all these examples, our leaders look to the support staff as a trusted group of eyes, ears and truthful feedback.

TEAM DYNAMICS

As with any team, the identity of a back-room staff can shift as people come and go. Each individual recruitment decision contributes to the evolving dynamic. Michael Maguire strives to put a small team together that possesses a 'mixture of skills and a blend of personalities'. Having utilised behavioural profiling, he looks for a 'blend of introverts and extroverts, different characters, otherwise you become too rigid to really engage the players, especially when you're in camp for a long time'. His back-room team is not as large as you might find in other sports and he prefers that approach. 'I think sometimes too many voices can mix messages. I like to work with a smaller team and be very thorough and identify what we actually require and be very good at that.' Maguire is secure in his method. He knows how he likes to work and the size of the team he needs in order to do that. For a leader who wants to be across the detail, a small team of support staff is easier to control and work with.

Because of this approach, Maguire has worked with staff 'that have had to slightly change how they go about things'. However, this is not a one-way commitment and Maguire has proactively educated himself and others 'in the knowledge of personality traits'. He takes the time to work with his staff and build relationships, acknowledging that, at times, they will all have to adapt. As a result, Maguire says, 'we are going to have a blend of things that need to mix but under pressure we always tend to go back to our core personality'.

Due to their ability to directly influence individual players, a leader's awareness of the characters and personalities within a support staff is just as important as their understanding of the athlete-group dynamic. Stuart Lancaster spends time talking to his staff, discussing their role within the culture and acknowledging that they are often better placed to provide insight into the 'psychology of individual players'. These relationships (between an athlete and staff member) are key elements of a team environment and a leader's awareness of their existence can enable effective and subtle flashes of communication. He continues, 'a masseur or a kit manager, the physiotherapists, or the strength and conditioners are usually very good sources of information because people often manipulate their image' to the leader. The 'image' to which Lancaster refers is essentially how a player looks to present themselves to the head coach and how they want to be seen in the eyes of the leader. At times this can be inauthentic as the player, acutely aware that the head coach is the one who makes key selection decisions, does not want to communicate their true feelings and strives to display the qualities that he or she thinks the leader wants to see. It may also be that a staff member has a stronger relationship with an athlete than the leader of the team, and that relationship is still just as crucial to the team dynamic. As long as the message gets through, the source is largely irrelevant.

On occasion, it can be more effective for a leader to allow a staff member to convey a message to a player. Sean Dyche, drawing again on his appreciation of behavioural profiling, will often ask his staff to communicate a message to a player instead of him 'because it will be better coming from them and the information will be better'. As well as ensuring the information is received, this can also avoid unnecessary conflict, helping to protect the leader-player relationship. This works both ways too; there are also some players with whom the Burnley manager prefers to deal directly because they are more receptive to his style.

In each example, irrespective of the size of the support team, the leader looks to remain abreast of the team dynamic without being too intrusive or divisive. Maguire's team, small in number, affords him a sense of order and control, and goes some way to ensuring a consistency of both method and message. As England head coach, Lancaster took charge of a more sizeable support unit which naturally means there is less control and more fluidity. He acknowledges the professional distance that can exist between player and leader, created by perceptions of hierarchy, and leans on his staff to provide a clearer picture of a player's personality and mindset. As for Dyche, this has become a routine, everyday aspect of his leadership. 'I try to think really simply. My first port of call is simplicity, logic – that is really a big thing for me in all of this.' He finds information to apply and is perfectly content to leave his ego at the door, trusting his staff to deliver messages appropriately.

DELEGATION

Overseeing a thriving sporting organisation across both a long- and short-term perspective invariably means that leaders will find it challenging to be acutely aware of all the detailed issues facing the team on a daily basis. As a consequence, effective delegation is a vital leadership strategy. However, an obstacle for many leaders across industries and sectors is their own desire and confidence in delegating and empowering the people around them. Some people are wary of weakening their own position by delegating tasks. In addition to this, a leader may feel internally conflicted as some of the attributes that have enabled them to be successful and reach this stage in their career may well be the same characteristics that cause them to find delegation challenging. Precision, high standards, control and perfectionism will at times be in conflict with the need to step back, let go of the detail and see a bigger picture. Part of this is the art and challenge of delegation, something which the leaders identity with, even if it does not always come naturally.

THE STAFF ARE PROFESSIONALS TOO

Michael Maguire is keen to let his assistants have 'the opportunity to actually coach'. He draws on his own experience as an assistant and recalls craving 'the opportunity to do a lot of hands-on stuff, I got a lot of enjoyment out of that'. It is time spent on the field with the players that allows Maguire to play to his own coaching strengths but, at the same time, he wants to provide his staff with opportunities for development and growth, as they find themselves in the same position that he was during the earlier part of his coaching journey. As is the case with players, support staff all aspire to their own career objectives. Like Maguire, Sean Dyche and Dan Quinn both held assistant coaching positions, absorbing knowledge from more experienced coaches, before being considered for the top jobs. This personal maturation and growth is evident across both sporting and business environments as leaders knowingly provide opportunities for others to develop, to the point where they are considered for leadership roles in their own right. Businesses often reference a hypothetical conversation between two parties. The first asks, 'What if I train them and they leave?', and the second replies, 'What if you don't and they stay?'

We have already discussed Thierry Henry's impactful role alongside Roberto Martínez. Upon leaving Belgium's international set-up, Henry returned to Ligue 1 in France, taking the job as head coach of the first club he played for as a professional, AS Monaco FC. José Mourinho benefitted from the guidance of the great Sir Bobby Robson and his successor at Barcelona, Louis van Gaal, before going on to be one of the world's most successful managers. More recently in the Premier League Mikel Arteta, Pep Guardiola's highly coveted assistant at Manchester City, left the Catalan's tutelage to become head coach of his former club, Arsenal. With the oval ball, Andy Farrell, the former Wigan Warriors and Great Britain rugby league player, has built a formidable coaching reputation in rugby union. Farrell, whose son Owen is England's captain and fly-half, was part of Stuart Lancaster's support staff with England, before the arrival of Eddie Jones prompted him to take on the role of defence coach with Ireland, where he worked under New Zealander Joe Schmidt. When Schmidt announced he would be stepping down following the World Cup in 2019, Ireland turned to Farrell as their new head coach.

An indisputable fact of leadership is that a *genuine* desire for developing others brings with it the inevitable fact that people will move on to pursue their own ambitions. More and more, we are seeing new generations of workers pursuing portfolio careers and craving a range of professional experiences. Of course, a leader would not want to lose a crucial component of their coaching unit. However, if development and growth truly are cornerstones of one's philosophy, an authentic leader will let them go, crucially with their blessing and ongoing support. Aside from remaining congruent with a people-focused approach to leadership, this maintains trust and the relationship between the two parties. You never know when you will work together again.

Ashley Giles echoes this sentiment. He wants to give his staff freedom and autonomy to do their jobs. However, he also indicates that he won't be far away should they not meet his own high standards, thus giving a glimpse of the personal conflict a leader can experience and an inability to resist the urge to dive in. Giles says, 'If the staff are doing their jobs we haven't got a problem. If suddenly I'm going around them to do their job then we've got a bit more of a problem.' Delegation is a golden leadership skill but, as Giles' words attest, it is not always congruent with a leader's natural style.

Stuart Lancaster, discussing his time with England, felt confident delegating to his three established assistants – Andy Farrell, Graham Rowntree and Mike Catt – while he 'managed the bigger programme', saying, 'I've never been one to be overly directive. They all have a big role in coaching the team. They have all got their own leadership qualities as well so it doesn't mean I should be front and centre all the time. So, I can step back and sometimes a change of voice is effective.' Getting his coaching staff 'on the same page and all believing in the same way of playing the game is important' because, he notes, 'if you get confusion between the coaches, you can guarantee you are going to confuse the players'.

Interestingly, when I talked to Lancaster during a follow-up interview, while he was enjoying success at Leinster, he talked about missing his time 'on the grass, developing players', something he has sought to address during his time in Ireland. Throughout his career, Lancaster has repeatedly proven himself to be an excellent delegator, a sense of modesty driving him to provide opportunities for those around him. During his time with England, he would regularly be seen leaning against the posts, observing sessions from afar. Yet this ability to delegate sometimes goes against his deeper love of coaching, which is built upon his passion for teaching, and the opportunity to spend his time improving players of all ages and standards. He seems to be able to flex his leadership style, consciously travelling along the continuum between on-field coaching and overall leadership.

Sean Dyche's tendency to let his assistants take training for part of the week has developed during their time together. Dyche is always there, observing, but allows his colleagues 'a bit of time to work with the players'. For Dyche, a new voice can have a positive impact and provide some variety whilst at the same time allowing him to have the one-to-one conversations that are so crucial, but so often overlooked. 'The players get enough of you, they don't want to hear you all the time. I am always around. Sometimes it is just horse whispering with the players, having a chat, two minutes here and there.'

Dyche's words – 'horse whispering' – might raise an eyebrow or a chuckle, but the similarities are clear. Horse whispering is about observing body language, creating trust, building confidence and developing a relationship between two parties. For Dyche, allowing someone else to take responsibility for a specific training session or meeting not only communicates a sense of trust in his people, but also allows him to add some personal touches to his leadership.

Peter Crouch, the former England international, played under Dyche during his final season as a professional in 2019. While the striker did not feature as often as he would have liked at Burnley, he talks highly of the support and backing Dyche offered during his transition from full-time athlete to the world of television and the media. When we step back, we see things we might otherwise miss, we are able to pay people some much-needed individual attention, and to have conversations at a deeper, more meaningful level.

INHERITING STAFF

Due to the aggressive and fast-moving nature of elite sport, head-hunting and staff turnover are inevitable. While leaders will often insist on the appointment of some loyal lieutenants, they cannot replace an entire staff. Upon taking up a new leadership role, the inevitable inheritance of support staff brings its own set of challenges for a leader. Giving the 'benefit of the doubt' was a common part of the process, as Lancaster describes his experience of taking over as England head coach: 'They were all pretty battered and bruised by that point but I knew they were good people and they just needed a bit of direction and support.'

Gary Kirsten believes that a staff must reflect the leader's own personal values. He recounted two contrasting experiences that he learnt from. 'I have inherited guys that have been fantastic and we've just got on with it and they have done a fantastic job, you know their values system lines up with yours. I have also found that one or two guys who I have worked with really don't line up with my values system. As the leader of the organisation, your support staff need to have similar values in terms of work ethic, managing players and the emotion of performance.'

Kirsten's words hint at the steeliness of his approach and remind me of the work of Jim Collins, author of *Good to Great*, who Stuart Lancaster also spoke to during his time with England. In the book, Collins examines the characteristics of elite organisations that sustainably out-perform their competition. Collins' well-known metaphor refers to an organisation as the 'bus' and the leader as the 'driver'. The driver's role is to ask 'first who, then what' and Collin's linear process for this is straightforward, but not necessarily easy to implement:

1. Get the right people on the bus.
2. Get the right people in the right seats.
3. Get the wrong people off the bus (with dignity).
4. Always put the 'who' before the 'what'.

Roberto Martínez faced the unique challenge of fusing an existing collection of staff at the Royal Belgian Football Association with his own long-standing and loyal back-room team – a situation with the potential for internal conflict. Martínez believes that the ability of the players and the opportunity to support such a talented group was the most powerful factor in achieving an effective working relationship and ensuring goal harmony within the group:

> Firstly we have people who are very good in their roles. We have role clarity, and we allow people to work. The aim, for us, is always to get better, to help this fantastic generation. I think having that at the forefront of your work allows the team dynamics to be very simple. The only thing that matters is to try to affect the players and help this super-talented generation to perform well.

During his time with Wigan Warriors, Michael Maguire retained most of his staff but was also allowed the freedom to make some crucial appointments: 'I always had someone there that I could bring in and start fresh in a certain way, so I've never really inherited a full staff and had to say, "Righto, this is what we've got."' In England, Maguire worked closely with Shaun Wane, 'an assistant coach that worked out extremely well. He has gone on and had some success there. I also brought a strength and conditioner who had very similar traits to myself. Once we came together, everyone else understood what was required.'

He goes on to describe the contrasting situation he encountered upon arriving at South Sydney. 'I basically moved all the staff except one. I didn't want the staff that were there because all they knew were the bad days, the losses. I didn't want that. I wanted a fresh start. So, you know what, we are going to turn this around by changing the way we think and do things.' Making well-informed decisions on existing members of staff is a vital part of the cultural assessment process that a leader goes through when arriving at a new organisation. Maguire provides two examples, from Wigan and Sydney, of cultural signposts that a leader might identify in their support team.

Maguire's relationship with Shaun Wane, a legendary former player at Wigan, throws up a unique leadership scenario. Almost immediately, it became abundantly clear that Wane wanted Maguire's job, another fitting example of an assistant's individual career goals. Despite the potential for conflict between two assertive characters, they dovetailed to great effect, winning both the Super League Grand Final and the Challenge Cup together. When Maguire left the club, Wane was unsurprisingly named as his replacement. He had bided his time and earned his opportunity, as Maguire recalls:

I knew he wanted the job. He didn't do it in a disrespectful way and I actually thought it was quite healthy. I hope that it inspired all my staff, I want them to aspire to be the best they can be because ultimately, I want to get the best out of them. When I was an assistant coach, I wanted to be a head coach. That's a natural thing. So, it was actually a really good working relationship. Sometimes you have to pull them back a little bit, but again it is the communication that you have and the honesty between your staff members. There's no better feeling than seeing him going on and being successful. I watch all the games, I see him stand up in exactly the same position I am, and I am just as proud to see him go about it as I am all my other staff.

Similar contexts can be found in teams across the globe – in politics, commerce and education – and it is easy for such issues to rumble on in the background, fuelled by gossip and hearsay. In this instance, it was somewhat inevitable that Maguire, a proud Australian, would return home, where rugby league is a bigger draw than it is in the UK. The certainty of the situation, combined with open and honest communication between the two coaches, neither being shy in speaking their mind, lent a sense of clarity to a potentially uncertain position.

Members of staff forge undeniably emotional ties with their clubs and teams. To them, these teams are more than a high-performing culture or organisation; they are a huge part of their lives, their identity and meaning. I have seen this first-hand in teams I have worked with, where staff members are also lifelong supporters of the club, sometimes even passing a role down through the generations of their family. This attachment adds a further layer of intense emotion to the potential issues a leader can face when starting out in a role or trying to impact a culture too quickly. They have to be careful to understand the emotional component to this situation, spending time getting to know the people and empathising with how long they might have been there and the service they have given.

Change can be difficult, especially for those with a deep-rooted affiliation to a club's tradition and heritage. Some individuals will struggle to respond to dynamic changes in an organisation. They might be committed to an existing series of behaviours and beliefs that a new leader is trying to shift, or they could be individuals who naturally crave the feeling of stability and security. Some will come round in time, and become key architects within the new culture as relationships are built and trust established. Others will ultimately end up moving on – or getting off the bus – should they fail to buy in to the vision of the leader.

CHAPTER 5: LEADERSHIP LESSONS

- Understand people first, and the role they play second. Ask 'first who, then what'. By developing the person, performance is more likely to follow.
- Relationships are a cornerstone of effective leadership. To build them takes trust, vulnerability and commonality. Some will come easier than others, but all are important.
- Time is precious, so reflect on how you spend it. Sometimes the unsung heroes need star-player attention.
- Recruit for both talent and character. Both can be developed. Trust your instinct. Do not be blinded by talent if the character leaves you cold.
- Consider the leaders of your team or organisation. They do not always have to be the most experienced, senior or vocal individuals. Look to establish a cross-section of leadership that represents your people. Plan for the long term and identify your leadership potential.
- Know the right time to give youth a chance; they might just surprise you.
- If you can't have both, take goal harmony over team harmony. Sometimes a spiky environment becomes a high-performance culture. Conflict and confrontation are acceptable if people are united by a common purpose.
- At times, you will need to prioritise your areas of focus to achieve short-term performances. That is the reality.
- Surround yourself with those confident enough to question you and tell you when you are wrong, but loyal enough to back you when the tough times come around. Dissent is an obligation.

- Be aware of the constantly evolving nature of team dynamics, the blend of strengths, traits and weaknesses. One change or decision can derail or inspire the status quo.
- Be willing to delegate. Losing some control is OK when people thrive on the opportunities they are given. You might have to go backwards before going forwards.
- Key team members *will* leave, it is a fact of leadership. Let them go. You never know when your paths might cross again.
- Change is challenging and requires balance. Tread carefully on emotional ties, but do not be afraid to make tough decisions.

CHAPTER 6

Responding to Specific Leadership Challenges

....

The origins of this book lie in a piece of academic research. One of the key objectives of that original study was to articulate a series of real-life and contextually grounded examples of how leaders respond to a range of moment-to-moment situations encountered within elite sport.

The context of each leadership role will differ subtly from the next. This might be due to the specific objectives of the role, the heritage of a team, the reality of the sporting context a team finds itself in, or the structure of the group. For instance, one leader may function primarily as a traditional 'head coach', spending the majority of their time working with athletes and operating in tandem with a director responsible for the recruitment of players and the overall direction of the wider organisation. Another leader may have a broader remit, operating as a performance director who is held responsible for both long-term and short-term success and, therefore, is constantly balancing the need for immediate performance with a big-picture view of the future. Irrespective of the role's technicalities, the need to respond effectively to challenge is a common factor of leadership positions.

Several common problems arose from the interviews. These ranged from managing maverick athletes, dealing with victory and defeat, and communicating with the media to managing up to board level, applying discipline and maintaining the performance levels of an unsettled team member. I was fascinated to get the leaders' first-hand accounts of how they navigated these critical moments, which mirror many situations you might encounter in workplaces around the world.

THE MAVERICK CONUNDRUM

Everybody loves a maverick. Those highly skilled yet unpredictable athletes who go their own way and have the ability to do things that others can only dream of. They think differently, they behave differently and generally have a significant impact on the identity of a group. Mavericks can win games, excite crowds and instil an unshakeable sense of belief in a team. Simultaneously and paradoxically, they can infuriate, anger and divide a team, especially when the expected results fail to materialise, causing relationships to fracture. Positively or negatively, these individuals leave a lasting imprint and often become the cultural architects (see Chapter 4) of a group. In terms of character and personality, a maverick is often a non-conformist, someone who does not wish to be hampered by policies and regulations. Indeed, their supreme talent regularly allows for a more flexible approach when it comes to the rules.

When Zlatan Ibrahimović arrived at FC Barcelona, he was told categorically by Pep Guardiola that players did not drive sports cars to training. The next day, Ibrahimović arrived in a Ferrari. He still delivered on the pitch. He hit his numbers and scored goals. That is enough for some teams, but not at the Camp Nou under Guardiola. Irrespective of the talent and the output, the behaviours just did not stack up. The relationship lasted just over a year before the Swede returned to Italy with AC Milan. Ibrahimović didn't hold back when sharing his thoughts, using typically 'maverick' language and referring again to sports cars, to describe his time in Catalonia:

It's simple – without a team I can't win anything. But I need space within the team so that I can come into my own. When you buy me, you are buying a Ferrari. If you drive a Ferrari you put premium fuel in the tank, you drive onto the motorway and you floor the accelerator. Guardiola filled up with diesel and went for a spin in the countryside. If that's what he wanted, he should have bought himself a Fiat from the start.[*]

In English rugby union, fly-half Danny Cipriani has long offered a tempting conundrum to his international coaches. Tempting because 'Cips', as he is known, possesses the talent and courage to play the sport in a unique way. His freethinking, risk-taking creativity means he has the ability to win a game almost, in arguably the most team-focused of sports, on his own. Yet this temptation is met by a lingering feeling of suspicion towards extraordinary talent, which conflicts with the system-based tactics that are commonplace in international rugby. The balance between creativity and control represents a fine line.

Somewhat typically of a maverick, Cipriani also has a back catalogue of personal and disciplinary misdemeanours that understandably cause concern to coaches who will always put a sense of team before any individual ego. By playing around the world in recent years, he has seemingly gone to great lengths to prove his own personal development and maturity. When given the rare opportunity to wear an England shirt, Cipriani has sparkled intermittently and, in any case, never let anyone down. Yet, the mud and labels still stick. Despite initially involving him in team camps, Eddie Jones, like Stuart Lancaster before him, opted to leave him out of major tournaments.

---

[*] Grossekathöfer, V. M. and Moreno, J. (2013). 'Ibrahimovic Attacks Guardiola.' spiegel.de/international, retrieved 20 January 2020.

Mavericks can be wilfully independent in both their thoughts and actions. They want to make their own decisions and have the freedom to express their single-minded opinions. With such strong opinions comes a tendency to be stubborn, argumentative and tenacious. They don't respond well to excessive supervision or 'micromanagement'. They do not want extreme detail; the big picture will suffice. To get the best out of a maverick, the leader must provide a sense of freedom that allows the player to express themselves, while simultaneously reinforcing the situational and cultural boundaries that must not be crossed.

My first interview with Roberto Martínez takes place during his time at Everton and we meet at the club's state-of-the-art training facility, Finch Farm. I am greeted by the man himself. He leads me up the stairs and with each step I pass images of the history and success of Everton Football Club. He enthusiastically ushers me into his sizeable office overlooking the training pitches, where a couple of first-team players are undergoing fitness tests ahead of the weekend's fixture. Upon meeting Martínez, you are instantly hit by his passion, energy and warmth for people. Slight in stature, he is by no means physically imposing yet his energy fills the room. The Spaniard is intense, his dark eyes narrow and darting around the room. He seems to have the ability and energy to manage multiple priorities, while still being fully focused and engaged in the present moment.

When I bring up the topic of mavericks, Martínez lights up and begins to tell me how he 'enjoys that type of player'. He accepts that on occasion a player 'needs different treatment because they have a different talent from the others'. This talent eliminates the possibility that the team can play to the same technical standard without him or her and this idea informs the rest of Martínez's view. He admits that he 'would probably give the maverick more flexibility than the others' and believes that these players need to be understood and to feel 'they are treated differently, but always within the boundaries that the group must accept'.

As potent as the talent may be, there do indeed need to be boundaries and forming a deeper connection seems to be the way to establish those. Martínez highlights the importance of developing a personal relationship and the need to 'be very strong whenever a player steps over the mark'. He offers a warning that 'there have to be real consequences to that', a sign that underneath the positive energy lies a willingness to make the difficult decisions. For all the excitement, a maverick's talent and presence can prove catastrophic if they go unmanaged.

As well as the relationship between the manager and the player, Martínez looks to confirm that the athlete's peers respect them enough to ensure the team environment remains unified, and the maverick's sense of ego is acknowledged:

> This is a team sport so, while this type of player needs to feel they fit in to the group and they are allowed to be themselves, if the others don't respect them then the maverick role isn't going to work in the team dynamic. It is very important that the relationship between maverick and coach is surrounded by the respect of the other players. The maverick needs to be treated carefully and maybe in a different manner, but unless this is respected by the rest of the group it will never work; that maverick figure will never have an effective role in the team.

There is also the issue of definition. Dan Quinn points out that the word 'maverick' can actually have different meanings to different people. For some the term engenders feelings of suspicion and impending trouble and, with this in mind, it is important to challenge our perceptions here. A leader must avoid making snap judgements about a certain individual based on the reputation that precedes them, instead making up their own mind from what they see, hear and feel. Quinn goes on to say, 'If a guy is loose or loud and outspoken at practice, that does not mean he is a maverick to me.' In his eyes there is no problem in having 'a free-spirited guy, as long as they are not disruptive to the club'. At the Falcons, it comes down to whether a player is 'willing to protect the team' and if people 'violate the guidelines' and the coveted Standard, then that is a problem that requires that individual to move on. Quinn views mavericks purely in the context of the team and, in many ways, puts the responsibility back on to the shoulders of the player. Idiosyncrasies are accepted and, if the player contributes to the culture, then they are part of it. If they detract from it, they won't be part of it for long.

Sean Dyche looks to ensure that there is a strong sense of rapport with the player. Ideally, this is with Dyche himself but could also be with a member of his back-room team. If the rapport is there, honest conversations can occur where Dyche looks to find ways to 'guide a player to their betterment' by outlining his expectations – 'this is what we need from you' – his strategy – 'this is how we are going to do that' – and the player's role – 'you are a big part of that'. He looks for the player to buy in but if they fail to do so, 'out they go'. He invests the maverick with responsibility and career ownership, and couples this with a personal connection.

For Dyche, 'no one player will be bigger than the situation or the team'. This is an interesting point to put to mavericks who, by default, are predominantly ego-driven. Using his 'talk-demand-drag' communication, he will always give players a chance to buy in to the overall direction of the group. Describing this approach, he tells me that he 'will talk to players on many occasions', then he will 'start demanding' and if they do not want to hear that, he will 'drag them towards it'.

'And if that fails?' I ask.

'If along the way a player has had enough, then off they go. That is just the way it works,' he replies. Dyche's approach provides a simple framework and strategy that allows him to manage this situation in an authentic way. He knows the different stages and signposts and, more importantly, his next step at each point in the relationship.

Stuart Lancaster brought the conversation back to the concept of culture, stating that if a culture is strong enough, then a maverick athlete can be absorbed: 'I think you can absorb someone who perhaps doesn't fit the norm. But you would only do that if you have a strong enough culture. There have been players who were considered difficult to deal with who have come into our culture and been fantastic. Under a different culture, they could have potentially caused more problems than they solved by coming into the team.' Anticipating that fit means fully comprehending the player, which Lancaster goes on to discuss.

How he deals with this type of athlete 'depends on how maverick is maverick'. He continues, 'If they are culturally dysfunctional and would rip the team apart I would not pick them. I think rugby is the ultimate team sport so you have got to consider that, because if they don't trust each other and they erode trust within the group, then you are done for.'

For Lancaster, the dominant cultural pillar of trust has to be protected from any maverick's behaviour in order to validate their selection. He has perhaps the strongest yardstick in this respect, but Ashley Giles also displays caution. He acknowledges that there is a place for this type of player within a squad but warns that 'you can only manage one or two'. 'You have got to be careful,' he tells me, 'any more than that, and you have got a critical mass. Too many and you lose your heart and soul. Too much rubbish going on.' While a leader must be consistent in many ways, Giles has learnt over several years that these players, at times, need to be managed differently. He goes on to give two real-life examples he encountered during his time at Lancashire.

EXAMPLE 1: THE BOUNDARY PUSHER

There are still guidelines, lines you don't cross. If one of these guys is late, he is late. So 'wind your neck in, make sure you're on time' but you might do that privately. But at the same time, one player you manage slightly differently because he is an off-the-wall Ausssie, a great cricketer, I know he will give me 100 per cent at the right time. But I also know, at times, he won't be that interested in training. I joked with him today because we played an internal T20 game yesterday and he was bowling nets and bowling well. He turned to me and said something. I just jokingly said – a couple of guys could overhear it and I wanted them to – I said, 'Nice of you to turn up today.' That is all I said, but he knows what I mean. I've not embarrassed him. The guys heard it. In some ways for me that is subtle management. They know I know, he knows I know, but I've let it run because I also know that on Saturday he will be ready to go.

Here, Giles is using an informal and seemingly spontaneous comment to deliberately send a message to both the maverick and their peers within the group. It forms as a note of caution to the maverick not to push the boundaries and to make sure on-field performances follow, and, at the same time a nod to the rest of the group that he is aware of the situation.

EXAMPLE 2: A LITTLE BIT OF LOVE

It is his first year, we had a meeting two weeks ago and I was quite straight with him because there was stuff I didn't like. He was quite straight with me and he actually thought, in simple terms, I didn't love him as much as other people. We got to the bottom of it and he realised that I did respect him. Of course I did because some of the stuff I saw from him, I saw one of the best players I have ever coached but I didn't see it consistently and I wanted to know why. We got to a point where we were clear. I've not got a vindictive bone in my body. The most important thing to me is that the team go forward, so I just wanted him to give more. In many ways I brought him closer. In the weeks that followed he would ask me questions, 'What do you think about this?' Now, when I see him running around the field like a blue-arsed fly, I say, 'That's fantastic,' or, 'That's superb,' you know. And at times you might give him a bit more, and publicly, so he goes, 'Thanks, I feel important now.' Some of them just need getting started, because these guys have got a lot of influence, and it's generally good.

In this scenario, Giles is praising the player in public and bringing him into the group. In his words, 'You forget sometimes, these guys play so much cricket, they need a bit of loving, even the ugly ones!'

The pressure and outcome-based focus of elite sport means tiny details can go unnoticed. Talent aside, a neglected or unloved maverick can be something of a ticking time bomb. Giles draws the players he worries about closer. He believes to get the best out of that type of player, 'you wouldn't necessarily put them in leadership positions, but you keep them close . . . some of them need motivating but it is just getting them started, initiating something, because they can really impact the group'. This is not a heavy-handed or meticulous approach – such a method would not go down well with a maverick – but rather the lighting of a 'touch-paper', after which the leader stands clear and allows the player to make their positive mark on the organisation.

A player often used as a standout example of the maverick athlete in cricket is Kevin Pietersen. Pietersen's brilliance played a key part in England's rise to the summit of the world rankings yet, despite their on-field success, he recalls how he was unhappy away from the game: mentally and physically fatigued and well on his way to falling out of love with cricket.* His performances on the field remained of a consistently high standard, however, culminating in an innings against South Africa at Headingley in 2012 which coach Andy Flower described as 'brilliant', 'angry' and 'one of the best you will ever see'. Pietersen seemingly possessed an ability to switch his performances on and off, yet after that demonstration of sporting brilliance came an emotional breakdown which saw him in tears in the team dressing room. Pietersen is an example of the maverick player who, on the surface, appears super confident and ego-driven, but underneath there lies a vulnerability that needs to feel a sense of belonging and value. It is to this example that Giles' approach lends itself.

In any team environment, a player's role and function within the overall dynamic will shift and fluctuate over a period of time. Consider a simple exercise where you plot an individual's position based on two key measures: their performance or output and their behaviours or attitude. In sport, output can be measured by statistics, such as fitness data, goals, assists, runs or touchdowns. In business performance is commonly evaluated by key performance indicators

* *The Edge*, supra.

including sales revenue, net profit margins, customer retention or reductions in cost. Behaviours are naturally a little harder to measure, but this is now done to great effect by organisations using a combination of surveys, questionnaires and 360-degree feedback. Consider the example of a commercial sales team, where an individual meets their financial targets every week, but constantly falls short of the team's agreed values, giving the leadership a decision to make.

While a maverick athlete would typically have the skill and ability to succeed, it is their behavioural contributions that really dictate their influence in a team setting. If the behaviours are in line with the culture to which the group is aspiring, then the maverick may well be one of the leaders on the field. However, if the behaviours are not deemed to be of the required standard, like in our Ibrahimović example, the maverick athlete can start to have a detrimental impact on the group. They will probably still hit their numbers in terms of performance, but their influence on the balance of the group may be so damaging that the decision is taken to facilitate the player's exit from the club. It is indisputable that a maverick *can* be a real burden on a group. Their nature dictates that they place more demands on a leader's attention and energy stores, and ultimately the leader must evaluate if they are worth the effort.

MAVERICK MOTIVATION

To ensure a maverick buys in to the direction he sets, Michael Maguire looks to really understand 'how that guy ticks'. When I ask him what he means by that, he refers to how that individual fits within the overall team dynamic: 'It is really about being able to understand personality and how they are embedded inside the team and the influence that they have, but then also the other parts of the team that influence him back.' From our discussions, I know for a fact that Maguire considers this for all of his players but naturally some require a more intense approach than others.

Maguire believes that 'everyone is different' and that mavericks 'are fundamentally good people', who a leader needs to 'tap into in certain ways' to enable that person to 'shift their thought pattern' and become part of the group. In this respect, a maverick offers Maguire a different challenge from his day-to-day leadership.

If required, he looks to his carefully selected on-field leadership team to pull a maverick 'back in line'. However, there have been times under his tutelage when a clear line has been crossed. Madge tells me that 'when it is affecting the culture of who you are as a team, or the values or standards you have . . . you have to make a decision and let them go'. He has seen, in past experiences, the 'values of an organisation deteriorate' and 'by moving on one or two of those people, you could have brought it back alive again, but they hung on and hung on, and sure enough it didn't come back around'.

While their individual approaches and techniques may vary, our leaders all agreed on the conundrum a maverick poses to an organisation. They bring a potential for both toxicity and brilliance in equal measure. Reflecting on his contrasting experiences of dealing with this type of player, Gary Kirsten sums up the leader's role with mavericks. On one hand Kirsten has managed athletes who 'have been fantastic individuals who have been a great asset to the team', and on the other he has seen players 'who are high performers but are destructive to the team'. For Kirsten, such a situation is not sustainable and, as a leader, 'you have to make a call':

I am happy to work with a maverick athlete if they are not pulling people along with them and trying to be destructive to the team space and they are just getting on with their own thing. But you do unfortunately get those individuals that, when things get tough in a team context, they want to take people along with them and pull them down. That is where you have got make some really big calls, because then I think it can destroy the team and ultimately, it is the performance of the team that is the number-one priority, not the performance of one individual.

Whilst Kirsten believes it is rare to see a maverick 'shift and become a great team man', he will look to use the talent of such an individual for the benefit of the organisation or team while, if needed, limiting their contribution to the team space:

'I would work with the maverick as much as I could. My view on mavericks who are not great team men is this: they are using the team for their advance, to further their own cause. Well I want to use the maverick to further our team cause. So, what we will do is use his performances, but we will isolate him from making the big team contributions.'

This is a new view, an honest 'what's-in-it-for-us?' approach that sets Kirsten apart. Utilising the maverick's main assets, depending on their ego, but isolating their impact on the team is, perhaps, a more transactional and ruthless win-win strategy.

Kirsten also highlighted the logistical challenges of recruitment in his sport, emphasising that not all leaders are in a position to simply move an individual out of the organisation. 'You have got to realise that in cricket you have got limited resource. You know, in the business context if you have a maverick you can get rid of them because you then you put out an application for a position and you get a hundred people asking for that job and then you run through the list and pick one. In sport, you have limited resources so if you have a maverick whose prestigious talent is better than anyone else, it is not a straightforward decision to say "we can get rid of him and replace him with someone", certainly not in cricket.'

Here, Kirsten presents another point of view, grounded in the brutal facts of elite sport. In the battle for results, sometimes necessity dictates that talent is, temporarily at least, king. Essentially, Kirsten concedes that the maverick does hold a large proportion of the cards, and the leader makes their decisions with that in mind. In my applied work, one leader I encountered (who is not in this book and will remain nameless) put it this way: 'The players can be *****s at times, but I need them more than they need me.'

Mavericks are often the individuals we remember and glorify long after they are gone. Cult figures who transcend sport, like Ali, Best and Maradona, all fit into this category. And yet there remains an overriding feeling of suspicion and fear surrounding the emergence of such precocious talents. The history of sporting excellence narrates spirited tales of comradeship, teamwork and loyalty. Perhaps then it is unsurprising that the maverick athlete who, with their non-conforming, unapologetic and ego-driven brilliance, seemingly contradicts these traditional virtues, is met with such scepticism.

Youth academies consistently produce good players with strong values and behaviours, but it is important to ask: where are the next mavericks, those who will see things others cannot and bring them to life in a flash of brilliance?

Every day, sport enthrals and intoxicates, bringing people together around the world amidst unpredictable moments of tension. The actors in these most dramatic of scenes are often the mavericks, the infuriating freethinkers in a dogmatic landscape. To that end, leaders must not isolate them, but rather embrace and encourage, managing them with a watchful eye to ensure cultural boundaries are not over-stepped. Sport as we know it would be a lesser place without them.

DISCIPLINARY SITUATIONS

In the world of social media, a player's every move has the potential to be captured on smartphones and broadcast and hashtagged across the globe. The athletes of today are widely expected to be role models, held up against the pinnacle of sporting performance and personal values, all under the public microscope.

In reality, athletes themselves are often only a few years older than those who look to them in admiration. Serena Williams was just twenty years of age when she claimed the World Number One spot for the first time. Usain Bolt was twenty-one when he won two golds at the 2008 Olympics in Beijing. Tiger Woods won his first major championship at the same age, having been earmarked for success throughout a well-documented childhood. Wayne Rooney scored on his Premier League debut versus Arsenal in 2001 – as a sixteen-year-old. They may do things we expect of adults but, in every other way, they are very much young people themselves. Once an athlete is into their thirties, in many team sports they are considered a veteran and a senior member of the group. Success is rapid and careers pass in a flash, and leaders should expect to manage maturity issues accordingly.

Leaders today are increasingly managing young, talented and ambitious people who possess a disproportionate degree of financial wealth. Considering this, it is not a surprise that all leaders could recall examples of their experience of dealing with a range of disciplinary issues. Across the conversations there was an overall theme of giving athletes 'the benefit of the doubt'. This is perhaps reflective of the scarcity of sporting talent and a leader's belief in and focus on developing people.

Roberto Martínez describes the clear-cut and pragmatic approach he takes to such situations within the restraints of competitive sport.

'When you get major disciplinary issues, I always try to give the benefit of the doubt. I accept everyone can make a mistake. If you make two mistakes, it is because you are stupid. After that, you cannot work with that person any more. That doesn't mean that you have to finish the relationship at that point because it may not fit in the transfer window and you don't have a replacement. But I would say that once they fail for the second time, you are already looking for a replacement.'

Any disciplinary issues are dealt with in-house under Martínez's guidance. 'As long as they want to listen and they are prepared to do things in order to help others', he will never come out and criticise a player publicly. 'I don't believe in that,' he tells me, 'I believe in behind closed doors, in between four walls, to tell people what is expected, what is not expected, what was right, and what was wrong. It is that private relationship, trust, and the safe environment really of making mistakes.'

It is striking that of all the elements of responding to challenges, an aura of trust, confidentiality and player respect prevails. As we have seen time and again, when a manager criticises players in public through the media, it is often the beginning of the end, and viewed as the ultimate betrayal of team trust.

Irrespective of personal relationships and second chances, however, the pre-eminence of the team prompts leaders to take a tough stance on discipline. Ashley Giles will, in his words, 'give guys a fair crack' but agrees that if there comes a time 'when people start questioning authority', then those people will leave the organisation – 'I can't have that in a group of people. If I think someone is doing that, then they are going to go. Simple as that.'

As Giles describes, at some point you simply have 'to draw the line'. However, the disciplinary process is not always straightforward and, as is the case in the world of business, employment law may prevent a leader from making a quick decision. 'Nowadays with employment law,' says Giles, 'you have to go through a process, so if it gets that serious you go, "Right, this is where we are, so this is your final warning, screw it up again, you're off." That is just the nature of the beast.' Whilst due process may slow a leader's action down, the ultimate decision remains their own.

Invariably performance, or 'the bottom line' Giles describes, also comes into the equation when making disciplinary decisions, offering a clear and factual guiding light for leadership:

> Some of the best teams have had difficult players to manage, and the job as the manager is to manage them, but there is always a bottom line with any player and it depends what that bottom line is. If the bottom line is he is still positive and he is scoring runs and you are managing to isolate some of their behaviours from the rest of the group, then you are OK. The problem with those characters is they become expendable very quickly. So, if they are not hitting their bottom line, that is when you are less forgiving.

Michael Maguire echoed this view, describing how, when a player steps out of line, 'it really hurts and they know it hurts'. He makes his thoughts clear, but this is always done behind closed doors. 'I do close ranks because no one really knows the actual truth in the outside world. I share my feelings and let them know the standards of our club.' He has no inclination to involve the media and offers a safe space from the scrutiny that surrounds his players. His tendency is to 'deal with the issue internally and then bring the player back'.

Maguire has an established reputation as a disciplinarian and taskmaster. Each morning, his players arrive at training to see their head coach finishing his morning gym session, a sign of the non-negotiable work ethic that was instilled in him from a young age. The reputation is not unfounded and he believes a lack of discipline will ultimately reveal itself on the field. However, we also know there is a caring, paternal side to Madge. Under his leadership, players will be given a chance, but rarely more than one:

> I know that young people will make mistakes, but if they make it twice they tend not to be part of our organisation. You are forgiving a little bit, but if the situation steps far outside the values of the organisation and what we believe in, they have got to move on. Unfortunately, they've just made bad judgements at the time, whether it is through alcohol or those sorts of things, but they also understand that if it happens twice then you part ways.

Maguire describes how sometimes these situations can, over the long term, bring people and teams closer together. 'Those times do bring us together. It is like family, the players become your kids so you do have that protective nature about them. But you've also got to be very disciplined about what is right and wrong and what we expect in our organisation.' This links back to the behavioural standards to which players are held accountable and that form a key component of the high-performance cultures we explored earlier (Chapter 3). Clear expectations mutually agreed provide a framework for a leader to fall back on when tackling disciplinary issues.

While frameworks and codes of conduct offer a sense of structure and control, at its core leadership remains a deeply human endeavour. In many examples, leaders take a case-by-case approach to their decision-making. Stuart Lancaster exemplifies a personal touch, explaining that while there can be guidelines in place, each decision is taken within its own specific context: 'Every situation is different depending on the person, the individual, the history behind it all, the scenario.' It is at these times when a leader refers back to their own philosophies, beliefs and values to make the call. 'You have got to use your gut feeling, intuition, and gather as much evidence as you can before you make your decision, make your decision timely and proportionate and do what you believe is the right thing for the long-term health of the team. It is difficult.'

In the build-up to the World Cup in 2015, Lancaster dealt with breaches of discipline from three players. Centre Manu Tuilagi, England's high-impact wrecking ball, was convicted of assaulting a taxi driver and two police officers. Hooker Dylan Hartley, a senior leader, was banned for four games for an on-pitch incident involving his international colleague and positional rival, Jamie George. Maverick talent Danny Cipriani, who had forced his way into the reckoning for selection, was arrested on suspicion of drink-driving just before the start of the World Cup camp. A series of challenges for Lancaster, who had built the culture of the team on respect and discipline, to ponder. The outcome? For differing reasons, including strong alternatives at each position, none of the players in question were selected for the World Cup on home soil.

The making of these decisions is, for Lancaster, 'the difference between leadership and management'. He summarises that 'management is discussing decisions', but leadership, a more overt and public function requiring bravery and confidence, 'is making them'.

Sean Dyche takes an objective view and needs the facts of a situation before making a decision – 'What level of discipline is it, you know, what have they done wrong? Is it outside the club or is it inside the club? Is it a private matter or is it a club matter?' He highlights the role of the media, both mainstream and social, in accelerating the intensity of such issues, making it difficult to keep things in-house. 'I find out all the facts first because it's terrible now. At Burnley we have been pretty fortunate but you can get a media story, then a Twitter story, then a phone-filming thing. The filming thing, we have all seen that one where what can look really bad is actually really innocent, so you have got to find out as many facts as you can.'

He highlights the specific contemporary issue he encountered when historic and controversial tweets from his centre forward at the time, Andre Gray, resurfaced online. Dyche acknowledges that the content of the tweets was both inappropriate and offensive but questioned how far into a player's past we can delve, highlighting how much a person can develop during that time:

> I thought that was really harsh. Five years ago? Do you not think we are all different from five years ago? How many years do you want to go back? Everybody talks about development, but Andre Gray, nobody wanted him to develop. So he has developed from five years ago, by his admission, by our admission, by everyone's admission who has ever dealt with him. We all talk about development, we all want people to develop. Development is a massive word now in schools, in business, it's in life, it is in conduct, it is in every part of life until it comes a time to go, "Oh no, we can't have that, we have to do him." So what is the whole point in talking about development? I thought it was bizarre because it was complete double standards. Football clubs should be developing players and people. We have done, and he still gets punished, so what is the point?

Not all cracks in discipline are as sensational as the examples discussed here. Arriving late for training, wearing the wrong kit, or being overweight or unfit are less dramatic, but cumulatively impactful nonetheless. During his time with India, Gary Kirsten was known to directly criticise players for their physical conditioning, body composition and nightlife.

Like Maguire, Kirsten exemplifies the qualities he looks for in his players. As a coach, just as he was as a player, he is supremely dedicated, tough, durable and possesses a relentless passion for the game. Unsurprisingly in this regard, he believes his job 'as a leader is to be watching players non-stop', enabling him to be zoned in to the behaviours of an individual athlete. If he sees that someone 'is doing damage to what we have created as a values system within our team, if they are going against our values as a team, I am going to check in with them. If they become a repeat offender on that, then we are going to have to take more drastic action.' While this approach may border on micromanagement, it can be valuable when working with young people on a rapid career trajectory, who are still very much in the learning process.

He acknowledges that 'everyone can make a mistake, everyone can do things that they didn't expect to do, or didn't want to do' and he will be 'very reserved' in his judgement on those occasions. Kirsten does not lead a group with a clear set of rules, preferring to emphasise the overarching role of the team culture:

> I believe that if the values system of the team is set up right and the culture is right, then people will want to do what the team needs because you are part of that team. It is my responsibility to get someone to feel an identity and a culture that sits within that team. If people are going to behave like idiots or break the rules or the informal rules that the team stands for, I'm going to check in with them and make them accountable to their teammates.

UNSETTLED PLAYERS

The perpetual movement and transfer of players has become a vital and inevitable part of the sports entertainment business. One only has to turn on the television during a Premier League transfer window to be faced with an incessant rumour mill from sources all around the world. 'Deadline Day' even has its own dedicated show, offering a minute-by-minute account of transfer dealings over the final twenty-four hours. In business, we might draw parallels with organisations going through change or restructures, where employees are uncertain regarding the security and stability around their role.

Roberto Martínez and Michael Maguire both described specific examples of high-profile players becoming unsettled due to interest from other parties and the potential to move from one organisation to another.

When Sam Burgess left the South Sydney Rabbitohs to join English rugby union side Bath in 2014 ahead of the forthcoming World Cup, it presented a significant loss to both the club and Maguire.

Burgess now enjoys legendary status at the Rabbitohs, having written himself into their folklore by playing through the pain in the Grand Final of 2014. In the first tackle of the championship match, he collided with opposition player James Graham, fracturing his eye socket and cheekbone. He continued to the final whistle and was awarded the Clive Churchill Medal for player of the match.

In 2010, the Rabbitohs had taken a chance on a driven young man from Yorkshire, who went on to become their leader. A big man who made big hits, with an even bigger influence, his iconic cup-final performance cemented his place in the club's history. For many, the embrace between Maguire and an emotionally spent Burgess is the abiding image from that euphoric night in Sydney. Maguire, who first met Burgess in an empty football stadium in Bolton, England, describes Burgess – now retired through injury – as 'one of the all-time greats of the game'.

While the loss of such an important player, on-field leader and cultural architect is difficult for any organisation to sustain, the reaction of the leader is crucial. At a critical moment, Maguire looked to change the perception of the situation, taking control and, instead of dwelling on the loss of a superstar, preferred to focus on the opportunities this created for other players:

> I actually think it gives growth to everyone else who is coming through. Younger players get to stand up and become someone like him now. That is opportunity. Sam obviously left a great legacy but for the younger kids who have seen how he has done it, they now have that knowledge, so go and do it yourself. We all want to be in that position, so I talk more about the opportunity. Losing key personnel is going to happen in every sporting organisation. Someone is going to move on at some stage and the next person is going to stand up.

Martínez, reflecting on Chelsea and Manchester City's pursuit of Everton's young English central defender John Stones, referenced his personal values and the importance of giving an athlete clarity about a situation and keeping him or her in the picture.

> It is very important to give a player clarity which means what is going to happen and what is the position at a given time. Give them a couple of scenarios, where if you behave in that manner [then] that could happen, if you behave in this manner [then] that could happen, and then give them the choice. If you

just look away . . . at those moments the players need information, they need help and if they get the wrong advice and the
wrong help it could escalate even further.

In his opinion, treating the person with respect means a greater likelihood of the situation being resolved in a satisfactory manner for all
parties.

Under the pressure and public scrutiny of player transfers, the
level of trust between leader and player can be tested to the limit. It
is at this time that the leader can look to withdraw against the 'credit'
of trust they have deposited into the emotional bank account (see
Chapter 5) of the relationship. In doing so, the player can believe in
what the leader is telling them, maintaining the respect between the
two parties. This also allows the leader to take ownership of the
narrative and offer the player some certainty in an uncertain world.

DROPPING AN ATHLETE

Many leaders would agree that dropping an athlete or cutting a player
from a squad is one of the toughest parts of the job. While sport may
be more high-profile, we can draw parallels with the business world
here, perhaps when firing someone or standing someone down from
a specific project or team. Nobody enjoys difficult conversations and
when you are telling a player that they have not been selected for a big
match, tournament or competition, you are effectively dealing with
their dreams. When a player comes so close to achieving that dream,
the reactions can be emotional and raw, meaning that the messages
become even more difficult to deliver.

Martínez believes that the most effective way to handle these situations is with honesty and by outlining with clarity what the player
can do as a response. 'I always feel that the player deserves to

understand why you are making a decision like that. I don't expect
for the player to agree but there is a big difference for him to understand what I am thinking and make him aware of what the next step
is. He will be wondering, "Have I got a future here?" or, "Can I do
things better to get into the team?" You have to outline a solution for
the player.' It is somewhat natural to want to avoid giving another
person bad news, and yet a leader must tread carefully, balancing the
delivery of tough messages and the facts of a situation with an effort
to relay hope and opportunity.

Stuart Lancaster believes timing is crucial and that delivering bad
news face-to-face is always the responsibility of the leader. This willingness to confront, rather than deflect or delegate to somebody
else, is a key ingredient to a leadership style built on authenticity and
honesty:

> Once you have made the decision, then it is a question of
> timing the communication of the decision to the player and
> doing it in an environment that is private, where the player
> feels he can voice his opinion, where I can give my opinion in
> a calm and accurate manner and the player feels he has got a
> right to reply. All of those conversations are done by me, rather
> than by text message, or turning over a flip chart to reveal the
> team or passing the buck to one of the coaches to do. It is the
> worst bit of the job.

In Lancaster's experience, there have been situations when delivering bad news in the short term has meant that the individual has
returned more determined to prove him wrong. Billy Vunipola, now
a bona fide superstar of world rugby, was dropped from the team
under Lancaster at the age of twenty-two. On reflection, the forward
admitted publicly that it was the right decision and acknowledged

that he had 'taken his foot off the gas'. As Lancaster believes, 'sometimes you have to take something away from someone in order to make them realise what they've lost'. Knowing the individual and what motivates them allows a leader to appropriately push and probe, delivering a message that results in the desired outcome for all involved.

I was curious to know more about the decision-making surrounding Sam Burgess' switch to rugby union and the seemingly common knowledge that he was aiming for a spot in Lancaster's World Cup squad. Knowing the controversy that existed, I approached this topic of conversation with some trepidation. Did it raise issues in terms of putting other people's positions under threat? Speaking back in 2015, Lancaster did not see it as an issue:

If Sam gets picked, he will have earned it by training well in the camp and playing well in the warm-up games, better than the other players in his position. The players respect him, get on well with him and, ultimately, he will have to earn his right to get in the team, as will everyone else.

As we know, England's 2015 World Cup campaign ended in disappointment as the team exited the competition prematurely, having failed to emerge from a difficult group. Burgess' role in the squad has been an ongoing point of contention within the game, the media and social media ever since. With the biggest of jobs comes the biggest of responsibilities, and leaders in sport will always endure intense scrutiny, delivered through lenses conveniently tinted by hindsight – for Lancaster, this particular moment was played out on the rugby world's biggest stage.

The relentless schedules of international sports, particularly cricket and rugby union, dictate that there will be times when senior players are absent from their club fixtures. In their absence other players step up to take opportunities but, upon their return, the international players inevitably regain their place. This can be challenging from a team-dynamic and ego perspective, as the understudies graft while the superstars globetrot, and it is a leader's responsibility to manage the situation. Ashley Giles recalls a situation where two of Lancashire's international players, Jimmy Anderson and Jos Buttler, were returning to the county side, meaning others would invariably miss out:

> Jos will come back into the side. He has not been around for most of the summer, but he is one of us, the guys know he is a good bloke. He was in practice today, fully committed, and does his stuff, very professional and the players have to accept that. He might win us the game. He might win us a trophy. All you ask from them, as I have just said, is when they come back in the environment, they are fully professional, one of the boys, buy into the team, do what everyone else does, not turn up half an hour late and leave an hour early. If they do that, then it is fine. I know the guys we've got; one has the club running through his blood and the other is a great lad.

Giles draws on a group's cultural foundations to provide the strength to sustain the evolving complexion of the team. He highlights the required behaviours, standards and values that he demands from everyone, superstar or otherwise.

REACTING TO VICTORY AND DEFEAT

On 2 November 2019, England's defeated rugby players trudged up to collect their World Cup runners-up medals. Having crushed the all-conquering All Blacks in the semi-finals, they had fallen at the final hurdle, being comprehensively beaten by an inspired South African team who possessed a fierce underdog mentality. Emotionally spent and devastated by falling short in the biggest game of their professional lives, only one player was seen to keep his medal on, the others removing them almost immediately. Furthermore, according to some reports, only one player visited their opponents' dressing room to offer their congratulations. Cue uproar from the world's media and fans. Claims of spoilt and entitled brats disrespecting the game reverberated around the rugby community. And yet the truth remains that we do not know who offered their congratulations privately, behind closed doors and away from the media. We do know that at the final whistle, while still on the field, the players can be seen shaking hands and embracing their opponents.

Removing runners-up medals is actually a fairly common occurrence in cup finals. After the Champions League final between Liverpool and Tottenham Hotspur in 2019, a number of the Spurs players chose to do the same. Players remove them, perhaps to avoid sending the message to their supporters that they are happy just to take part. Whether this automatically means they are disrespecting their opponents, the competition and the sport is up for debate.

Poor reactions to defeat are not looked upon favourably by virtuous notions of respect, spirit and honour, and yet it happens. As I have said countless times before in this book, athletes and leaders are human beings who, at times, struggle to control their emotions and reactions in the heat of competition. In 1991, the Detroit Pistols, known back then as the 'Bad Boys' of the NBA, walked off the court in their decisive play-off game against Michael Jordan's Chicago Bulls, so as to avoid having to shake hands with their vanquishers. Myriad coaches, including Bill Belichick, José Mourinho and Arsène Wenger, have failed to shake hands publicly after particularly tempestuous encounters. Once again, we are rarely privy to what happens where the cameras cannot tread.

Victory and defeat are the most inevitable and unpredictable realities of elite sport. It is a harsh and fierce results business. This is not the WWF, where there is a script to be followed for the sole purpose of entertainment. Nobody enjoys defeat, but the handling of these two extremes reveals character and delivers important lessons for sport and life.

EXPLANATORY STYLES

When working with individuals and teams, I encourage them to consistently reflect on each performance, irrespective of the result or outcome. Typical questions might include 'What was good?', 'What needs to improve?', 'What did you learn about yourself and the sport?' and 'What actions will you take as a result?'

Now, this process is rarely so clear-cut and, if timed poorly, can cause irreparable damage. You have to take the sporting context into account. To attempt this in the immediate aftermath of a significant defeat would be tantamount to professional self-destruction. The England rugby team, for instance, would not take kindly to being posed such questions in Japan. At the time, head coach Eddie Jones' reaction was to say,* 'After we have a few beers today, we will probably have a few more beers tomorrow and maybe Monday, and then maybe we will have to pull up stumps.' In other words, leave it, lick your wounds, then take the lessons. That is difficult to do when you have to wait four years for another attempt at the summit of the sport.

---

* Morgan. T. (2019). 'Beer, beer and more beer': How England team plan to console themselves after defeat.' *The Guardian*, 2 November.

However, this process of reflection, if timed appropriately, can help to maintain a sense of perspective, establish the lessons that can be taken from the entire spectrum of sporting experiences, and promote honesty and accountability, as well as reducing the prevailing tendency to overanalyse. A life in sport brings extreme highs and devastating lows. Both are inevitable. It is the reactions to such emotional experiences, from both the team and the leader, that contain the key to sustained success. The leader must embody this way of thinking too, which is often achieved by finding time for challenging self-reflection (solo or with a mentor), which encourages a flexible and rational mode of thinking.

In psychological terms our reactions to events sit neatly in one of two distinct camps: pessimism and optimism. Of course, we know that in reality the human experience is never quite so orderly; we all stray into both categories as we encounter a range of events.

Pessimists are often more likely to 'give up' in the face of adversity. A key facet of a pessimistic approach is what Professor Martin Seligman referred to as 'learned helplessness', or the perceived lack of control over our situation. Optimists, by contrast, are more likely to respond favourably to challenge and see benefits in terms of health, motivation and performance. Seligman encourages pessimists to switch their thought processes around adversity. They do this by challenging their self-talk and reframing this with a sense of 'learned optimism',* based on the theory that optimism can be cultivated from pessimism. Seligman contends that we can go a significant way to achieving this is by keeping our 'explanatory styles' in check.

The concept of explanatory style can be split into four distinct elements, which enable us to directly challenge our self-talk, mindset and leadership approach:

* Seligman, M. (1998). *Learned Optimism*. New York, NY: Pocket Books.

1. *Personalisation:* pessimists internalise negative events and blame themselves. Learned optimism encourages them to think about the external factors leading up the event.

2. *Permanence:* pessimists may develop a fixed and permanent way of thinking (e.g. 'it will always be like this'), while learned optimism points towards a temporary mindset (e.g. 'this is tough, but it will pass').

3. *Pervasiveness:* pessimists are more likely to generalise adversity in one area (e.g. 'we can't defend'), while an optimistic mindset is more specific ('we need to do better at one-on-one situations'), leading to clear and agreed actions moving forward.

4. *Perception of control:* this is the perceived lack of control that we mentioned when discussing learned helplessness – a mindset of 'there's nothing we can do about it'. This is contrasted with a learned optimism viewpoint of asking, 'What can we do?' and identifying appropriate actions.

SPORTING CONTEXT

Roberto Martínez described how each defeat or setback must be considered in its unique context, thus impacting his team's response to the result:

It is an interesting one because there are many different types of defeat. There are defeats where you feel you are beaten by a better side, which then is very straightforward to cope with. Then there are others where you as the manager haven't helped the team enough. I am always the first one to try to see what we as a staff could have done differently. And the third one is where we feel we let ourselves down and because of that

we couldn't beat the opposition, and if that is the case, if someone hasn't done enough, then you need to find solutions.
When it is the other two, it's just purely finding answers, I
need to find the answers myself of where we are going next.
The moment I find the answers of why we lost and what we
are going to do about it, I'm fine, I can cope with anything at
that point.

In looking within himself first, Martínez displays a leader's tendency
to internalise a team's performance. His structured thought process,
an attempt to discover the perceived source of a defeat, allows him to
move more rapidly from a problem-based way of thinking to a solution-based approach.

In dealing with defeat, the leaders look to the group to take
responsibility for the performance, and to offer their own opinions.
It is important that athletes have significant input when debriefing a
performance. High-performing teams and individuals do not back
away from failure. They proactively face up to it and learn from the
experience. While this is a deeply uncomfortable process, the best
teams possess a willingness to confront the reality of their performances. Ashley Giles wants his players to communicate honestly, to
the point that he will often ask them to take control of the post-game
debrief. However, he also notes the cyclical nature of cricket and the
potential impact that such conversations can have. A sense of timing,
therefore, is crucial:

> We play so much, we don't play once a week and get two days to
> suck it up and look at the tape and analyse it, then debrief it and
> start practice for the next game. We play one night and start
> again the next day so you have got to choose your words and
> messaging very carefully. You are looking to take the emotion

out of it if you can, so let's not talk about emotional things like, 'He doesn't care . . . he doesn't try . . . you were shit.' There is a time and a place for the odd hairdryer, but you have got to look at actions. So, if you analyse it sensibly, 'What did we do wrong?', rather than get hot-headed. We have all done that at times and then you walk away going, 'Actually, you know what, the opposition played bloody well. We trained well, we were ready, and we practised.' Sometimes, it just doesn't happen.

While acknowledging that leaders do not always respond in a rational and effective manner, Giles strives to detach somewhat from the emotional impact of results. The aim is to eventually conduct an intelligent and logical analysis, viewing circumstance and events, before responding to them.

Stuart Lancaster described how the presence of trust within a group drives a willingness to be vulnerable that enables players to speak up in response to defeat. This type of conversation does not come easily and there is a layer of delicacy to its establishment:

'You have got to create a sense of mutual accountability and trust that we are all in it together and avoid [assigning] personal blame [in a public setting]. Ultimately you have got to be careful not to completely damage morale when you have a defeat because you've got to try to pick them up and get them to believe they can win the next week.' His teams 'review together, avoid blame, but focus on accountability' meaning that 'people are prepared to put their hands up and say, "I made an error there."'

Michael Maguire described the hurt that comes with defeat and, referring to a semi-final defeat, how he looks for his teams to use that raw emotion to improve:

Without a doubt, it hurts. Hurt always makes you stronger. That hurt is something that you never ever want to go back to. That is the growth and it's making sure that the players understand that your window is very short in your sporting life. How you end up and how you go through that is how you are going to be remembered. It's understanding that, when you get so close, or whether you're going from the bottom up, we are all in it for one reason. Otherwise, why would you do it? What is the point of turning up and training as hard as you can and then turn up and want to finish in mid-table? It is the whole reason why we do it.

You learn from every loss you take because to have that feeling is the last thing you want. Nobody goes out to say, 'I am going to lose'; we are there to win. You use that pain of loss of 'How are we going to get better?' and 'What are we going to do?', especially when you get so close. You can nearly touch it and then all of a sudden it disappears on you. There is a lot of pain in that.

Losing, or even the thought of losing, can have a galvanising impact. The experience or threat of pain can at times act as an inspirational negative. At half time in the 1999 Champions League final, with his Manchester United team trailing FC Bayern Munich, Sir Alex Ferguson used the emotional power of impending defeat in his speech:

Lads, if you lose you will have to go up there and get your medals. You will be six feet away from the European Cup, but you won't be able to touch it, of course. And I want you to think about that fact that you'll have been so close to it and for many of you it will be the closest you'll ever get. And you will hate that thought for the rest of your lives. So just make sure you don't lose. Don't you dare come back in here without giving your all.*

In 2017, the Atlanta Falcons lost the Super Bowl to the New England Patriots in dramatic fashion, having been on the wrong side of the greatest comeback in NFL history. The Falcons led by twenty-five points in the third quarter but the Patriots recovered to level the scores at twenty-eight points apiece, force an extra period, and shock the world when they emerged victorious. After the disappointment faded enough to allow for reflection, Quinn's reaction was the same as it would be for any setback, Super Bowl or otherwise. Quinn uses the analogy of an ascent of Mount Everest to reinforce his message:

We hoped, when we look back, we could create a programme that means we could always take shots at a summit, as opposed to going all the way down so our reference was, 'Hey man, let's go back to base camp.' We have got a number of good players, we have got a real style about how we play, so it was never that we were trying to go into a rebuilding mode. Let's go to base camp, reconnect to the things that got us up there near the summit. In football we can go take our shot every year, so we did the same thing the following year, we ended up losing in the play-offs but we felt like, going into the play-offs, we would be as hard to deal with as anybody. It didn't happen for us but, going in, we felt comfortable in that environment for sure. So we didn't feel

* Crick, M. (2003). *The Boss: The Many Sides of Alex Ferguson*. London: Simon and Schuster.

like we were going all the way down to the bottom of the mountain.

The Everest analogy fits the leadership narrative here perfectly. After the disappointment of 2017, the Falcons did not need a complete reboot; they did not need to retreat to the villages that lie deep in the foothills of the Himalayas. The foundations had been laid and the effort and energy expended in reaching 'base camp' remained valid. Retreating further would be undoing all of the progress they had made to date. They were acclimatised to the dizzying altitude of elite sport and trusted their environment. They had proven to themselves how close they were, and that their methods were working. For any climber, the image of summiting Everest is one of ultimate inspiration. A failed summit does not diminish, but intensifies, the goal. For the Falcons the Super Bowl was, and remains, Everest.

Martina Navratilova, one of the greatest tennis players of all time, once said, 'The moment of victory is much too short to live for that and nothing else.' Time does heal and a leader must be willing and able to compartmentalise, but not deny, the past. Quinn is focused on giving each team he leads his complete attention, rather than allowing the group to be haunted by ghosts of the past. 'This team of 2018 deserves all of our focus, all of our attention,' he says, pointing to a clock on the wall. I look at the clock which, at first glance, looks like any other. But on closer inspection it is not a normal clock. At each point, instead of a number, it simply says 'now'.

The make-up of an NFL roster changes so frequently that each specific group only gets a fleeting opportunity for glory. 'The players get a short window to go for it. We get a longer window, but that doesn't mean we don't put everything we can into this year. We are not thinking of the 2021 season, it is just focusing on right now and going after it. I think that is a fun part of being on a team. It is just this year. It is going to be a hard road, we need to battle for it, and then take our very best shot at it. Then go do it again . . .'

The dynamic nature of the NFL cultivates a persistent sense of urgency in its teams, something that is mirrored across sporting cultures, especially international sport. By contrast, in corporate and non-sporting organisations, the leadership challenge can be more about maintaining momentum and running long-term projects. Quinn notes that for regular team sports the reaction to defeat is potentially easier, as they will usually have another opportunity to achieve the summit the following year. He contrasts that with the Olympic sports:

It would be hard to be in the Olympics, you know, where it's like, 'OK, four years from now . . .' – I know you have competitions along the way and there are markers for you, [but] our Olympics [the Super Bowl], fortunately, is every year, and so we get to go battle like hell for it to say, 'Go win the gold again, no we got silver last year, now we are going for it again,' you know so, yeah, it sucks losing but it also is the life of a competitor. It doesn't make it easier to take. It's not like I don't think about it or it doesn't have a bad mark on me, within my heart, but it doesn't drive me to the next moment. It is all for this team, for this season.

While defeat is often assumed to be the more challenging leadership situation, Gary Kirsten discussed issues raised when dealing with both success and failure in a sporting sense, and described the need for a consistent approach. Leadership has hugely emotional components and stability, he says, is 'shown by allowing that process of emotion to unfold'. In both victory and defeat, he highlights the importance of the team, rather than specific individuals. His approach is about cultivating steady emotional states and measured responses, meaning any egos are kept in check:

When the team has done well, I do not like an over-focus on any one individual. The media force us to focus on what an individual did to allow the team to be successful. So, I will always pull the team into that context. When things haven't gone well I won't isolate individuals either and I will want to debrief with the team in terms of how we can take steps forward. If there needs to be an individual conversation around success and failure, then we will have those conversations. I am very mindful not to criticise in the media, [not] to criticise in front of other team mates, [nor] to praise too much in front of the media and [not] to praise too much in front of their teammates. For me, I look for consistency in terms of behaviours . . . get back on the journey, enjoy the success for a night and celebrate, and then move on in a very mature and respectful way going forward.

Sean Dyche strives to maintain a sense of perspective within the group following a poor result or performance. 'We make sense of it and remind them of the good things we can do to correct it. That is one of the big things. I think the trick is not losing sight of where you are at because often, the hardest thing in management . . . is if you haven't won, people are demanding, "Why are you doing that?", "Why don't we do this?" And you go, "Hang on a minute . . ." sometimes the strongest and hardest thing to do is not change anything—we go, "No we are on the right lines here." It just needs a tweak, and a twist, a bit of luck, and some slightly better performances, and we are not a million miles away.' There is a fine line between a consistency of approach and unyielding stubbornness, yet the solidity of Dyche's approach speaks volumes. At Burnley, if the team finds themselves on a run of disappointing results, they maintain an enduring belief that the tide will turn. Today's sporting leaders must be able to resist the modern phenomenon of instant reaction, and avoid making reactive comments or changes in order to accommodate recent events.

It was enlightening to hear the emotive accounts of how these individual leaders handle the inevitable successes and failures that are part of elite sport. Gary Kirsten describes the inner turmoil a leader experiences amid a run of bad results: 'When you start losing games, oh boy it starts to eat you alive, and you don't know how to turn it around.' He is referring to the cyclical nature of sport and goes on to describe how negative momentum can spread: 'The games you are meant to win you've lost and the ones you're meant to lose you are losing! So, you are picking up very few wins. It can accumulate very quickly.' In these situations, the media lens magnifies the issues and leaders must hold firm against a sea of speculation and doubt.

Kirsten reflected on his role as head coach of the Delhi Daredevils in the Indian Premier League. The IPL is an intense and vibrant cauldron of sport. Players are acquired by making themselves available for the competition's player 'auction' and can also be traded between teams during specific time periods. As is the nature of the international cricket calendar, preparation time is limited. In New Delhi, tens of thousands of passionate fans flock to the stadium to watch the Daredevils take on the opposition under the floodlights, surrounded by the buzzing humidity of the Indian capital. Exciting, fast-paced and unforgiving, immediate results are a must in this environment. There is no time or patience to build a long-term culture. You cannot claim progress is being made if the results don't stack up. In the IPL, performance always comes first:

It was interesting, one season we had a good lead-up to the tournament, probably one of the better lead-ups that any team could have, because you have only got ten days. We were ready to go but we lost our first two games straight out. They were tight games and we probably should have won both of those. Had we picked up one win out of those, it would have got everyone to buy into our new thinking and say, 'OK, we're on track,' the players get a bit of confidence, now we can go. But we were always just fighting to get enough wins under our belt, always on the back foot.

Victory and defeat are among the few guarantees of a leader's experience in sport. The conveyor belt of fixtures dictates that reactions to both situations are a continuous and significant part of the job. It is commonplace and understandable to spend more time picking over defeats than victories, yet there are lessons to be had in both outcomes. The reflection, mindset (and explanatory style) of the leader are key starting points here, setting the tone for the group, and impacting their reactions to outcomes. Amid the chaos of results, a leader must strive to stay balanced. A short-term result may leave you wanting to react quickly, but the hardest thing to do may be to stand firm behind your vision and approach, reinforcing the sense of belief and confidence in your people.

MANAGING THE MEDIA

In high-profile sporting environments, every word of a leader's interactions with the media are constantly scrutinised. The importance of delivering the right message to players and fans is a crucial and significant part of a leadership role, and one that at times leads to conflict with the media. From a psychological perspective, press conferences and interviews are almost as interesting as the sport itself, revealing leadership techniques, subtle messaging and the character of the leader.

The sports media are intense no matter where you are in the world. In Australia, where rugby league makes the front and back pages, Michael Maguire warns that the media and the messages he communicates via that medium are elements of his leadership that have to be managed carefully. He is speaking to the media, but there is a constant underlying awareness that his players are viewers too, and this represents an opportunity to reinforce key messages:

> You have got to use the media in the right way. What I am saying on camera, one of my players can take that the wrong way. And they go, 'Well, hang on, he is talking about something that he just spoke to me about,' and you might not have that knowledge that [the player] has seen it in that way and, really, whenever you are putting something out on camera, your players are watching, or your community is watching. I am aware of that each time I go out and speak to them.

This was further substantiated by Gary Kirsten's guarded approach to the media:

> I have always tried to keep an incredibly low media profile and I understand that some sports or some media environments don't allow for that, but I have certainly tried to do that as much as I can in cricket because my work sits behind the scenes, not in front. If I have to do my bit, the key for me is to be incredibly generic, be unemotional in my responses, not criticise my players in any way, take on the responsibility for the losing and just shield your players in that space. There is

nothing that can destroy a team culture more than a comment that gets taken out of context and can go on to become a cancer that starts in your team culture that takes a long time to repair.

There is a deep-lying sense of severity in Kirsten's words. He is warning us about the media and the toxic influence it can leak into the sacrosanct team culture.

As expected, some of the participants felt more at ease than others in front of the cameras and the microphones. Maguire certainly does not enjoy the experience. 'I can tell you now, when I walk in front of a camera I am never ever comfortable. Because once it is out there, it's out there.' His private and protective character means he is not one to put on a show for the cameras and he knows 'a lot of the media probably do not feel comfortable' around him. He keeps his distance, strives for privacy and overtly acknowledges the often fickle motives of the media. He continues, 'It is just the family thing. I like to stay internal. I know they get frustrated with me. But ultimately, at the end of the day, I do that because I am protecting the people inside. When you have success, people want to pull you down. Some of them will push you up, but people want to tear you apart, so it is protecting your own kingdom, I guess.'

Contrasting experiences of the same beast lead to different reactions. Roberto Martínez has some empathy with the media, as a result of his time working in television, meaning he got 'to know the way the business works'. Consequently, he tells me, 'You don't feel it is personal, you do not feel that they are making a personal attack on you.'

Stuart Lancaster recognises the important role of the media and the need for mutual respect. 'The press have got to feel that you are not trying to be deceitful or devious in the way you operate. You give them respect for what they are trying to achieve and you've got to keep your patience at times.' He accepts that a leader's job comes with an unavoidable element of the spotlight and 'inevitable criticism' from the media, which often leaves the leader with 'no right of reply'. Lancaster outlined that 'a lot of the information that gets put out there is not necessarily accurate' and muses that a leader cannot always 'tell the actual truth regarding the reasons why they have made certain decisions'. According to the former England coach, this would mean 'hanging players out to dry in the media', which in turn would inevitably 'affect the team culture and the trust of the players'.

Depending on their history as players or otherwise, all leaders will have certain factions of the media that they will need to be mindful of. A key theme of the leaders' approach to the media was to be 'as honest as you can up to a point' (Martínez) and to be 'open and transparent, you have got to give them something' (Lancaster). Ashley Giles said, 'Most of the people I have worked with would say, "He is open, he doesn't shut down, he might be a sensitive soul but we like him."'

The word 'media' now goes far beyond the traditional avenues of newspapers, radio and television. There are countless social media sites, blogs and YouTube channels with thousands of subscribers. Going a step further, organisations like the New Zealand All Blacks, Manchester City, Tottenham Hotspur and a host of NFL organisations have actually allowed camera crews behind-the-scenes access for predominantly commercial and brand-building purposes. The media is not going away, so the management of such powerful forces is an inescapable and potentially troublesome element of leadership.

MANAGING UP: RELATIONSHIPS WITH STAKEHOLDERS

Such is the nature of elite sport, a leader's role is rarely focused exclusively on the coaching and management of athletes. Wider commercial and boardroom demands are common place and include board meetings, contract negotiations and sponsor commitments. This can prove challenging and tiresome for some leaders, whose predominant skill-set is centred around the improvement and development of players, yet the ability to understand the specific needs of the organisation – to 'manage up' and forge relationships with key decision-makers – is crucial, as outlined by Gary Kirsten:

> You have got to be able to manage upwards as much as you have got to manage downwards as a coach or a leader. You've got to build relationships with people but you also have to understand the need of the owner or the organisation, whether that is an international governing body or a team franchise.

The owner of the Atlanta Falcons is American businessman and co-founder of The Home Depot, a major American home improvement retail company, Arthur Blank. Dan Quinn's approach to building their relationship is to continuously provide information about the team: where they are in terms of practice, injuries, mindset, health, succession planning, recruitment and staff changes. Across sectors, leaders need to communicate with their stakeholders, and in this respect, sport is no different. A leader who ignores this obligation is unlikely to be in the job for long.

Quinn's relationship with Blank was tested in 2019, when the Falcons' regular season form prompted concern amongst their supporters and the media. Having reached the Super Bowl two years earlier, the pressure was on the head coach and calls were made for him to be replaced. The possibility crossed Blank's mind, and he admitted as much in an interview on the Falcons' own website.[*] However, drawing on his vast experience in business, he decided to back his head coach and publicly stated his five reasons why he was retaining Quinn's services.

Blank's first reason was Quinn's willingness to adjust coaching roles – including his own – partway through the season 'to free himself up and have more ability to be all of the things that he needed to be as a head coach'. This flexibility and lack of ego went some way towards saving Quinn's job. Blank also noted other reasons, including the development of a simpler defensive system and putting 'round pegs in round holes' in terms of positions on the field. Critically, the owner cited the players' buy-in to Quinn's leadership and the concept of brotherhood as a significant factor in his decision: 'I think most importantly is that the players actually believe it, the players actually live it and the players have really supported the organization, the franchise and each other.'

The fifth and final reason that Arthur Blank gave is indicative of a head coach's position as part of a wider leadership unit and the necessity to manage stakeholders effectively. The Falcons' spectacular new home, the 'Mercedes-Benz Stadium', opened in 2017 and the responsibility for the project had fallen to CEO Rich McKay. This had effectively, in Blank's words, sidelined McKay, a former general manager within the league with vast football experience, 'for probably five years or so'. The stadium project has been a roaring success, voted number one for fan experience over the last three seasons, but the shifting priorities of a key stakeholder had left gaps elsewhere in the leadership dynamic. Ahead of the new 2020 season, Blank has

* McFadden, W. (2019). 'Five factors that influenced Arthur Blank's decision to retain Dan Quinn.' atlantafalcons.com, retrieved 30 January 2020.

asked McKay to spend more time working with Quinn and General Manager Thomas Dimitroff, offering 'a sounding board, a source of knowledge, a source of wisdom and some guidance'.

Quinn's relationship with Blank, his major stakeholder, is testament to his leadership approach and ability to communicate and establish buy-in from those around him. All parties are on the same page and while it does not guarantee a job for life, Blank buys in to a consistency and stability of method. In a recent interview[*] he highlighted the role of consistency in building successful NFL teams and gave an insight into the leadership dynamics at the Falcons:

> If you go back and look at the history on this, and we've done studies on this, including recent history, those franchises that have been able to keep their general managers and head coaches in place for a long period of time are the teams that historically have been able to perform at a high level on an ongoing basis. So, the notion of the coach of the year, flavour of the month, whatever they may be, is very unhealthy for an organization, it truly is. If you have the abilities, the creativity, the leadership, you have the personnel making the right decisions, you have the coach providing the right leadership and you have other coaches on the field making a difference technique-wise, you can win in this league and you can win better than most teams can. We need the ability to do that, and I think the combination of Thomas and Dan, together with the supervision of Rich [who is] directly involved on a day-to-day basis, he's going to be pretty much living in Flowery Branch, and I think that triad will work very effectively for us going forward.

[*] 'Five factors that influenced Arthur Blank's decision to retain Dan Quinn', supra.

Quinn clearly has an understanding of what Blank looks for in a head coach. The ability to understand the specific and changing needs of an owner or board in a given situation is further emphasised by Roberto Martínez:

> There are owners that want to know what is going on every day. Others don't want to know. Others, they just want to let you know that when there is a major moment they want to be part of it. I think you need to find out what the owner feels comfortable with and from that point, I have just found they've been very open and very honest. I make them part of the whole process and try to be quite level-headed – not being over-confident when things are going well, or too negative when things are not going too well. I think it is important as well that you are not there to fight with the owner, you are there to understand what the owner is giving you to work with and get the best out of it and then, from that point, make them aware as well what could be the next step to improve the club.

Again, a level head and a thorough understanding of an owner's motives and values is a precursor to a fruitful professional relationship.

A leader and their stakeholders, be that a board of directors, a governing body or an individual owner, must be aligned on both an outcome and a philosophical level. Leaders need to establish this early on in negotiations and see the selection process as collaborative rather than a typical interview. Ashley Giles described meeting the chairman of Lancashire and asking, 'Well what do you want to achieve? What do you want from me?' This congruence is important because, as he describes, 'I can tell you everything I want to do, like build legacy, but if you just want to win then we're not matched up because that is not me.' Giles exemplifies how important it is for a leader to have clarity in what they stand for and a willingness to act upon it, irrespective of the sense of opportunity that lies before them.

Intriguingly, two of our leaders, Giles and Kirsten, encountered one another in a potential leader-stakeholder dynamic, when Kirsten was encouraged to apply for the head coach role with England. Giles, having moved on from his role at Lancashire, was on the panel in his position as the ECB's director of cricket. Despite Kirsten being favourite for the role, the ECB opted for English coach Chris Silverwood, preferring an English coach and the element of continuity that Silverwood, who was bowling coach under predecessor Trevor Bayliss, would provide.

Referring to his relationship with a high-profile owner at the Rabbitohs, Michael Maguire describes how he kept actor Russell Crowe, a passionate supporter and figurehead, up to date but also at a distance:

> 'I would like to think they respect what I do for them and I respect what they do. We don't really have a lot of conversation at all. I believe if I can show that we are moving forward as an organisation, he can just sit back and enjoy what he is doing. He might have his two bobs' worth and I will accept it or disagree with it but, ultimately, at the end of the day we set those boundaries when you first walk into an organisation.'

Maguire is not one to be intimidated or impressed by celebrity status, preferring instead to make his judgement based on character. Whoever the stakeholder, a leader must remain steadfast to the non-negotiable aspects of their approach.

When Sean Dyche arrived at Burnley, he had not long been sacked by Watford owing to a change in ownership, having been in charge for just one relatively successful year. In light of that experience, he decided he was not going to move his family, meaning that while Dyche would relocate north to Lancashire, he would also regularly travel back to the family home in Northampton. By stipulating this from the beginning, Dyche was able to manage both the stakeholder and family dynamics:

> The board here are really good about that and always were. When I first got here we had a tough time for the first six to eight months. They never questioned, 'Oh, you weren't here, you weren't there' – none of that, they have always let me work and believed in me, which has been really helpful.

Dyche admits he has not experienced a great deal of conflict with the board at Burnley, but perhaps that is down to his approach to leadership rather than good fortune. As expected, their relationship is based on honesty: 'I have always told them things with absolute honesty, they've accepted that honesty, mostly. You always have that odd rumble here and there, but not many.' The owners trust Dyche and allow him to work. On the job, Dyche possesses a sought-after combination of ownership and freedom:

> They have allowed me to work which I thank them for on a regular basis because they don't stick their nose in. They ask opinions, they ask about different things but they never intrude. You get the feeling at some clubs that the board are expressing to the manager that 'You shouldn't be doing this, that and the other' and asking, 'Why aren't you doing this?' Here, they are more interested in what my reasoning is, things like that, so we have a very open relationship. That has been really helpful because it allows me the chance to work and the staff to work, so there is good trust and openness.

As well as being unaffected by profile, some leaders purposefully seek out the higher-ups within an organisation. Gary Kirsten looks to build one key relationship within the wider organisation, preferably with the primary decision-maker. 'You need one champion at the top who buys into your thinking and he becomes your go-to guy. When the results aren't really stacking up, he can stand up at board level. That is a very important component to leadership because, especially when you are trying to shift a culture, if you don't have that relationship and then the results don't go your way, it is very easy for them to move on to the next coach.' As with Quinn and Arthur Blank, positive relationships with senior stakeholders can prove invaluable.

In addition to dealing with owners or chairmen, leaders are often tasked with attending sponsor events as part of a club's commercial obligations. Maguire describes how he is 'selling the club every day, who we are as a club, speaking to those who want to get involved with the club', and acknowledges that 'the more involvement you get from the corporate world, the stronger your club is going to become and, realistically, that is what I want, I want a stronger club'. While Maguire would prefer to be either on the grass with ball in hand or enjoying time with his family, he reframes his commercial obligations as an opportunity to increase resources, therefore making his job easier and increasing the likelihood of success.

He makes an effort to get to know everyone involved with the club on a commercial level, seeing them as a key part of the Rabbitohs family. 'I am happy to talk to them and happy to be associated with them and things like that because, once they come into our organisation, I see them as part of our family. If you don't have them, you don't have the strength as an organisation. So it's a matter of utilising that as something that we do as we keep moving forward.'

Different sports place different demands on a leader. Leading international teams also means managing the important relationships with the clubs who employ the players on a daily basis. Stuart

Lancaster was proactive in his approach to building these relation-ships, taking on the responsibility himself rather than choosing to employ a team manager:

> I go out of my way, and I go to clubs and visit them. I try to give ground to gain some trust, I communicate as effectively as I can, I'm fair and I do what I say I'm going to do and as a consequence I think clubs respect the fact that, whilst they might not all agree that taking their best players is good for their club, they will support it.

In New Zealand and Irish rugby, players are centrally contracted by the governing bodies but, in England, they are owned by the clubs. Due to a clash of domestic and international priorities an element of conflict here is inevitable. The clubs rightly want to protect their assets, but inevitably the national sides want to field their strongest teams and ensure they are on the same page in terms of training load and injury rehabilitation. To alleviate this, Lancaster looked to build trust by communicating transparently and identifying commonalities between parties. Enhancing England's international programme should, in the long term, bring increased funding and spotlight to the domestic game. By improving relations with the clubs, players' perceptions of their club and the experience of joining up internationally should also, as a by-product, be increasingly and resoundingly positive.

When leading a team or organisation that is essentially run by a national governing body – in this case the Rugby Football Union (RFU) – there are several forces at play that must be managed, as described by Lancaster, who proactively looks to 'manage up':

> There is the board, council, CEO relationship, other members of the international performance department, and the

management team and the executive team. So, you are naive if you don't influence up and try to educate them as to what you are trying to do with the team and where you are going. So, professional game board, you name it, I'm on it, and I go into it because they are the people who ultimately will make the decision on whether you are going to be in the job and the team are going to be successful in the future.

Managing up means that leaders will at times have to step out of their professional comfort zones. For Lancaster, managing myriad stakeholders presented both a challenge and an opportunity for further personal development. Since leaving his role with England, he has taken seats on numerous advisory boards, utilising these broad and unique skills.

The success of a leader in sport can depend equally on both their ability to empower, challenge and motivate their athletes, and the skill set required to simultaneously maintain a constructive dialogue with varying stakeholders. A leader must balance the needs of the team, their bosses (owners, shareholders, governing bodies, boards), and the entire organisation, while developing people and driving the on-field performance that supports organisational growth. Mixing with suits, as well as tracksuits, is becoming the norm. This is undoubtedly no easy task, but the leader's ability to respond to both the foreseen and unexpected challenges that come with a life in elite sport, will set them apart from the crowd.

CHAPTER 6: LEADERSHIP LESSONS

Mavericks:

- The contribution of a 'maverick' must outweigh the cost. Be careful not to glamorise them too much. Evaluate their talent and skill alongside their behaviours and attitude.
- Understand that some people are different and need to be managed as such. Balance creativity with control by combining an element of freedom with clear boundaries.
- It can be tempting to persevere with rare talent. Be ready to accept it's not going to work and move them on if they become detrimental to the team.
- Observe them in a team environment. The leader-maverick relationship is important, but so is acceptance by their peers.
- This goes back to understanding the person, their character, background and drivers. The person who appears super-confident on the surface can be sensitive underneath. There might be more to them than meets the eye.

Discipline

- Establish the facts and context of a situation personally. Do not rely solely on the accounts of others.
- Look for the good in people but be prepared to move them on if the time comes when a line is crossed.
- Be ready to take tough decisions to remain aligned with your approach.
- The team always comes first.
- Discipline does not just mean grave errors of judgement; the gradual accumulation of bad habits and losing behaviours has a potentially toxic effect.

Unsettled players

- Give people as much information as you can regarding their situation.
- Don't shy away from conversations. If you don't have all the facts, then tell them that.
- Draw on the emotional bank accounts, relationships and trust you have developed as a leader.
- Even if you don't agree on the outcome, maintain the relationship. You never know when your paths might cross again.
- If you lose a senior team member, be prepared to take the initiative and reframe the narrative. A departure can provide opportunities for others to step up, and ultimately improve the team dynamic.

Dropping players

- It is the leader's responsibility to – communicate the decision in person.
- Timing is crucial. Balance a need for clarity and positivity with an avoidance of delivering false hope.
- Honesty is always the best policy. Clear communication means no blurred lines, and whether someone agrees with a decision or not, they will invariably respect it.
- Sometimes short-term pain is the trigger for long-term development.
- Turnover and movement are inevitable. Monitor the team dynamics as people come and go, drawing on your cultural foundations to maintain consistency.

Responding to victory and defeat

- Use reflection regularly, as an individual and as a team. There are lessons to be had, some bigger than others, in every performance.
- Timing is crucial. Allow people the time to lick their wounds if need be.
- Create an environment where it is encouraged – not frowned upon – to speak openly. It will take time, but should increase accountability and responsibility.
- Monitor your explanatory style as a leader. Embody this way of thinking and cascade it through the team. It will drive the mindset of the group.
- Motivation does not always need to be positive. The threat of a negative result, timed appropriately, can have a real impact.
- When facing a setback, a cultural reboot is not always the answer. Trust your approach and instincts. Retreat to base camp and prepare to go for the summit again. Consistency can transmit confidence to the players.

Managing the media

- Use the media and social media wisely. You are always on display and cannot fake being genuine.
- Look beyond traditional media. All of your communications (in person, the press, social media, emails, texts) have an impact on others. Be aware of your audience and the messages you are sending.
- Be mindful to keep criticism in-house. Don't lose the dressing room.

Managing up

- Consider your relationships with your stakeholders. Could these improve? How do they like to be communicated with? You might need them.
- Consider your 360-degree relationships; manage up, down and to the side.
- Before taking a role, check the alignment between your values and approach, and the objectives of the stakeholders.
- There might be parts of your job you don't like. Manage and reframe your own narrative of these demands. Board meetings, corporate events, networking and time with commercial partners, rather than being a drain on your personal resources, can offer genuine opportunity.

Conclusion

In October 2015, Stuart Lancaster could only watch as Adam Ashley-Cooper broke free of the English defence and passed for Matt Giteau to score, delivering the final agonising blow as England exited their home World Cup under Twickenham's floodlights, at the hands of Australia. As the exhausted players shook hands at the final whistle, the camera panned to a crestfallen Lancaster. He stood, arms folded, at the entrance to the players' tunnel, knowing he had to remain but wanting with every fibre to escape to the sanctuary of the dressing room. His post-match interview came with a heartfelt apology to the fans and a call to arms to back his young players. Less than twelve hours later, having watched the game back, he faced the media again. Another apology and an acknowledgement that this team 'were not ready to win'.

In the years that have passed, Lancaster has spoken publicly about the emotion of these moments and the fact that he will never truly come to terms with the disappointment. Lancaster, who succeeded in laying solid foundations for the future, is both a thoroughly decent man and a world-class coach, but in that moment he found himself at the bottom of the volatile sporting pit.

Fast-forward to May 2018. Lancaster is stood in the San Mamés stadium soaking in the atmosphere as Leinster defeat Racing 92 in the European Champions Cup final. After the game, his son Daniel and wife Nina join him for a photo on the pitch with the coveted trophy. Five minutes later, he FaceTimes his daughter Sophie at home in Leeds. They were there to support him amid the raw emotion of 2015 and they are here now to share the moment of triumph. While Lancaster is keen to point out that Leinster's 2018 European and domestic double was more about repaying the club's faith in him than it was professional vindication, some point to that success as the conclusion of Lancaster's story of redemption.

However, leadership is a journey rather than a destination. One of the only things that can be expected with any degree of certainty is that it will bring moments of both joy and despair, and countless other emotions in between. Every leadership position has its ups and downs and the world of business can be equally brutal and cutthroat. Steve Jobs, one of the most celebrated business leaders of recent times, was ousted from his own board at Apple. He went on to co-found a small animation studio called Pixar, before returning to Apple to build perhaps the best-known brand in the world. J.K. Rowling's tale of a boy wizard was turned down by a dozen publishers before going on to build the magic global brand of Harry Potter. Tim Waterstone was fired by his early employers, WH Smith, prompting him to go away, start a bookshop in 1982 and sell it eleven years later for £47 million – to WH Smith. Resilience is an essential ingredient for anyone who wants to not just survive the journey, but thrive.

In our leadership sample, Stuart Lancaster is not alone in experiencing such sharp sporting contrasts. Roberto Martinéz went from the indignation of being fired from his role at Everton to being one game away from a World Cup final, beating the legendary green and yellow of Brazil on the world's biggest footballing stage. Michael Maguire brought glory back to the South Sydney Rabbitohs, winning their first Premiership for more than forty years and securing his place in the club's folklore. Two years later, he was out of a job. As in life, nothing in sport is permanent.

To offer a concise definition of an ideal leader would be a convenient conclusion to a project like this, but it would also fail to do justice to myriad factors at play in such unpredictable team environments. Leadership is, at its core, a deeply human endeavour, and so it follows that leaders must adapt and flex their approach to the specific needs of teams and organisations. While there may be certain traits or characteristics that lend themselves more frequently to positions of leadership, there is no perfect leader or ideal philosophy. The accounts in this book reflect this, while highlighting some common themes.

While each leader has their own unique upbringing, style and personality, the presence and application of resilience is a constant theme in their individual journeys. A key attribute of high performers is an almost obsessive reaction to challenge and setbacks. Their early lives and sporting careers are stocked full of examples of this quality, be it recovering from crushing defeats, being released from a club as a youngster, retiring prematurely due to injury, or dealing with the complexities of family life.

Another ever-present theme has been the importance of relationships: the leaders' ability and genuine desire to understand the human beings they encounter along the way. It is a fact of elite sport that talent will come and go; players will join and leave organisations. Irrespective of the time an athlete spends as part of a team, a leader should always strive to understand the individual and make a genuine human connection. It is this interaction and empathy which impacts a leader's philosophy and, ultimately, how an individual deals with the many and varied leadership challenges they will face.

If you were to ask a truly elite athlete to reflect on even their best performance, they will almost always find something to improve upon. This introspection is a common characteristic of the nature of talent and the unending quest for perfection. Our leaders all embark on quests of both personal development and reflection in their own way. Tied to this is a willingness to be vulnerable and open to learning – another aspect of elite leadership. Indeed, one person cannot build a culture, and if they attempt to do so, they risk finding themselves increasingly isolated. In building their support staff, our leaders sought to create a combination of loyalty and a desire to think differently and challenge the status quo.

Culture is a much-discussed concept across contemporary industry. That is perhaps why its various components make up the lengthiest section of this book. It is undoubtedly a precursor to high performance and its presence enables the execution of both tactics and strategy. It is true that talent needs culture, and culture needs the talent. It is the leader's role to consistently embody a culture and regularly reinforce its key values. The challenge here, however, is the constant balancing act they execute between big-picture concepts such as purpose and legacy, and the unequivocal need for short-term results.

The lessons and themes of this book can be applied across industry. While framed in the context of sport, these messages find their origins in human behaviour and thus are universal. As a reader, you may not agree with them all. You may have preconceptions and opinions of the individuals depicted in these pages, but I hope you can take those points that resonate with you and apply them to your own behaviour, be that in business, sport, education or family.

Fittingly, I will leave the final word to each of our contributors. This is, after all, their book as much as it is mine. At the end of each interview, I asked the leaders to provide three points that they would use in a leadership masterclass. Their answers are below:

LEADERSHIP MASTERCLASS

ROBERTO MARTÍNEZ

- Be yourself, do not act or pretend.
- Anticipate as many situations as you can; the more that you can expect things, the more you can be prepared for.
- Be a dreamer. The leader needs to come up with dreams to achieve big things. If you are too conservative as a person, you will never, ever overachieve. It's impossible.

ASHLEY GILES

- A good culture.
- The right people.
- Hard work.

STUART LANCASTER

- Know yourself.
- Be yourself.
- Be clear on your philosophy before you go into your job. Do not try to learn and adapt on the job, particularly at the sharp end.

MICHAEL MAGUIRE

- Know exactly what you want to achieve and build a clear vision towards it.
- Work harder than anyone to achieve that.
- Have great people around you.

GARY KIRSTEN

- Presence and credibility. You need to win the changing room and have a way about you that is endearing to other people.
- Consistency. You need to be consistent through the results; don't let your emotions run with the results.
- Really care. People want to see that you genuinely care about them regardless of the results.

SEAN DYCHE

- You will have to make decisions. Be prepared to make them because everyone is looking at you.
- Deal in 'positive realities': know what the challenge is, take it on, take the realities on and try to be positive with it.
- It isn't going to be easy, so be ready: you have got to be ready to take the hits because you are going to get some hits and they are going to hurt sometimes. It sounds negative but it's just the reality.

DAN QUINN

- Have energy for relationships with the people you are leading.
- Have a clear vision of what you want to accomplish and clearly communicate it.
- Constantly assess your progress and what changes need to be made.

Acknowledgements

....

This book would not have been possible without the love, support and patience of my wife Lucy, who has backed me every step of the way, in this project and everything else I set my mind to. A special note to our two children, Bella and Henry, who have shared their daddy with this project for too long now, and my parents, Alison and Dave, for their support through the years, and for giving me the love of writing and sport respectively.

I must also thank those people who have supported me personally and professionally during my career: Michael Finnigan, Dr Martin Eubank, Dave Edmundson, Simon Clarkson, Alison Wood and Matt Whyatt. I have enjoyed expert and patient support from both my editor Tom Asker and agent Melanie Michael-Greer, who took a chance on me and have guided me throughout this entire process. I would also like to thank Tom Smith, Richard Evans, Isa Nacewa, Tommy Fleetwood and Thomas Bjørn for giving their own valuable time to this project.

Of course, the final thank you is reserved for the seven contributors to the book, the Leaders, without whom this book would certainly not be here today. Stuart Lancaster, Gary Kirsten, Roberto Martínez, Ashley Giles, Michael Maguire, Dan Quinn and Sean Dyche all gave their time generously. They have not always been easy to pin down but they have all provided a unique insight into their worlds, where they lead teams on a daily basis. It has been a privilege to act as their scribe and narrator.

Index